The Conditions of Paradise

AZURE DREAMS

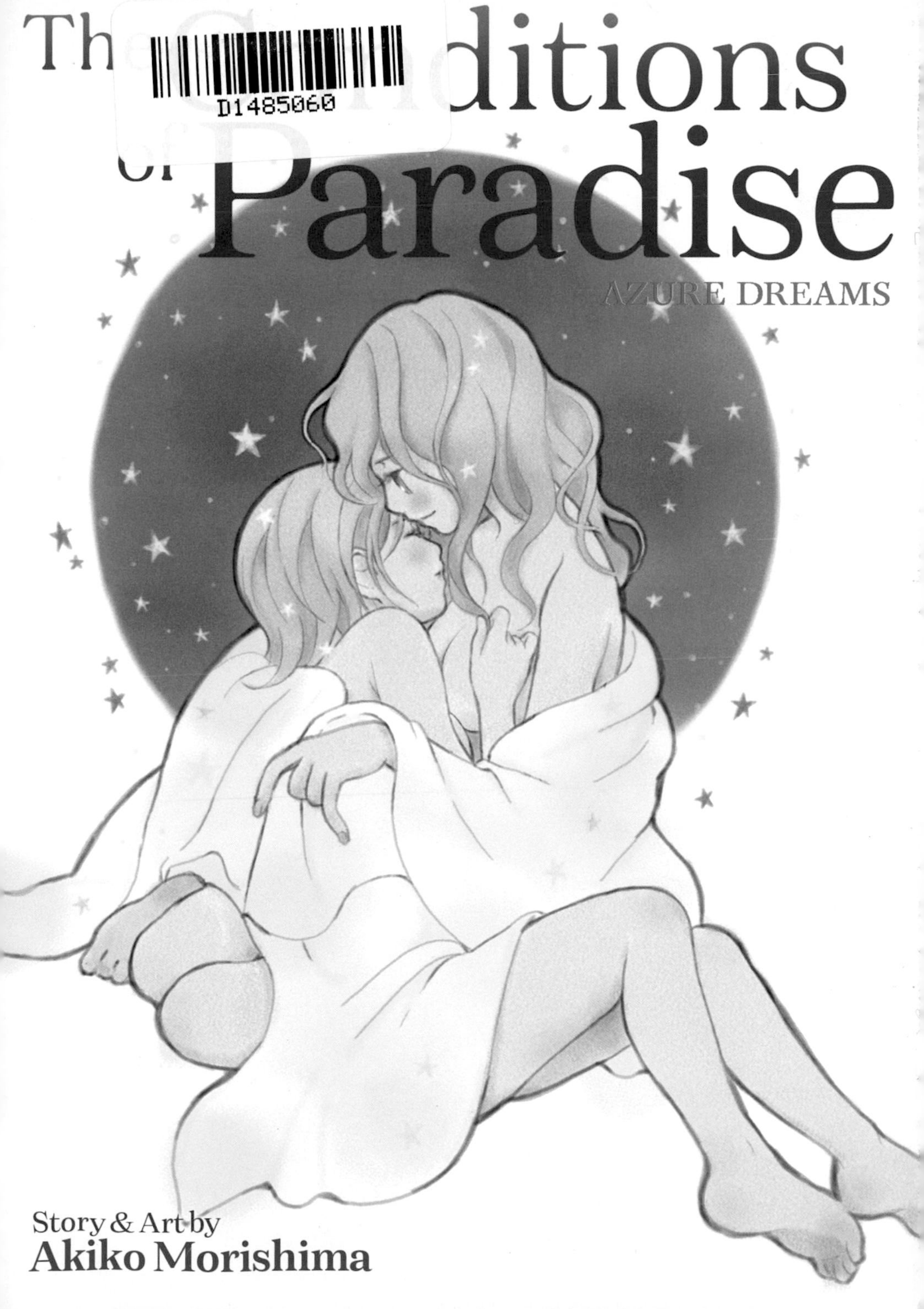

Story & Art by
Akiko Morishima

CONTENTS

Azure Dreams 3

The Star Princess 27

Honey and Mustard 35

Reminiscence: Nostalgia 67

The Season of the Twenty-Year-Old Virgin 101

Under a Full Moon 125

Incomplete Fujoshi 135

Afterword 148

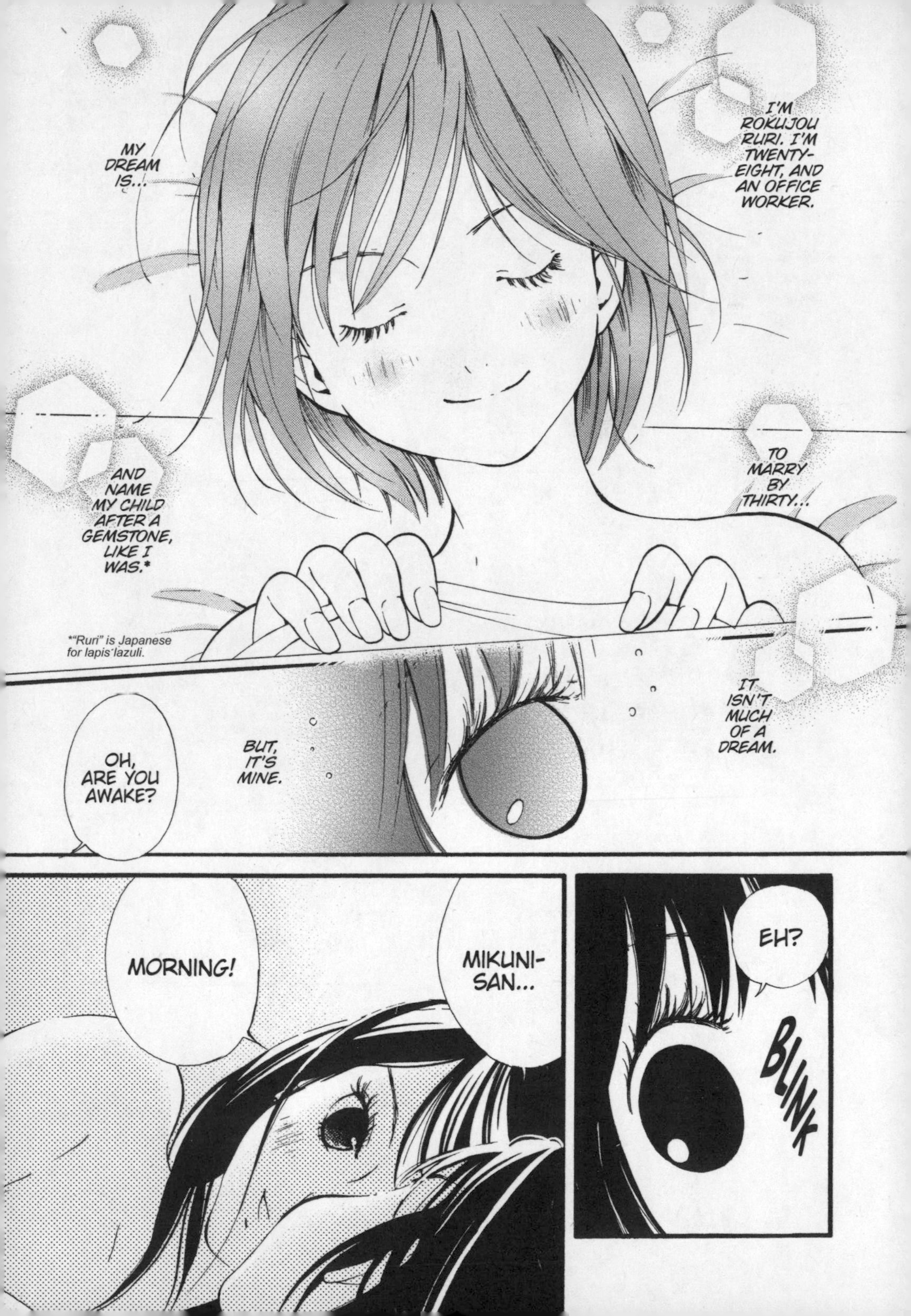
I'M ROKUJOU RURI. I'M TWENTY-EIGHT, AND AN OFFICE WORKER.
MY DREAM IS...
TO MARRY BY THIRTY...
AND NAME MY CHILD AFTER A GEMSTONE, LIKE I WAS.*
IT ISN'T MUCH OF A DREAM.
BUT, IT'S MINE.
OH, ARE YOU AWAKE?
EH?
BLINK
MIKUNI-SAN...
MORNING!

*"Ruri" is Japanese for lapis lazuli.

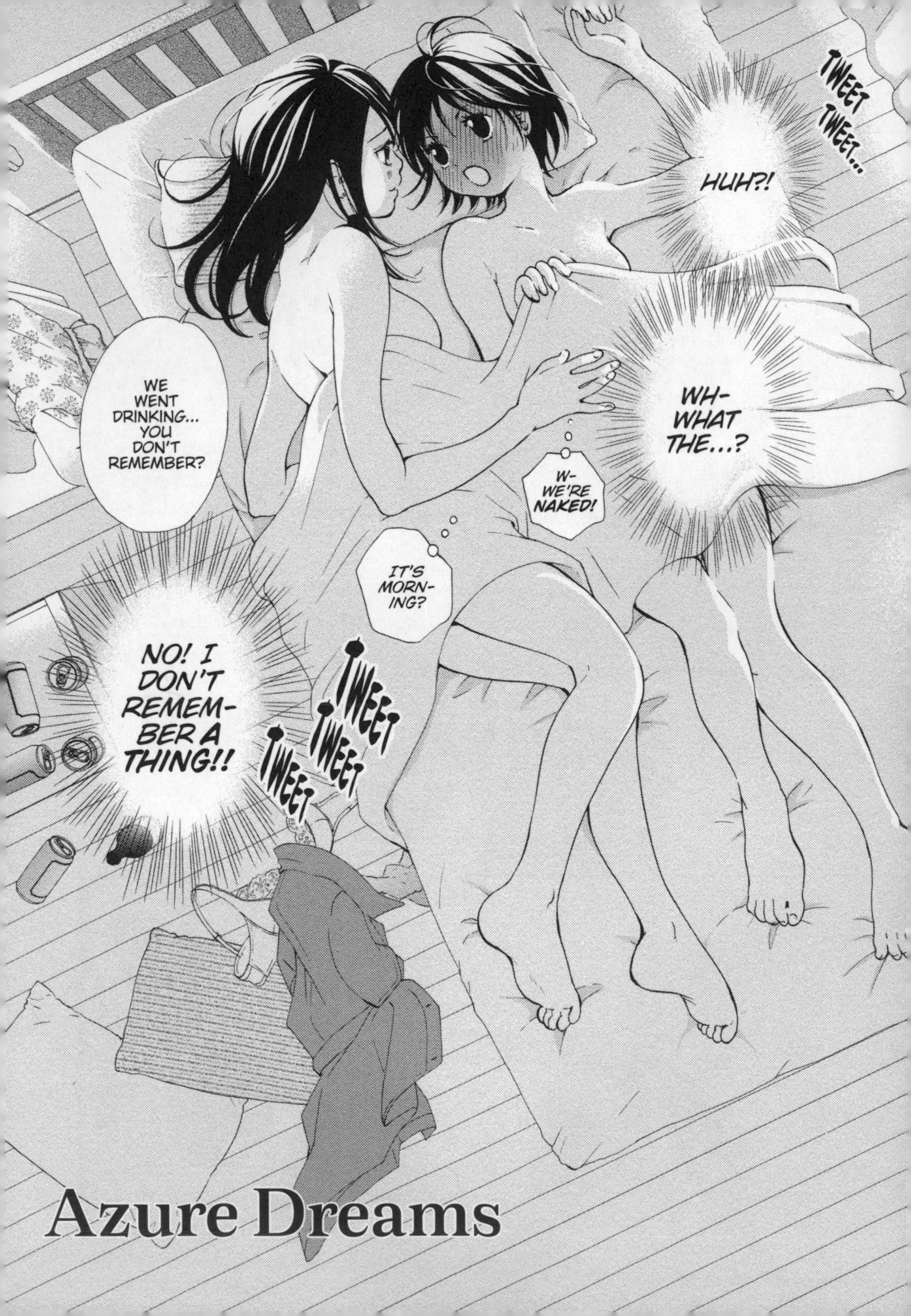
TWEET TWEET...
HUH?!
WH-WHAT THE...?
W-WE'RE NAKED!
IT'S MORNING?
WE WENT DRINKING... YOU DON'T REMEMBER?
TWEET TWEET TWEET
NO! I DON'T REMEMBER A THING!!

Azure Dreams

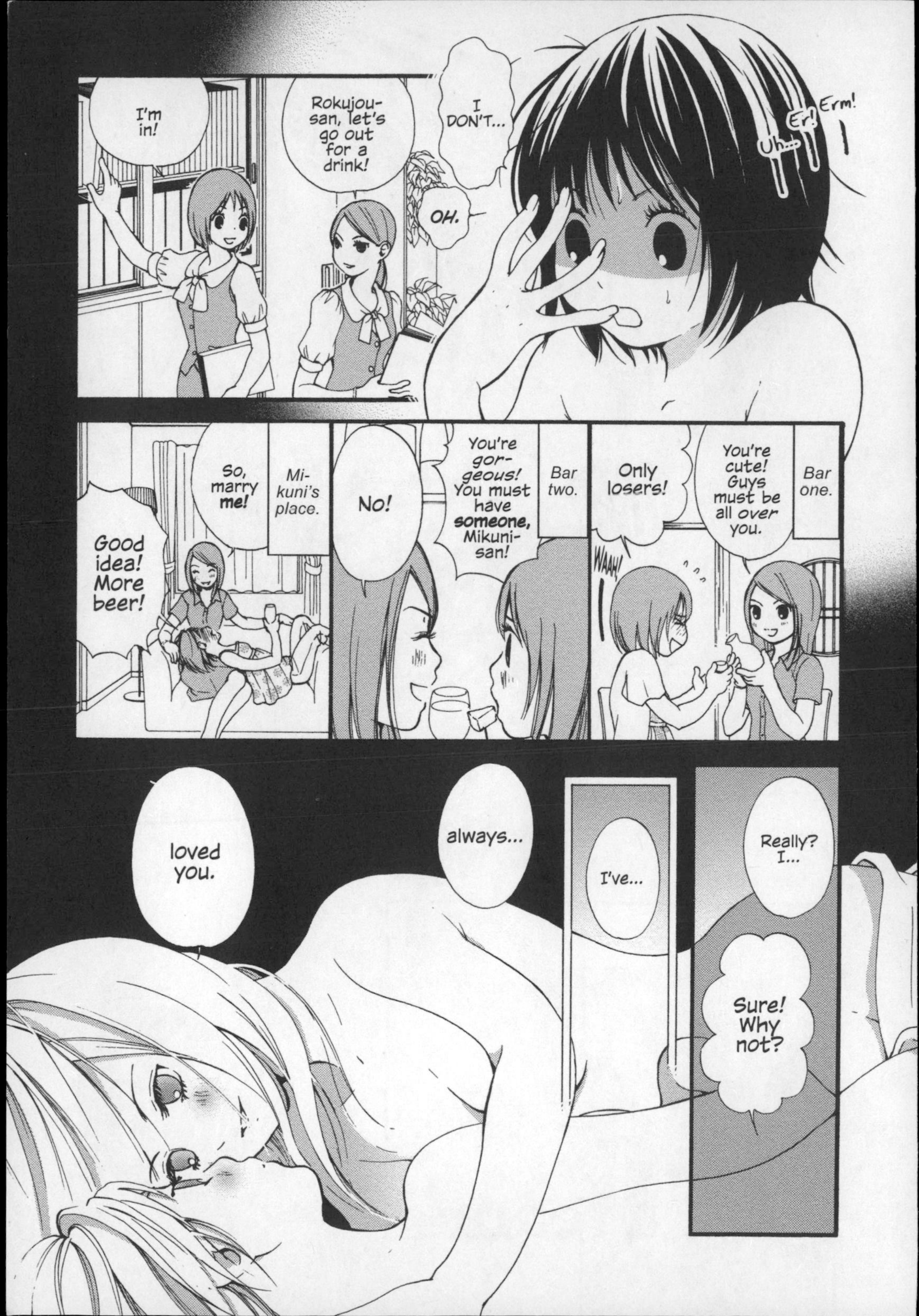
Erm!
Er!
Uh...
I DON'T...
Rokujou-san, let's go out for a drink!
OH.
I'm in!
Bar one.
You're cute! Guys must be all *over* you.
Only losers!
WAAH!
Bar two.
You're *gorgeous!* You must have **someone,** Mikuni-san!
No!
Mikuni's place.
So, marry **me!**
Good idea! More beer!
Really? I...
I've...
always...
loved you.
Sure! Why not?

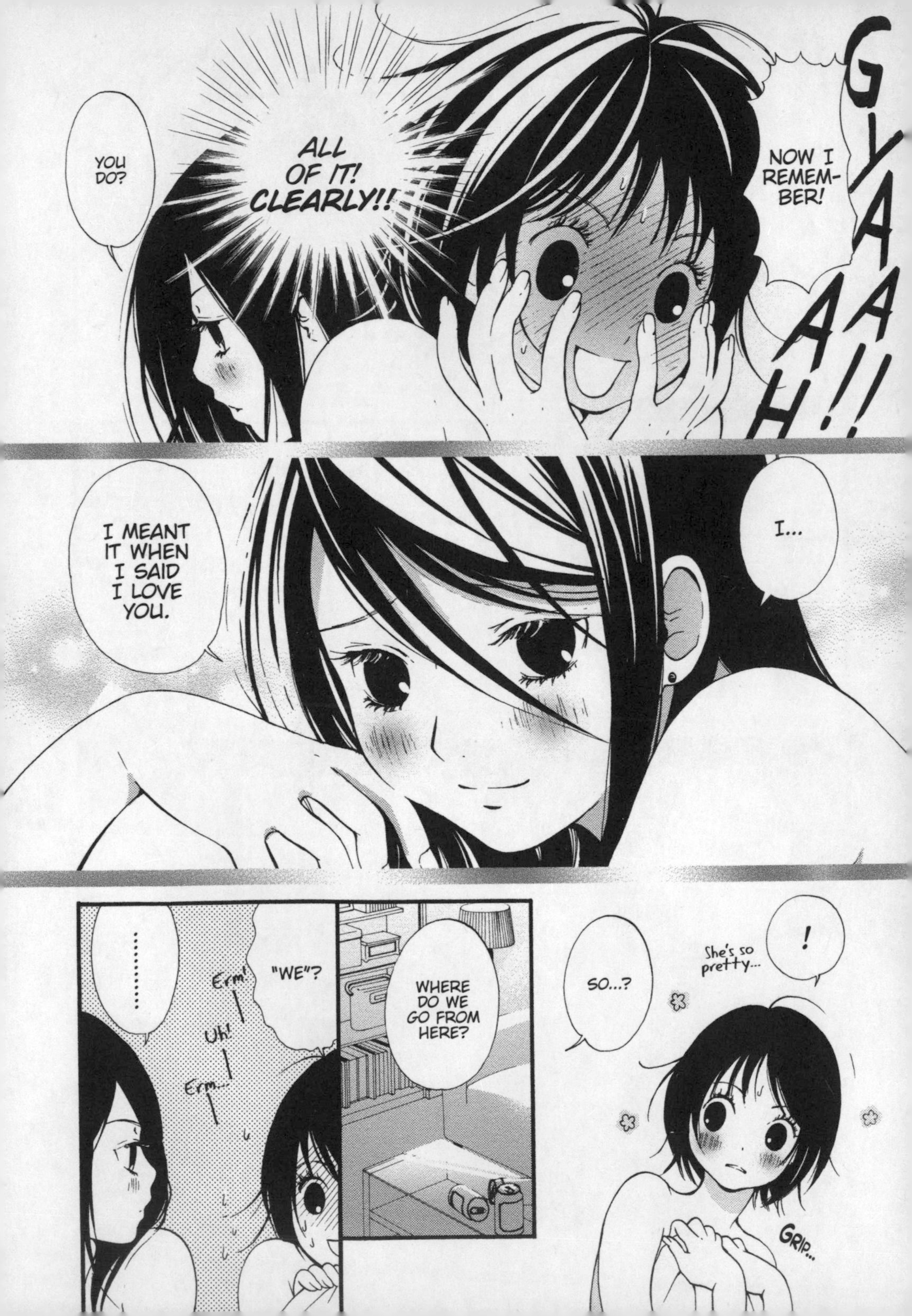
GYAAAAH!!
NOW I REMEMBER!
ALL OF IT! CLEARLY!!
YOU DO?
I...
I MEANT IT WHEN I SAID I LOVE YOU.
!
She's so pretty...
SO...?
GRIP...
WHERE DO WE GO FROM HERE?
"WE"?
Erm!
Uh!
Erm...
....

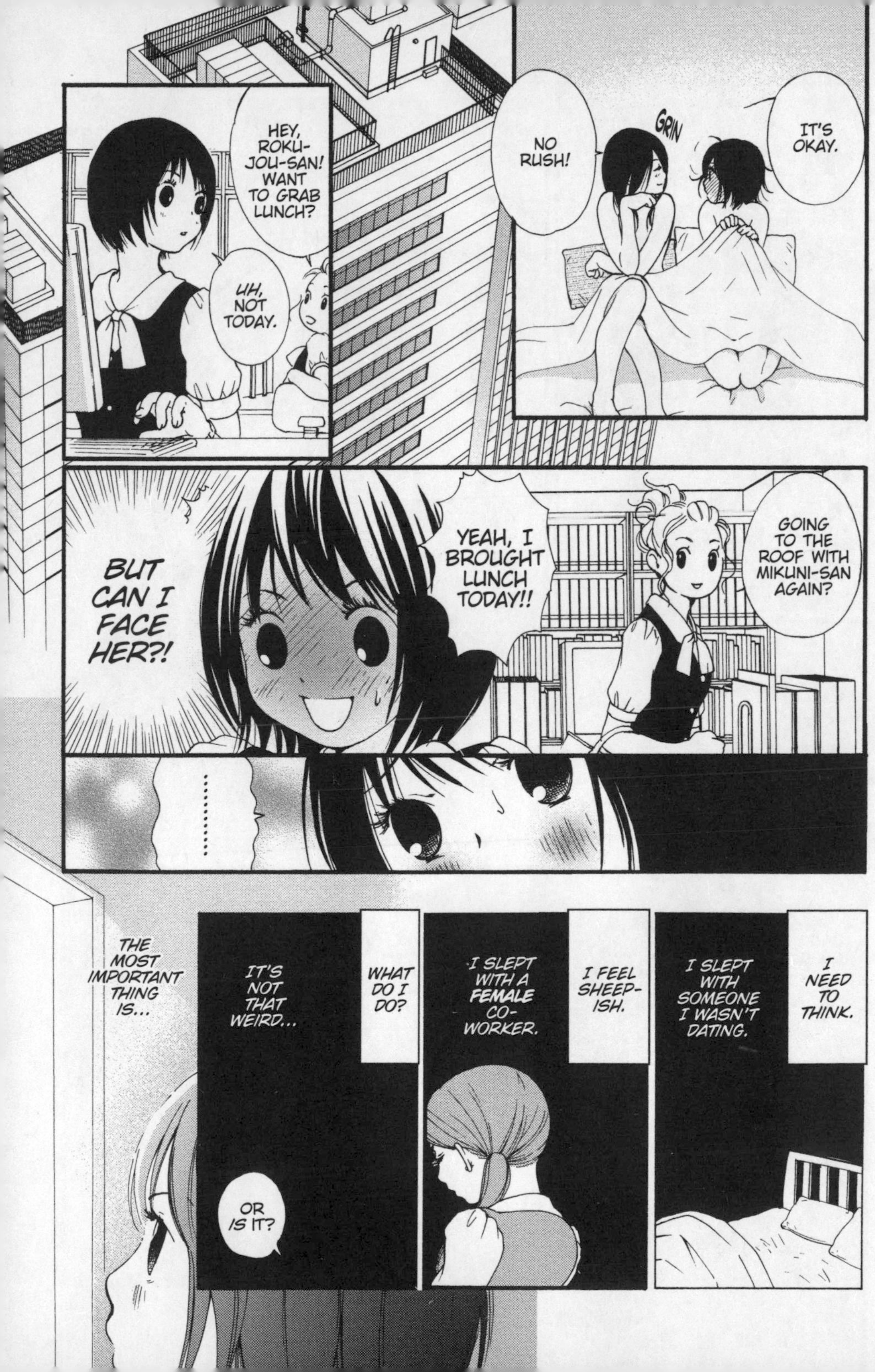
IT'S OKAY.
GRIN
NO RUSH!
HEY, ROKU-JOU-SAN! WANT TO GRAB LUNCH?
UH, NOT TODAY.
GOING TO THE ROOF WITH MIKUNI-SAN AGAIN?
YEAH, I BROUGHT LUNCH TODAY!!
BUT CAN I FACE HER?!
......
I NEED TO THINK.
I SLEPT WITH SOMEONE I WASN'T DATING.
I FEEL SHEEP-ISH.
I SLEPT WITH A FEMALE CO-WORKER.
WHAT DO I DO?
IT'S NOT THAT WEIRD...
OR IS IT?
THE MOST IMPORTANT THING IS...

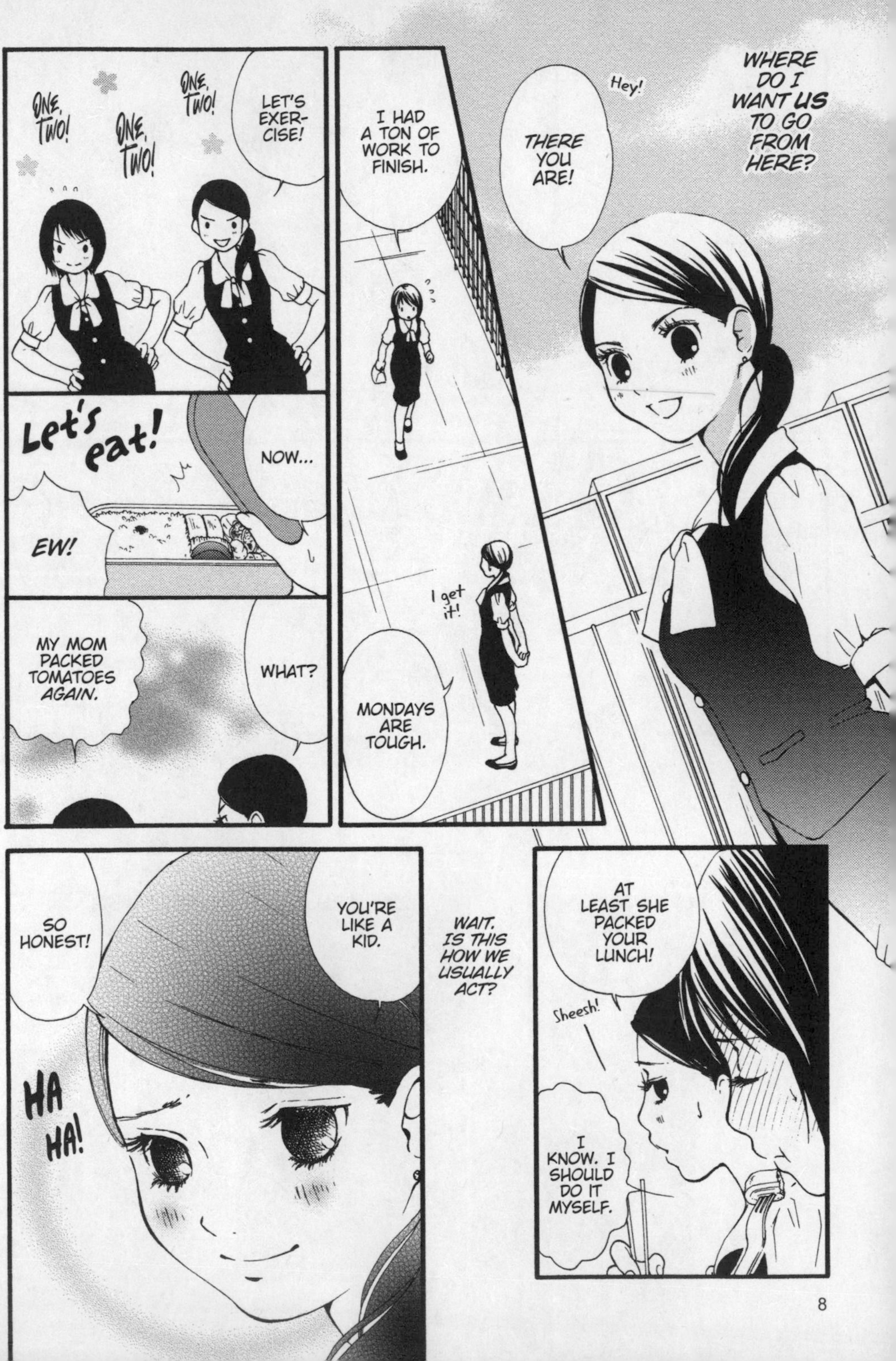
WHERE DO I WANT US TO GO FROM HERE?
Hey!
THERE YOU ARE!
I HAD A TON OF WORK TO FINISH.
I get it!
MONDAYS ARE TOUGH.
LET'S EXERCISE!
ONE, TWO!
ONE, TWO!
ONE, TWO!
NOW...
Let's eat!
EW!
WHAT?
MY MOM PACKED TOMATOES AGAIN.
AT LEAST SHE PACKED YOUR LUNCH!
Sheesh!
I KNOW. I SHOULD DO IT MYSELF.
WAIT. IS THIS HOW WE USUALLY ACT?
YOU'RE LIKE A KID.
SO HONEST!
HA HA!

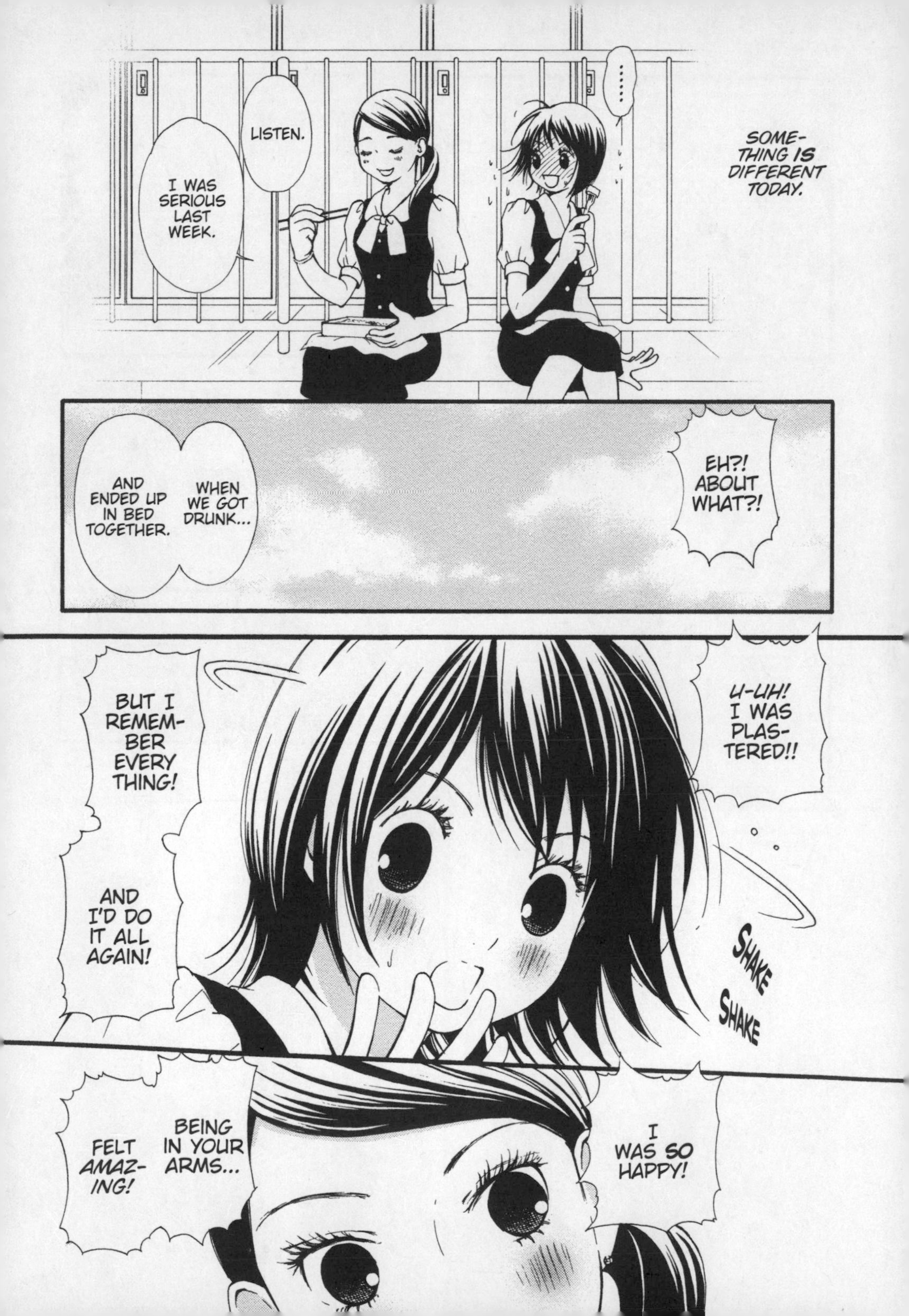
SOMETHING IS DIFFERENT TODAY.
......
LISTEN.
I WAS SERIOUS LAST WEEK.
EH?! ABOUT WHAT?!
WHEN WE GOT DRUNK...
AND ENDED UP IN BED TOGETHER.
U-UH! I WAS PLASTERED!!
BUT I REMEMBER EVERY THING!
AND I'D DO IT ALL AGAIN!
SHAKE
SHAKE
I WAS SO HAPPY!
BEING IN YOUR ARMS...
FELT AMAZING!

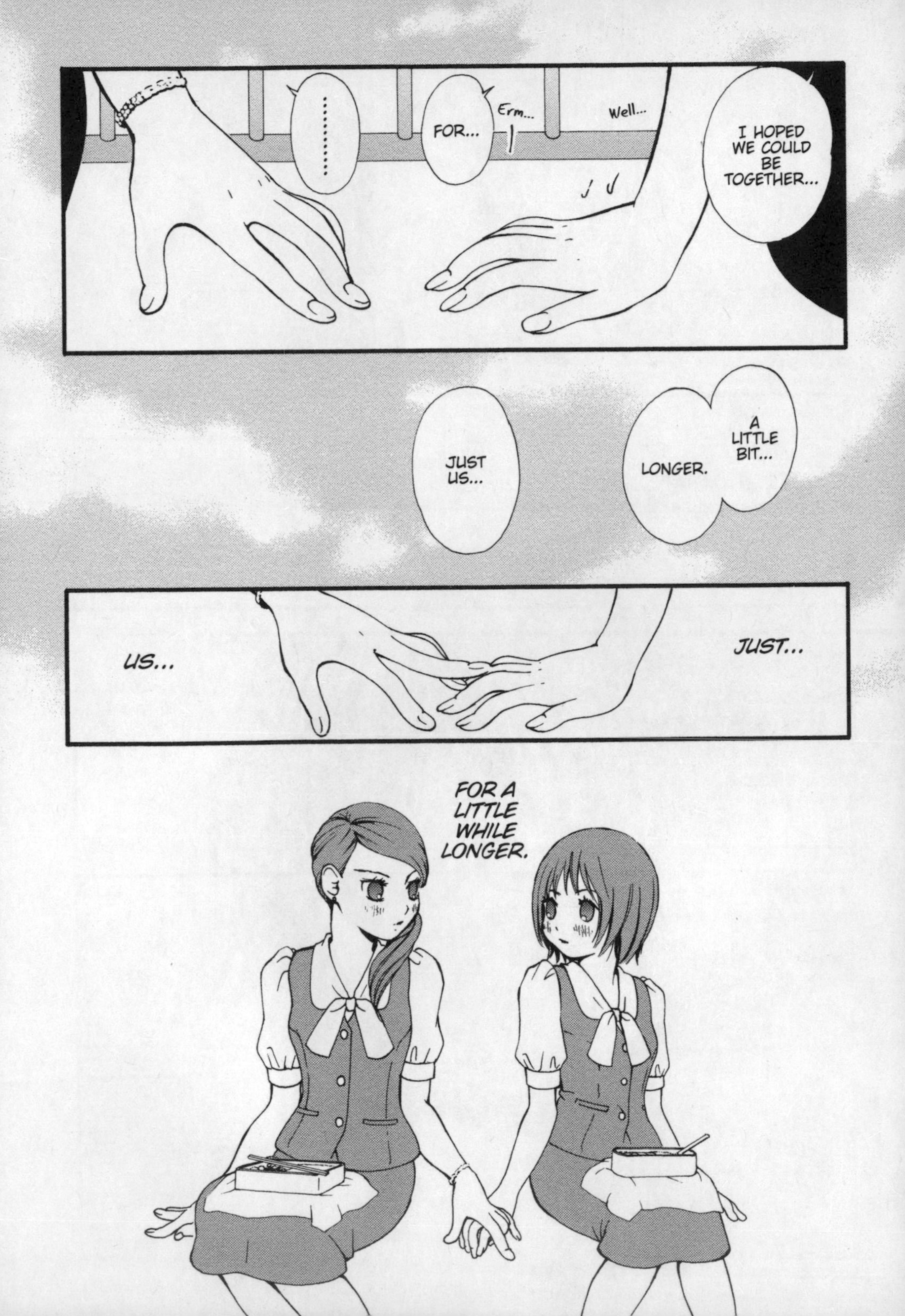
I HOPED WE COULD BE TOGETHER...
Well...
Erm...
FOR...
......
A LITTLE BIT...
LONGER.
JUST US...
JUST...
US...
FOR A LITTLE WHILE LONGER.

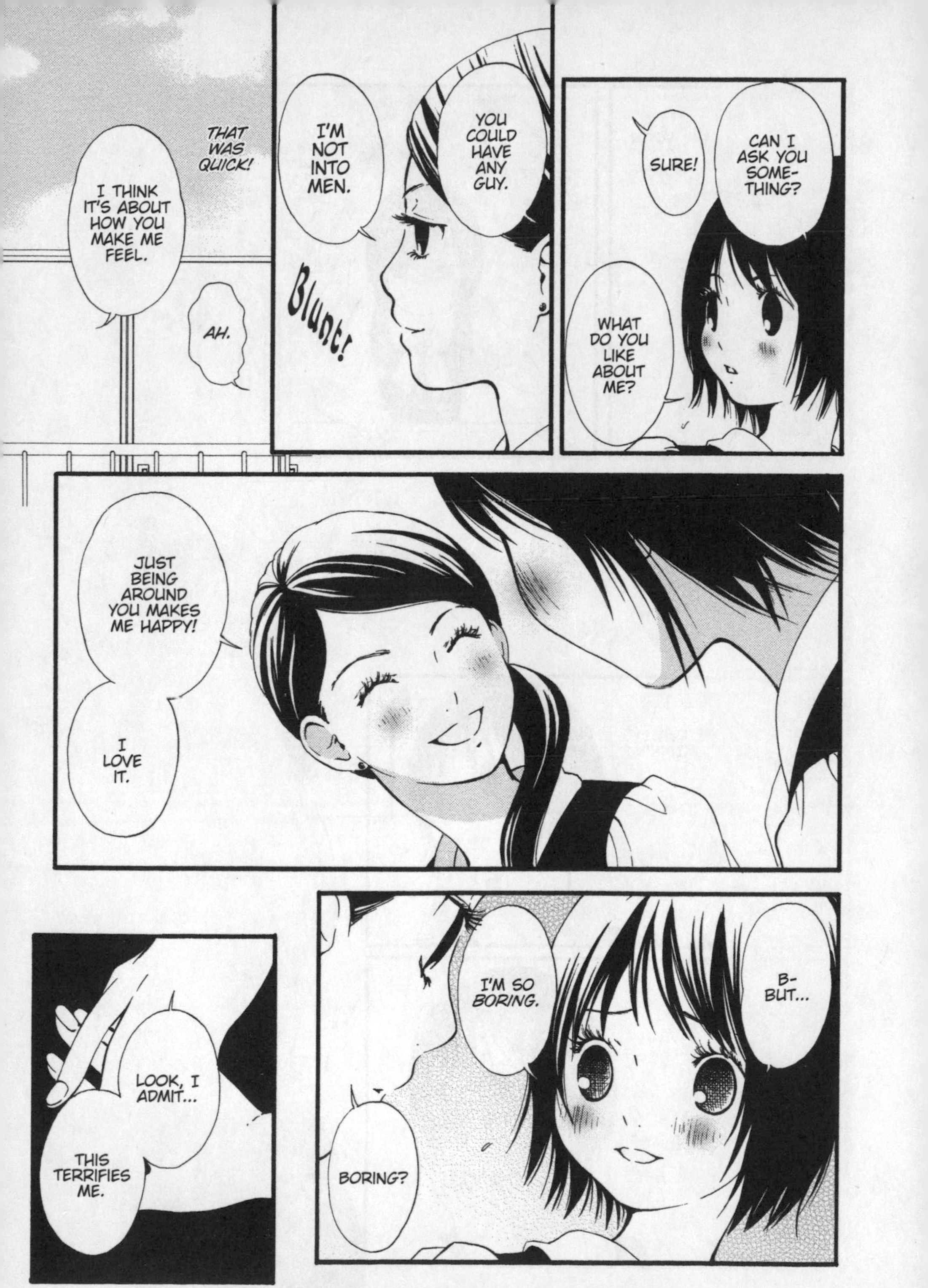
CAN I ASK YOU SOMETHING?
SURE!
WHAT DO YOU LIKE ABOUT ME?
YOU COULD HAVE ANY GUY.
I'M NOT INTO MEN.
Blunt!
THAT WAS QUICK!
I THINK IT'S ABOUT HOW YOU MAKE ME FEEL.
AH.
JUST BEING AROUND YOU MAKES ME HAPPY!
I LOVE IT.
B-BUT...
I'M SO BORING.
BORING?
LOOK, I ADMIT...
THIS TERRIFIES ME.

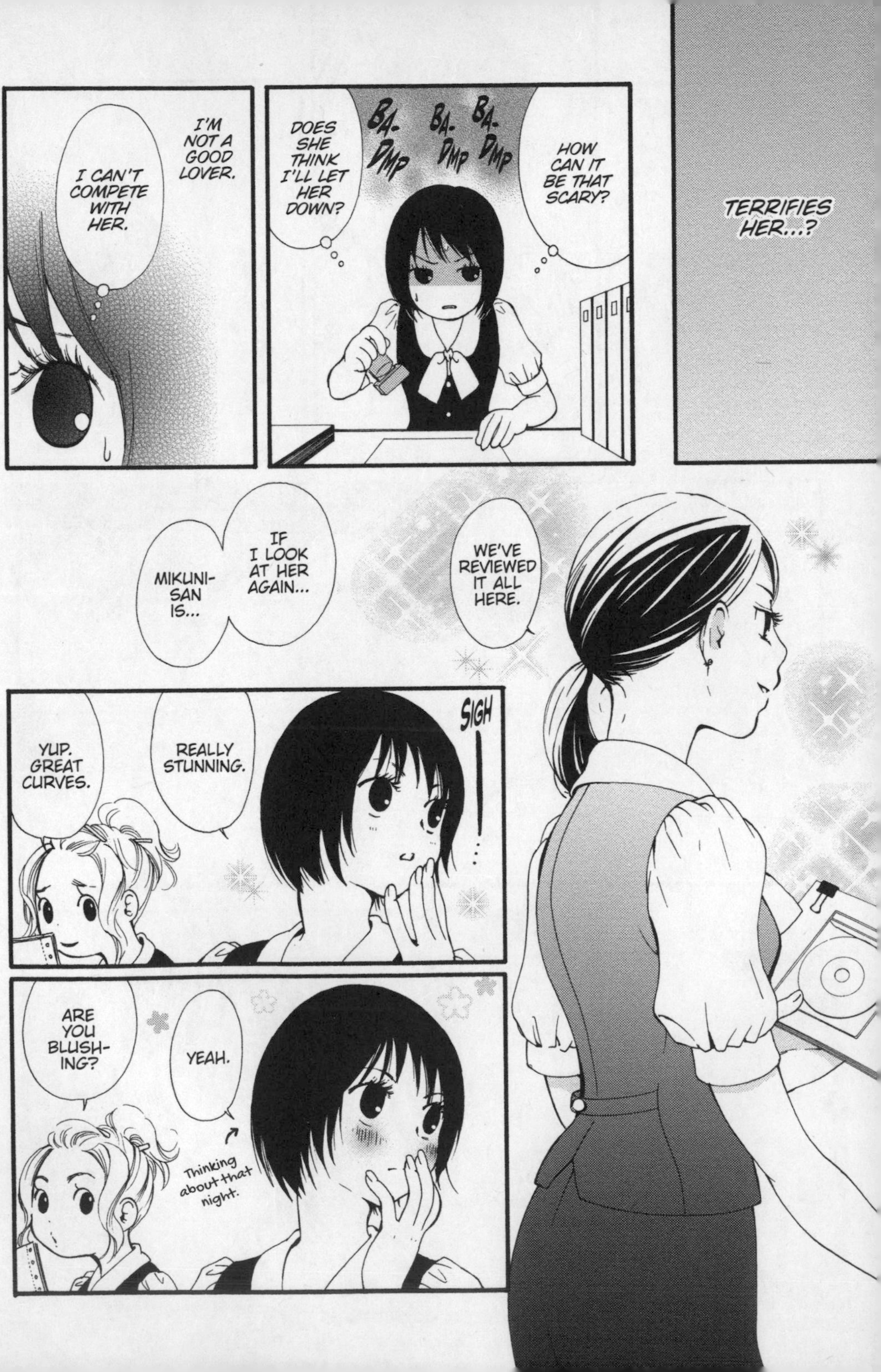
TERRIFIES HER...?
HOW CAN IT BE THAT SCARY?
BA-DMP BA-DMP BA-DMP
DOES SHE THINK I'LL LET HER DOWN?
I'M NOT A GOOD LOVER.
I CAN'T COMPETE WITH HER.
WE'VE REVIEWED IT ALL HERE.
IF I LOOK AT HER AGAIN...
MIKUNI-SAN IS...
SIGH
REALLY STUNNING.
YUP. GREAT CURVES.
YEAH.
ARE YOU BLUSHING?
Thinking about that night.

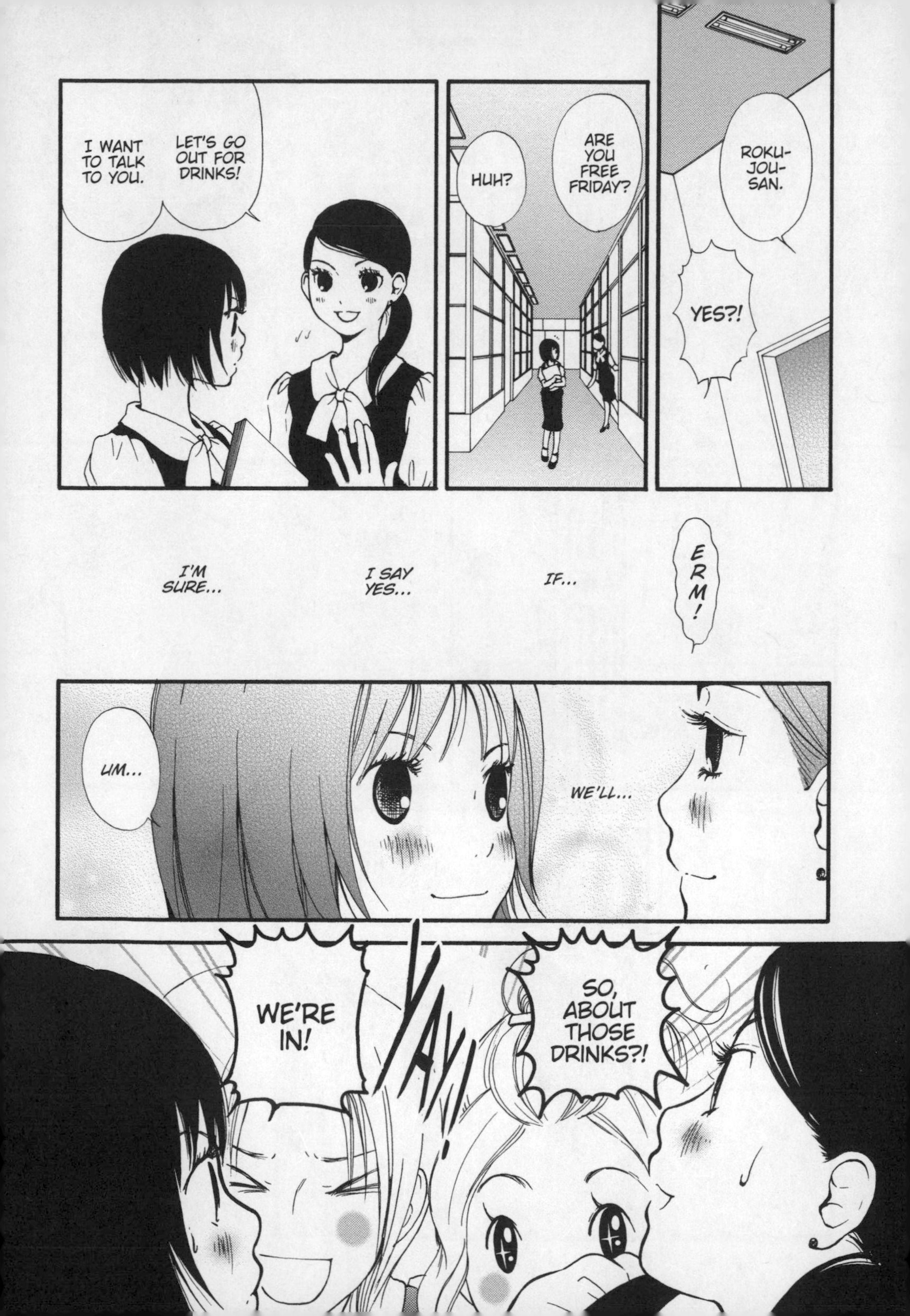
ROKU-JOU-SAN.
YES?!
ARE YOU FREE FRIDAY?
HUH?
LET'S GO OUT FOR DRINKS!
I WANT TO TALK TO YOU.
ERM!
IF...
I SAY YES...
I'M SURE...
WE'LL...
UM...
SO, ABOUT THOSE DRINKS?!
YAY!
WE'RE IN!

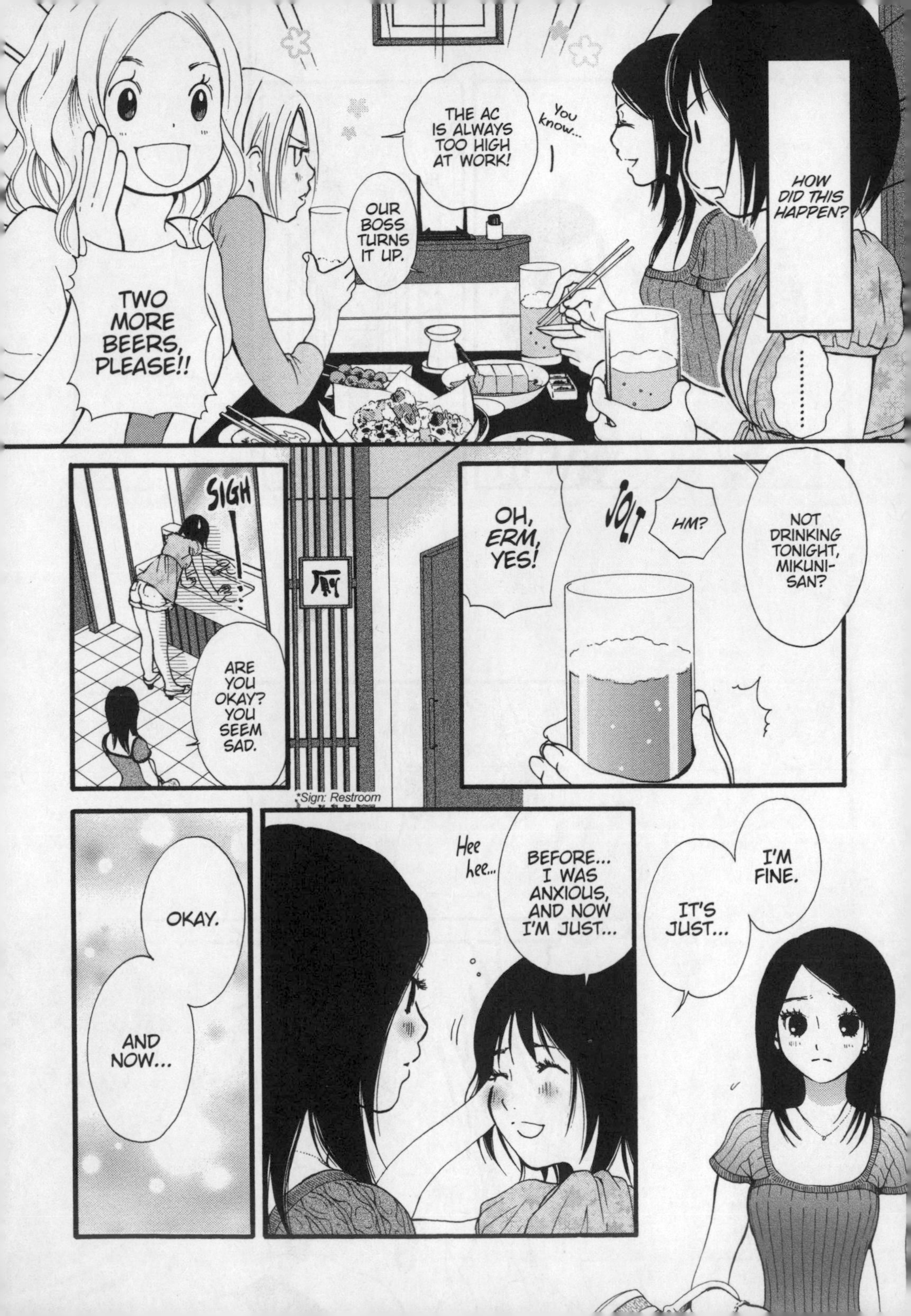
HOW DID THIS HAPPEN?
......
You know...
THE AC IS ALWAYS TOO HIGH AT WORK!
OUR BOSS TURNS IT UP.
TWO MORE BEERS, PLEASE!!
NOT DRINKING TONIGHT, MIKUNI-SAN?
HM?
JOLT
OH, ERM, YES!
SIGH
ARE YOU OKAY? YOU SEEM SAD.
*Sign: Restroom
I'M FINE.
IT'S JUST...
BEFORE... I WAS ANXIOUS, AND NOW I'M JUST...
Hee hee...
OKAY.
AND NOW...

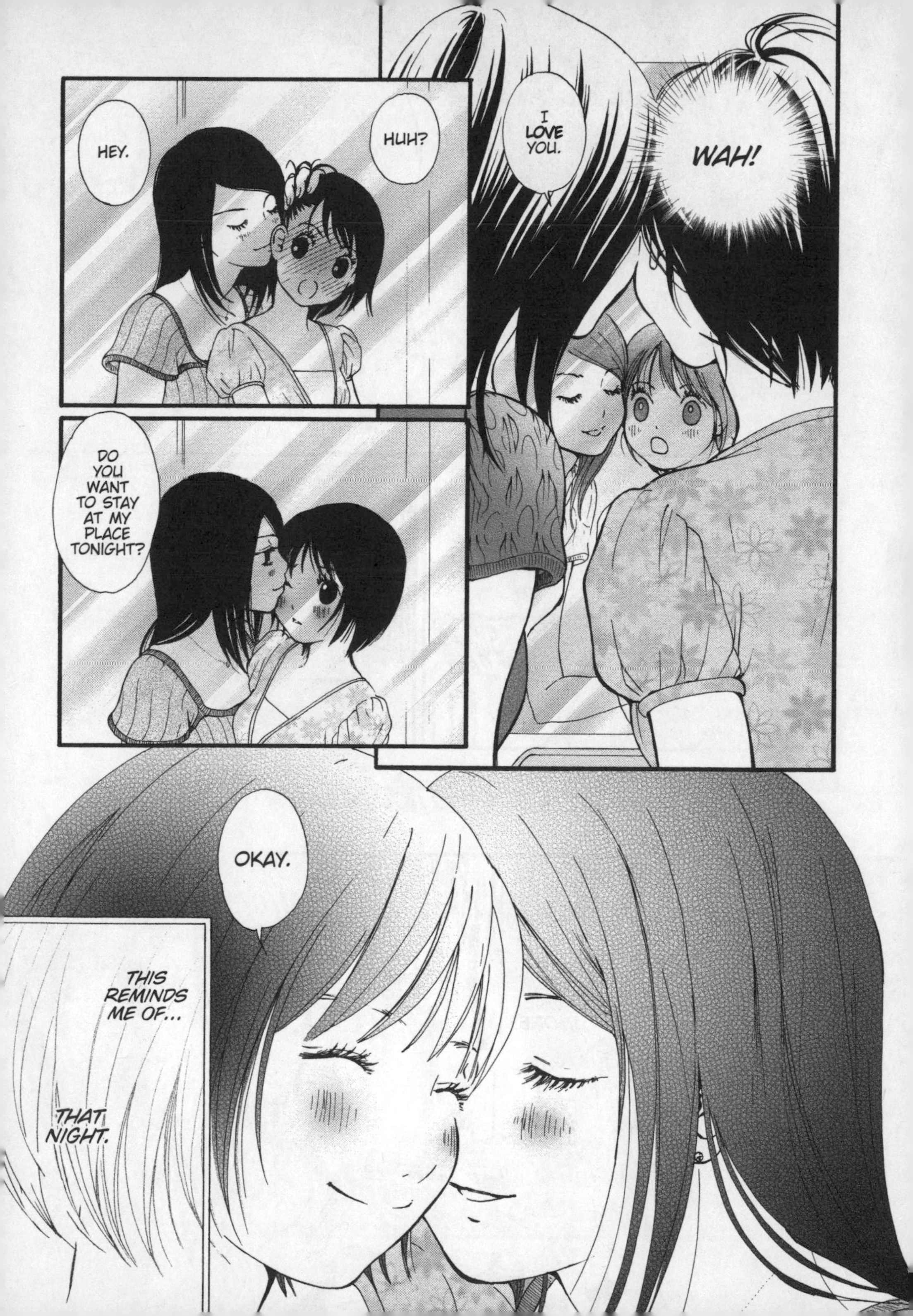
HEY.
HUH?
I LOVE YOU.
WAH!
DO YOU WANT TO STAY AT MY PLACE TONIGHT?
OKAY.
THIS REMINDS ME OF...
THAT NIGHT.

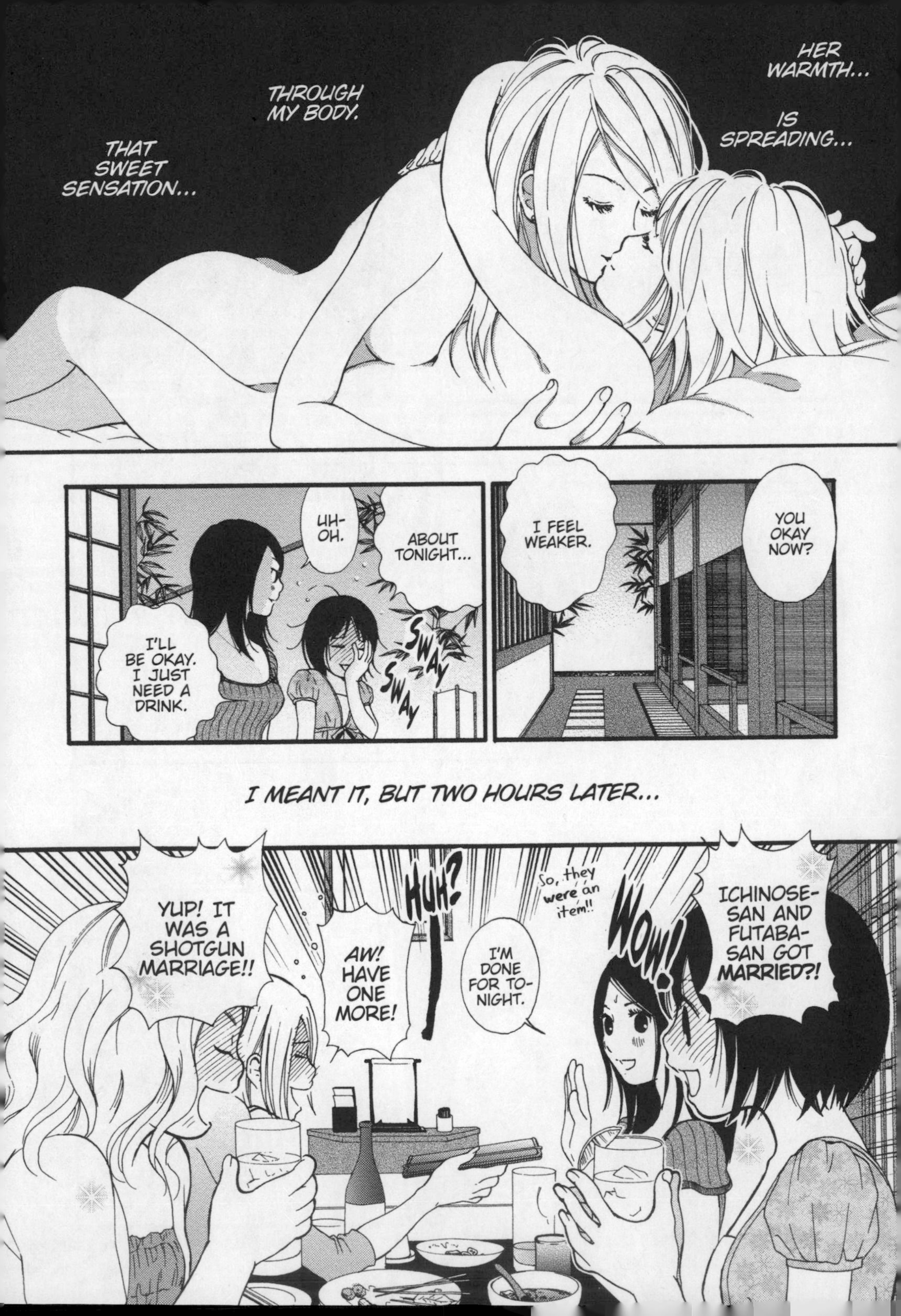
HER WARMTH...
IS SPREADING...
THROUGH MY BODY.
THAT SWEET SENSATION...
YOU OKAY NOW?
I FEEL WEAKER.
ABOUT TONIGHT...
UH-OH.
I'LL BE OKAY. I JUST NEED A DRINK.
SWAY SWAY
I MEANT IT, BUT TWO HOURS LATER...
ICHINOSE-SAN AND FUTABA-SAN GOT MARRIED?!
WOW!!
So, they were an item!!
I'M DONE FOR TO-NIGHT.
HUH?
AW! HAVE ONE MORE!
YUP! IT WAS A SHOTGUN MARRIAGE!!

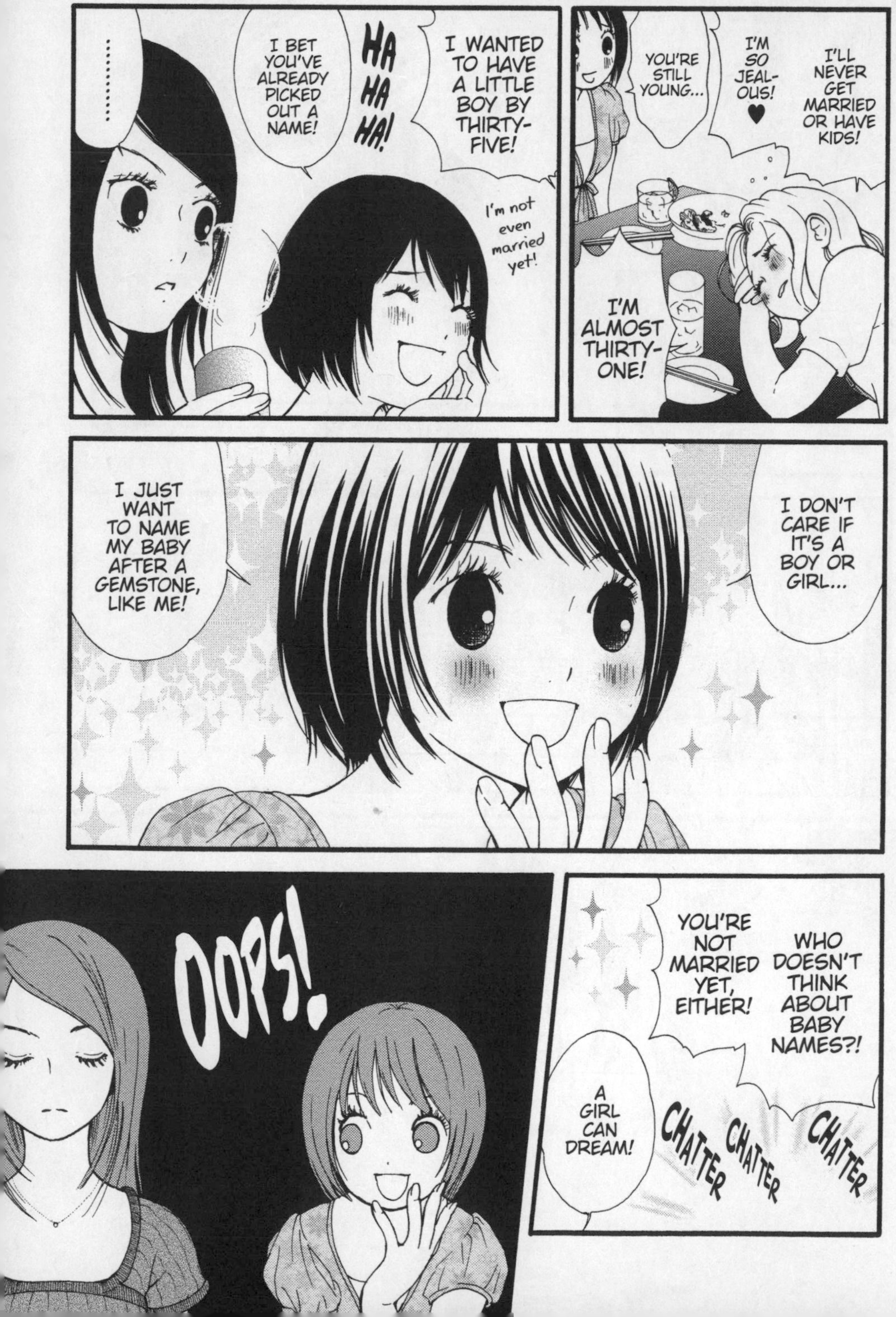
I'LL NEVER GET MARRIED OR HAVE KIDS!
I'M SO JEAL-OUS! ♥
YOU'RE STILL YOUNG...
I'M ALMOST THIRTY-ONE!
I WANTED TO HAVE A LITTLE BOY BY THIRTY-FIVE!
HA HA HA!
I BET YOU'VE ALREADY PICKED OUT A NAME!
......
I'm not even married yet!
I DON'T CARE IF IT'S A BOY OR GIRL...
I JUST WANT TO NAME MY BABY AFTER A GEMSTONE, LIKE ME!
WHO DOESN'T THINK ABOUT BABY NAMES?!
YOU'RE NOT MARRIED YET, EITHER!
CHATTER
CHATTER
CHATTER
A GIRL CAN DREAM!
OOPS!

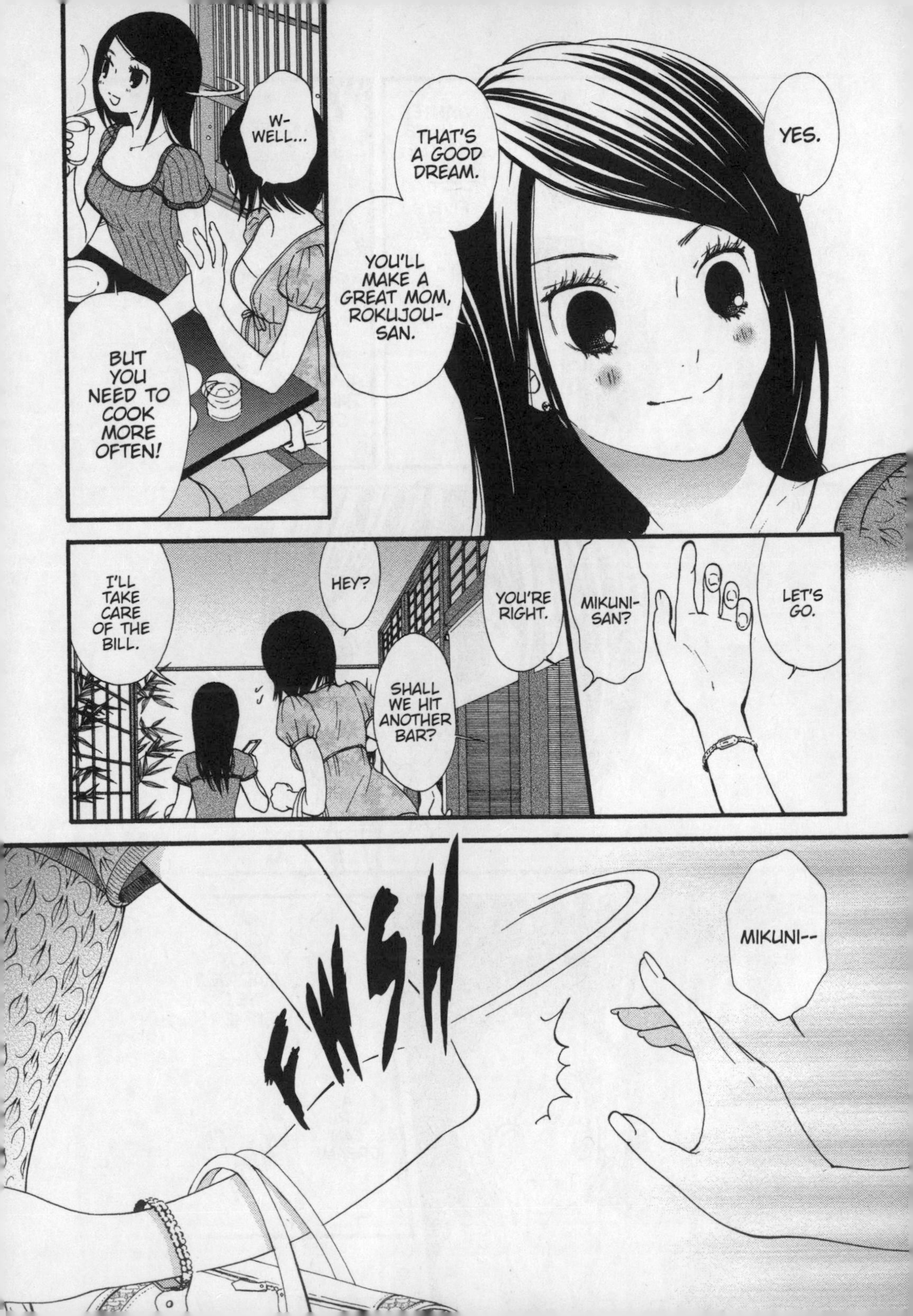
YES.
THAT'S A GOOD DREAM.
YOU'LL MAKE A GREAT MOM, ROKUJOU-SAN.
W-WELL...
BUT YOU NEED TO COOK MORE OFTEN!
LET'S GO.
MIKUNI-SAN?
YOU'RE RIGHT.
HEY?
SHALL WE HIT ANOTHER BAR?
I'LL TAKE CARE OF THE BILL.
MIKUNI--
FWSH

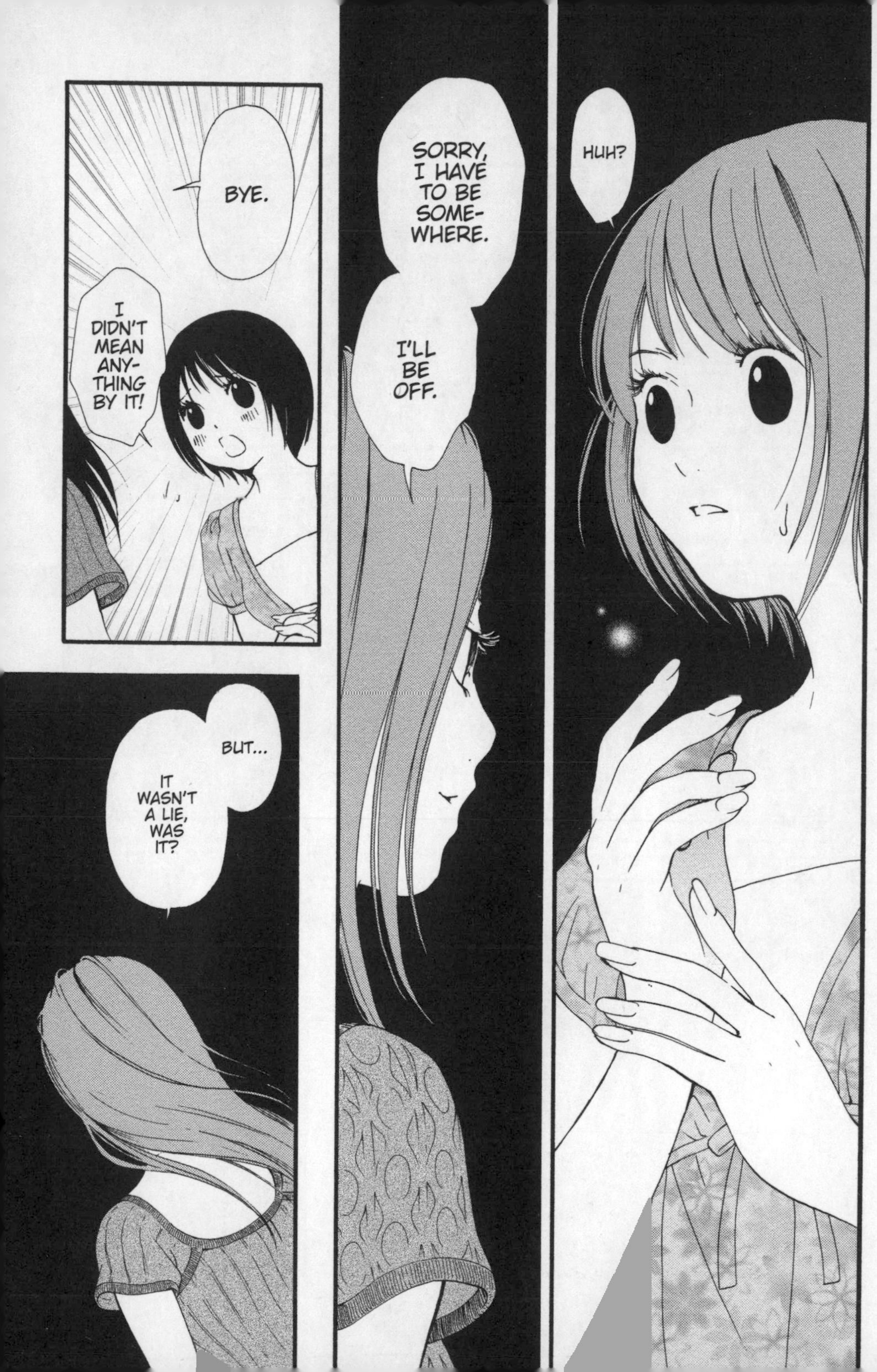
HUH?
SORRY, I HAVE TO BE SOME-WHERE.
I'LL BE OFF.
BYE.
I DIDN'T MEAN ANY-THING BY IT!
BUT...
IT WASN'T A LIE, WAS IT?

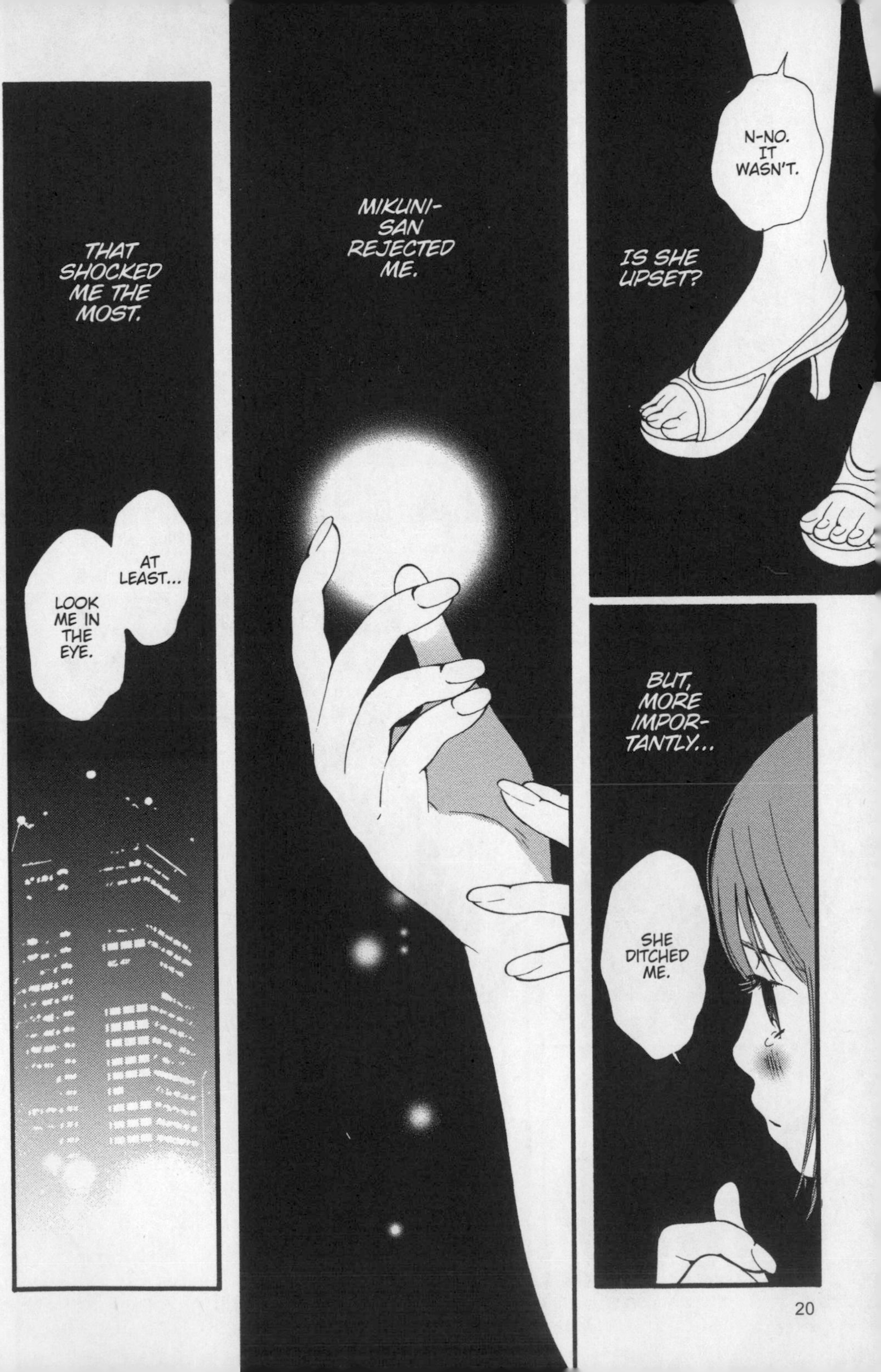
N-NO. IT WASN'T.
IS SHE UPSET?
BUT, MORE IMPORTANTLY...
SHE DITCHED ME.
MIKUNI-SAN REJECTED ME.
THAT SHOCKED ME THE MOST.
AT LEAST...
LOOK ME IN THE EYE.

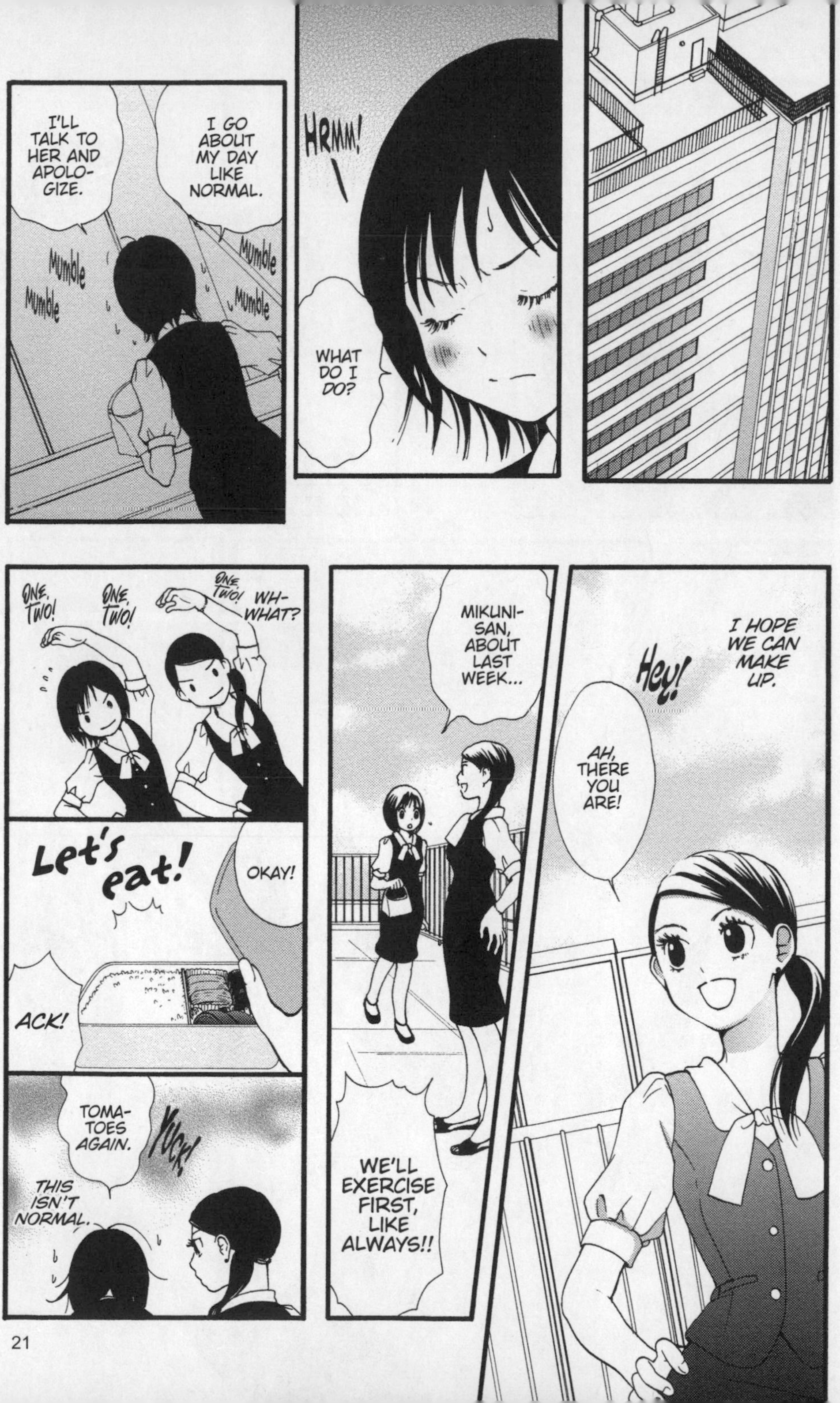
HRMM!
WHAT DO I DO?
I GO ABOUT MY DAY LIKE NORMAL.
I'LL TALK TO HER AND APOLO-GIZE.
Mumble
Mumble
Mumble
Mumble
I HOPE WE CAN MAKE UP.
Hey!
AH, THERE YOU ARE!
MIKUNI-SAN, ABOUT LAST WEEK...
WE'LL EXERCISE FIRST, LIKE ALWAYS!!
WH-WHAT?
ONE, TWO!
ONE, TWO!
ONE, TWO!
OKAY!
Let's eat!
ACK!
YUCK!
TOMA-TOES AGAIN.
THIS ISN'T NORMAL.

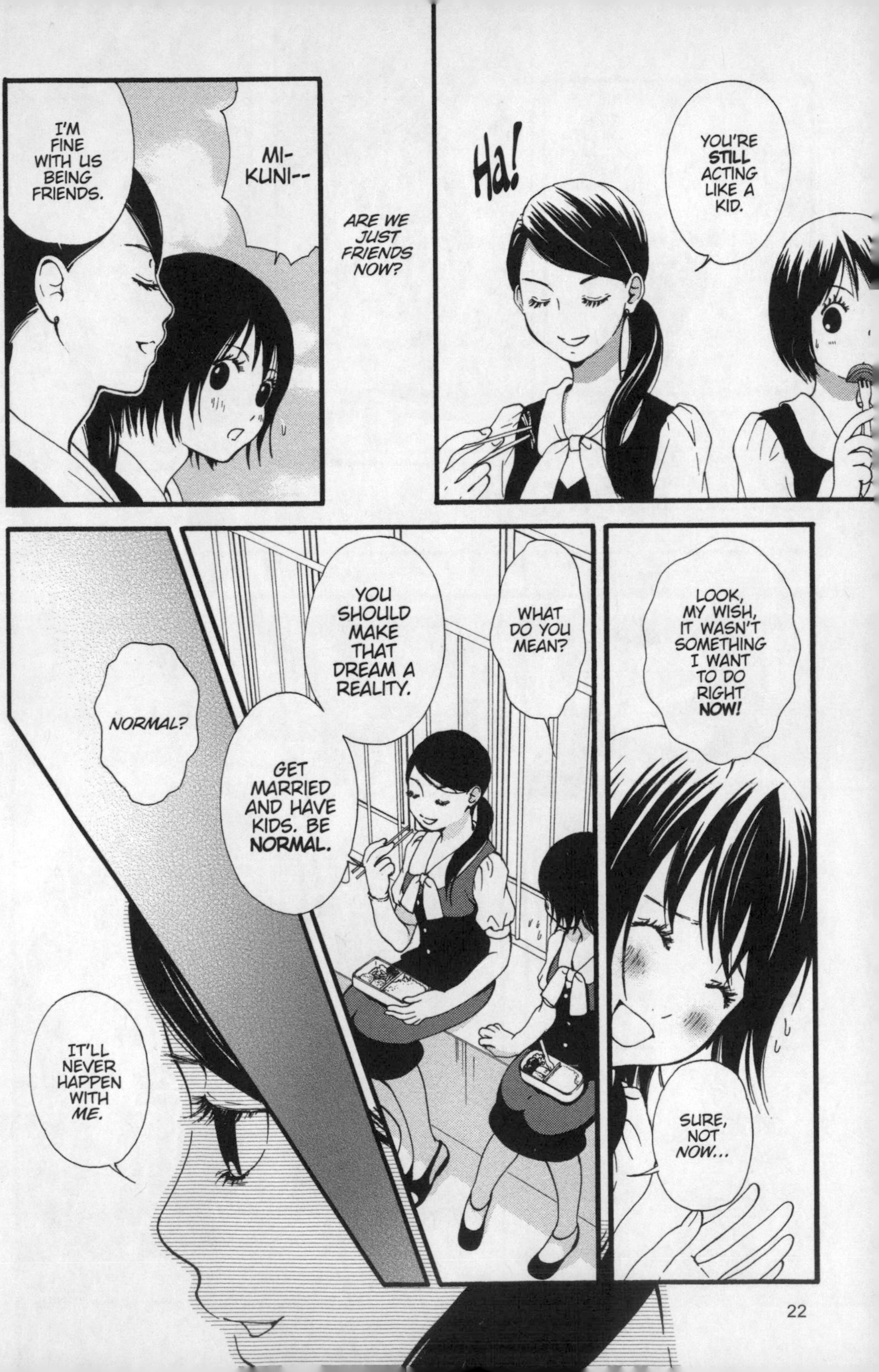
YOU'RE STILL ACTING LIKE A KID.
Ha!
MI-KUNI--
I'M FINE WITH US BEING FRIENDS.
ARE WE JUST FRIENDS NOW?
LOOK, MY WISH, IT WASN'T SOMETHING I WANT TO DO RIGHT NOW!
SURE, NOT NOW...
WHAT DO YOU MEAN?
YOU SHOULD MAKE THAT DREAM A REALITY.
GET MARRIED AND HAVE KIDS. BE NORMAL.
NORMAL?
IT'LL NEVER HAPPEN WITH ME.

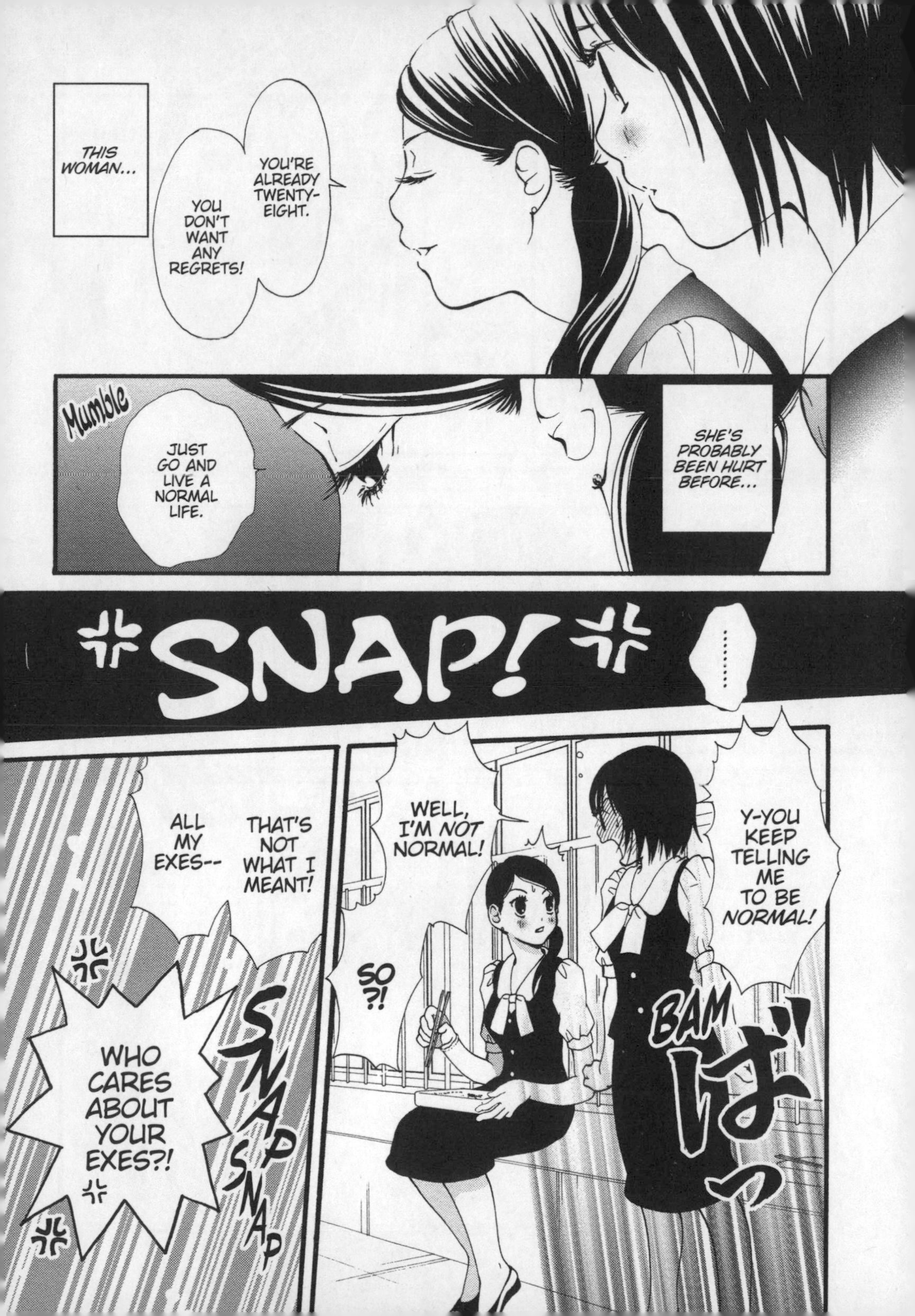
YOU'RE ALREADY TWENTY-EIGHT.
YOU DON'T WANT ANY REGRETS!
THIS WOMAN...
SHE'S PROBABLY BEEN HURT BEFORE...
Mumble
JUST GO AND LIVE A NORMAL LIFE.
......
SNAP!
Y-YOU KEEP TELLING ME TO BE NORMAL!
BAM
WELL, I'M NOT NORMAL!
SO?!
THAT'S NOT WHAT I MEANT!
ALL MY EXES--
WHO CARES ABOUT YOUR EXES?!
SNAP SNAP

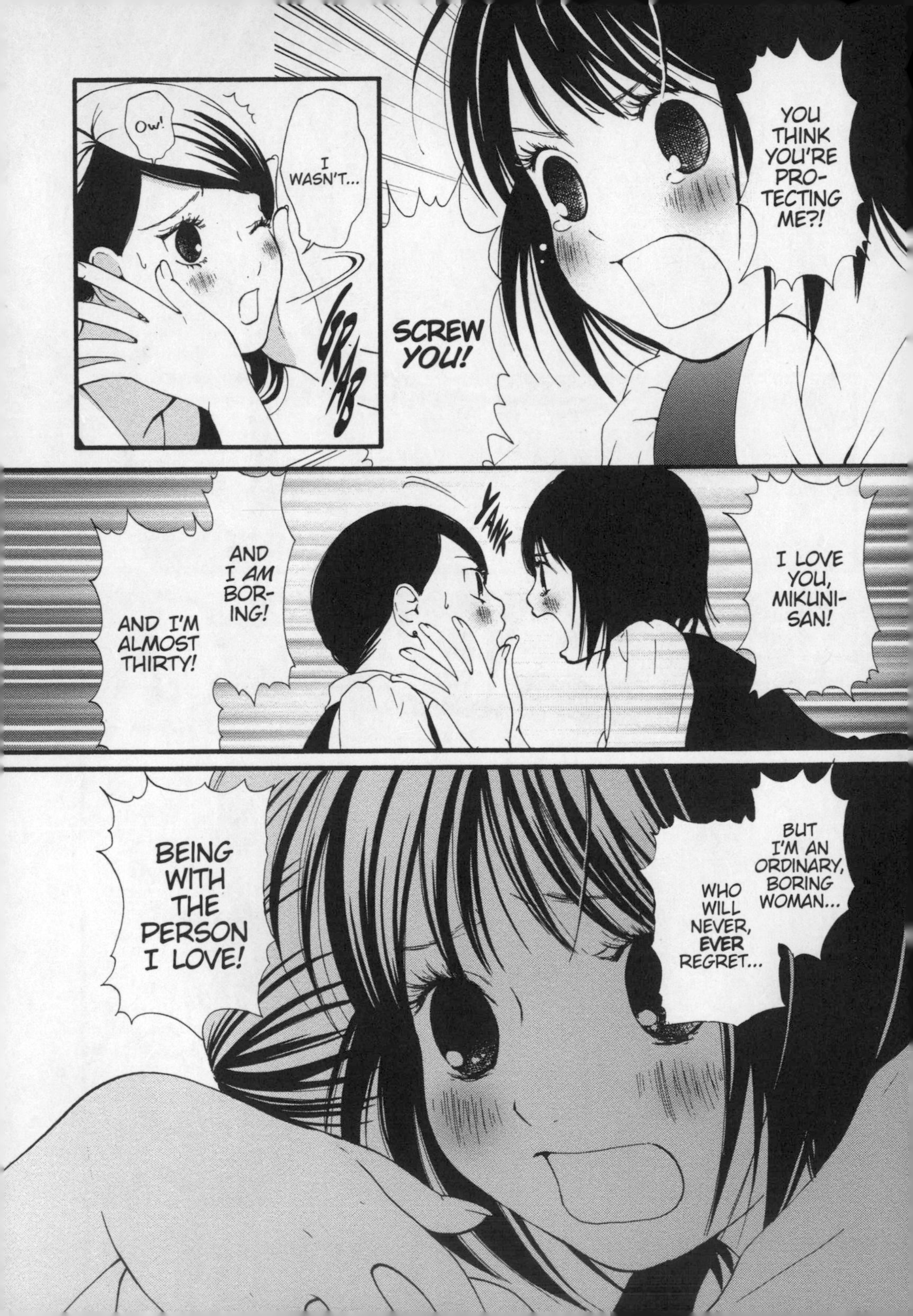
YOU THINK YOU'RE PRO-TECTING ME?!
SCREW YOU!
I WASN'T...
Ow!
GRAB
I LOVE YOU, MIKUNI-SAN!
YANK
AND I AM BOR-ING!
AND I'M ALMOST THIRTY!
BUT I'M AN ORDINARY, BORING WOMAN...
WHO WILL NEVER, EVER REGRET...
BEING WITH THE PERSON I LOVE!

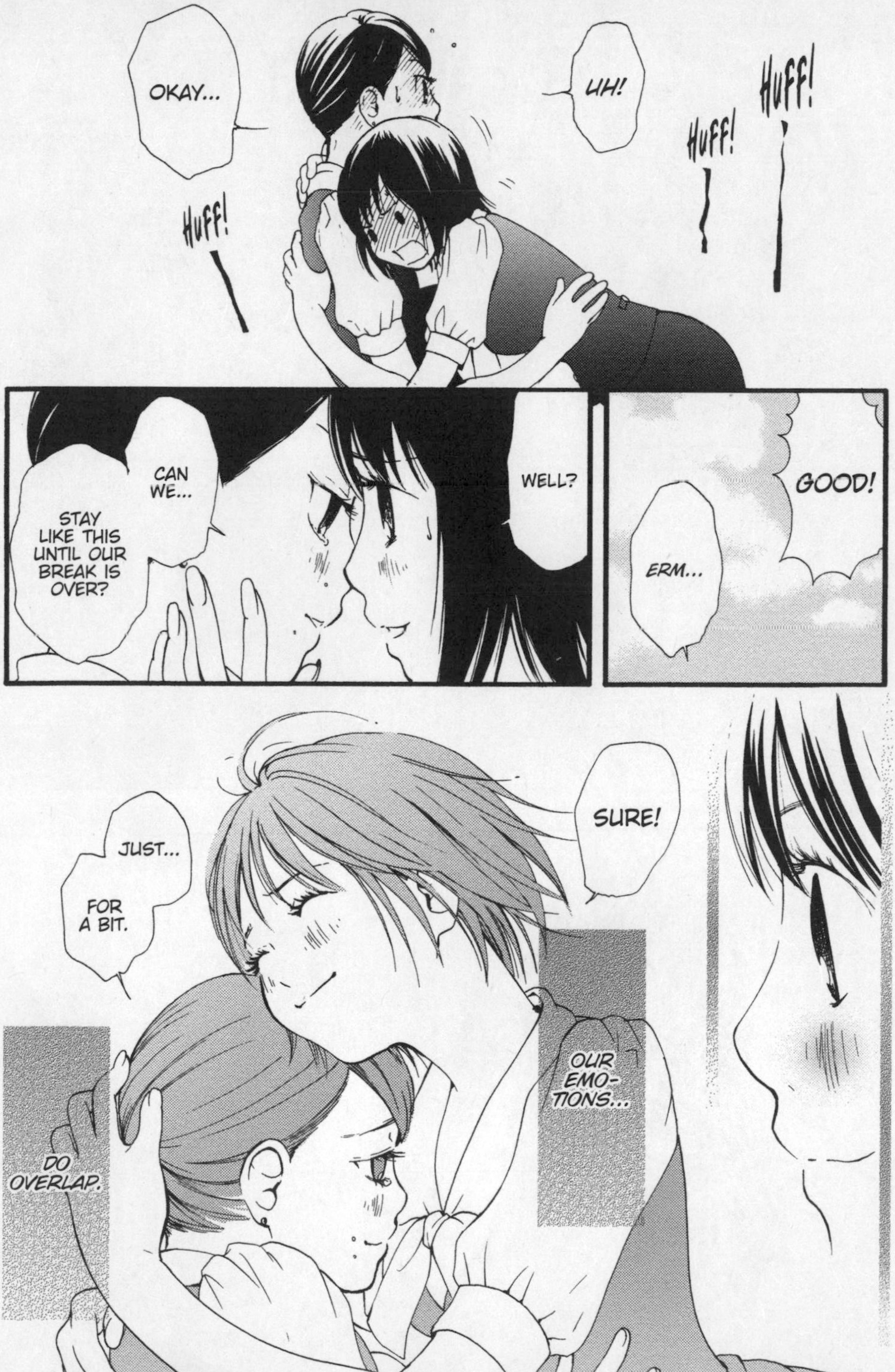
HUFF!
HUFF!
UH!
OKAY...
HUFF!
GOOD!
ERM...
WELL?
CAN WE...
STAY LIKE THIS UNTIL OUR BREAK IS OVER?
SURE!
JUST...
FOR A BIT.
OUR EMO-TIONS...
DO OVERLAP.

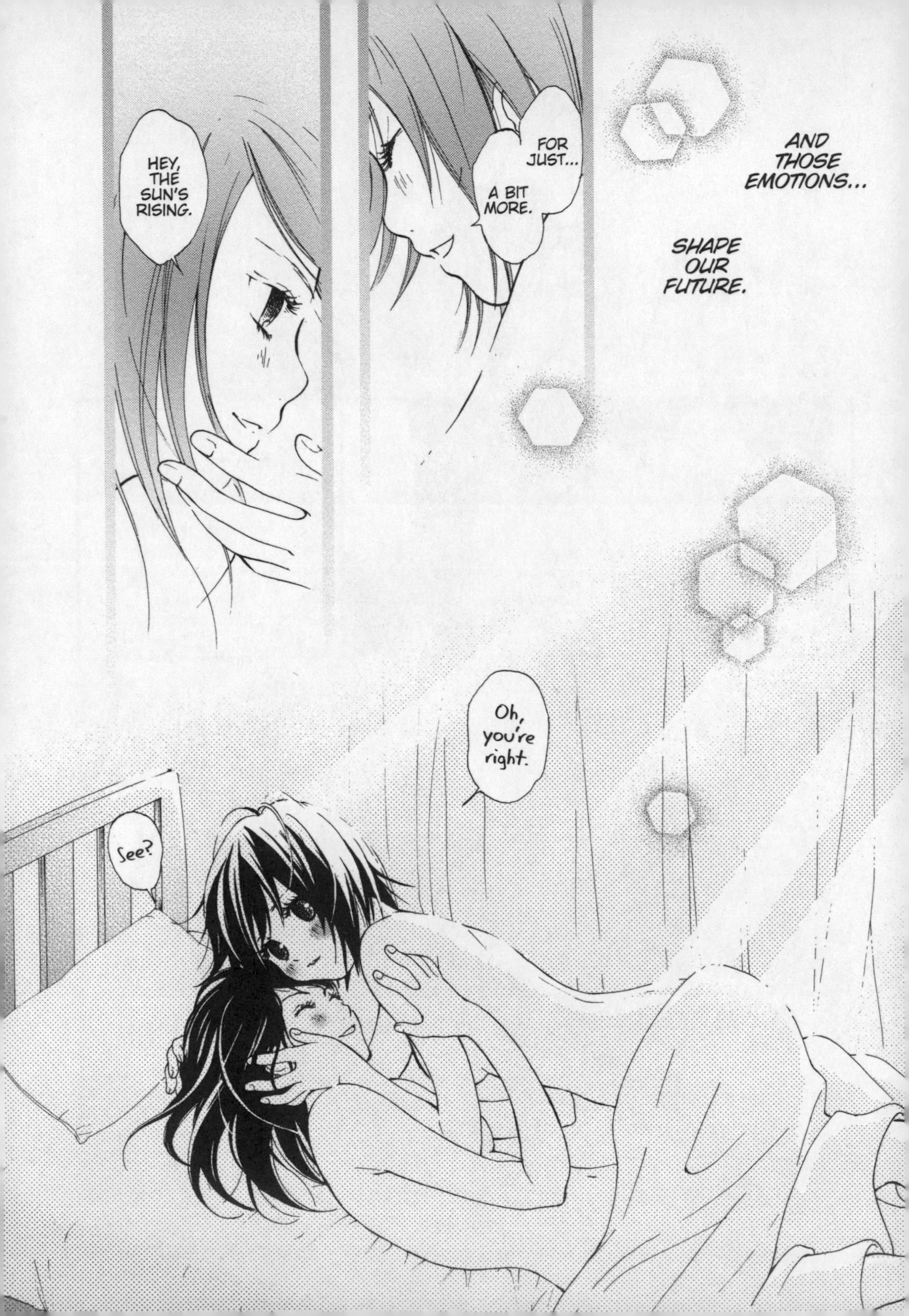
AND THOSE EMOTIONS...
SHAPE OUR FUTURE.
FOR JUST...
A BIT MORE.
HEY, THE SUN'S RISING.
Oh, you're right.
See?

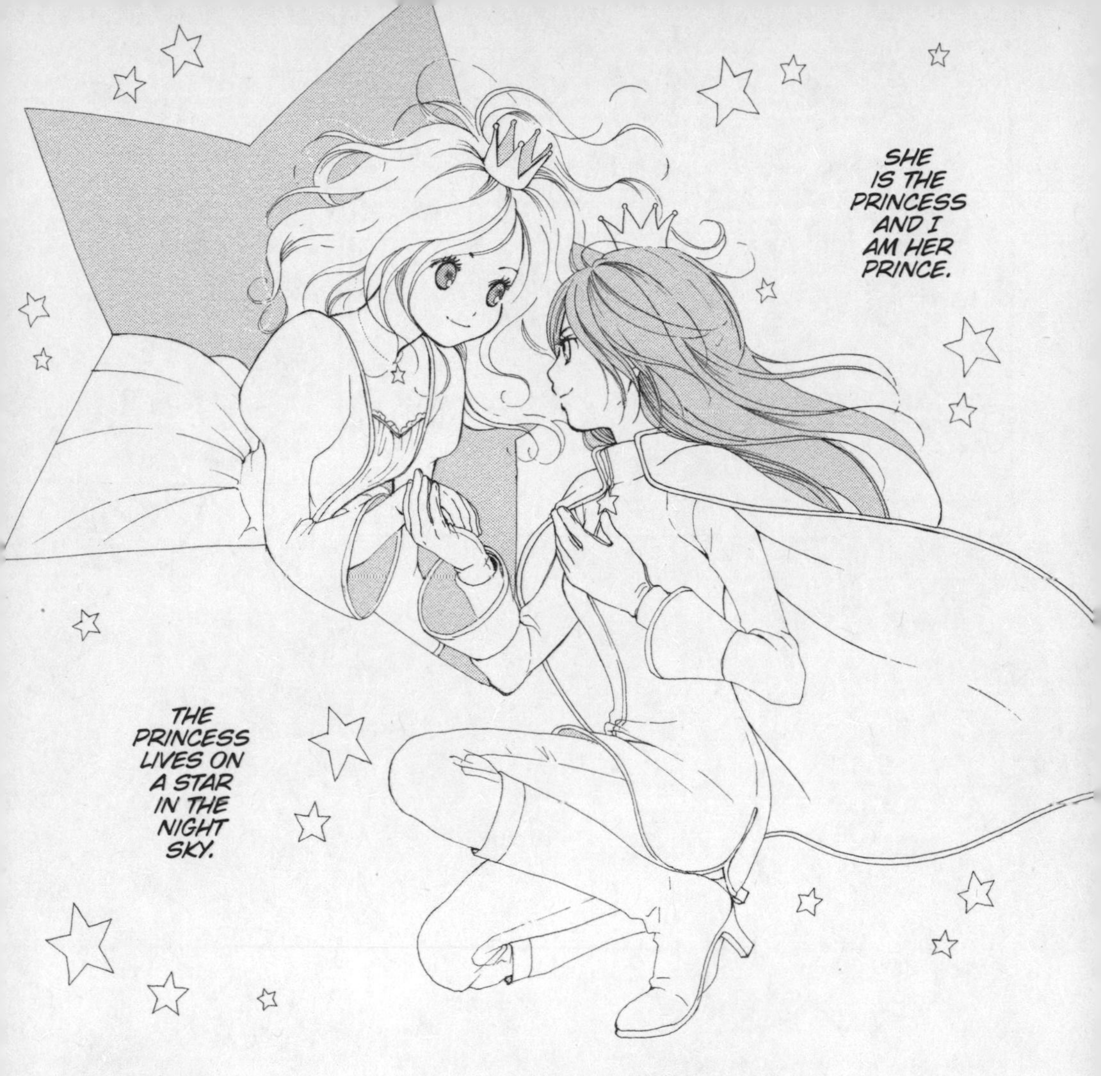
SHE IS THE PRINCESS AND I AM HER PRINCE.
THE PRINCESS LIVES ON A STAR IN THE NIGHT SKY.

The **Star Princess**

IF WE WERE TO EVER FALL IN LOVE...

THE WORLD WOULD...

SHINE IN DREAMY COLORS.

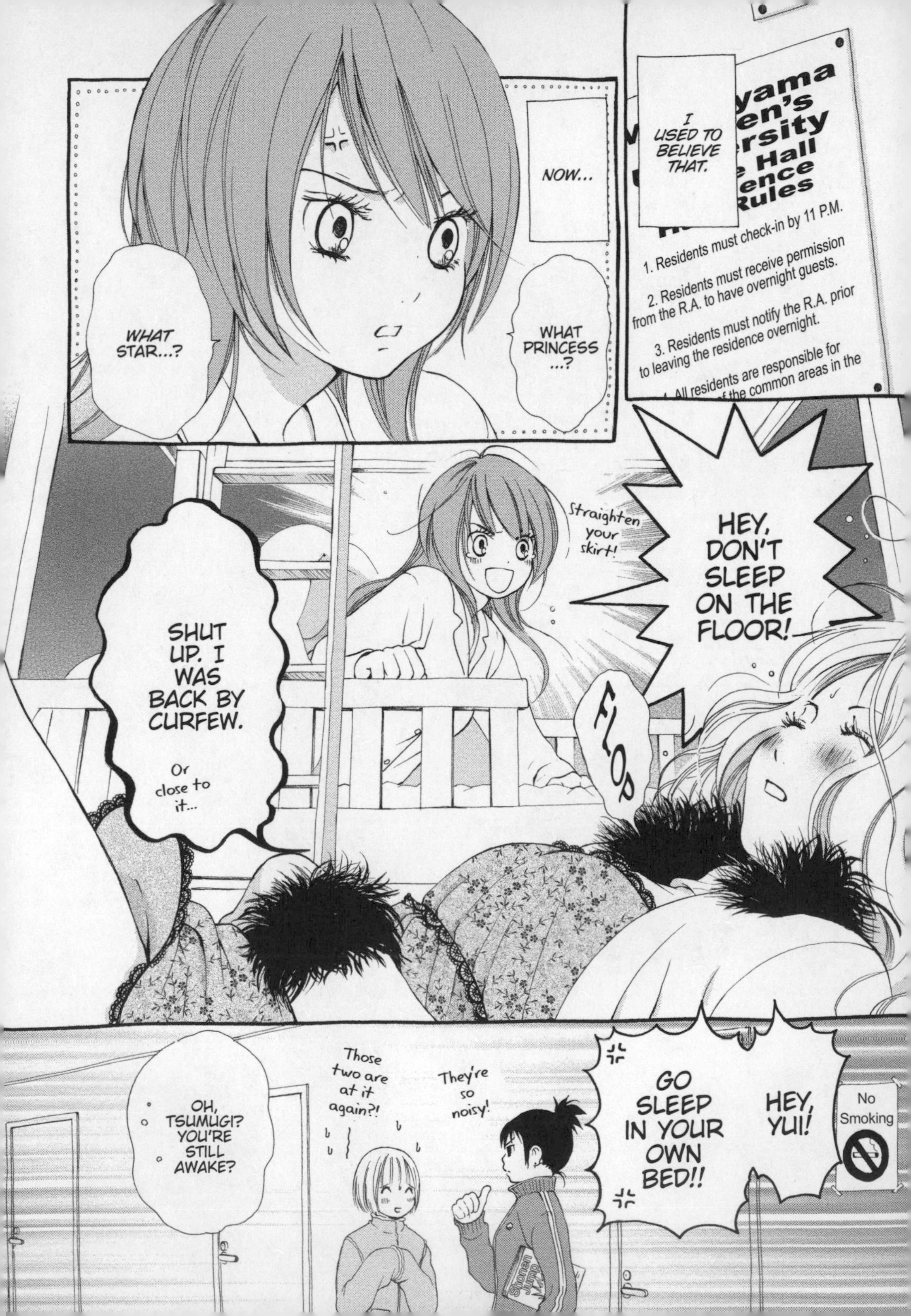
I USED TO BELIEVE THAT.
1. Residents must check-in by 11 P.M.
2. Residents must receive permission from the R.A. to have overnight guests.
3. Residents must notify the R.A. prior to leaving the residence overnight.
NOW...
WHAT PRINCESS...?
WHAT STAR...?
HEY, DON'T SLEEP ON THE FLOOR!
Straighten your skirt!
FLOP
SHUT UP. I WAS BACK BY CURFEW.
Or close to it...
HEY, YUI!
GO SLEEP IN YOUR OWN BED!!
No Smoking
They're so noisy!
Those two are at it again?!
OH, TSUMUGI? YOU'RE STILL AWAKE?

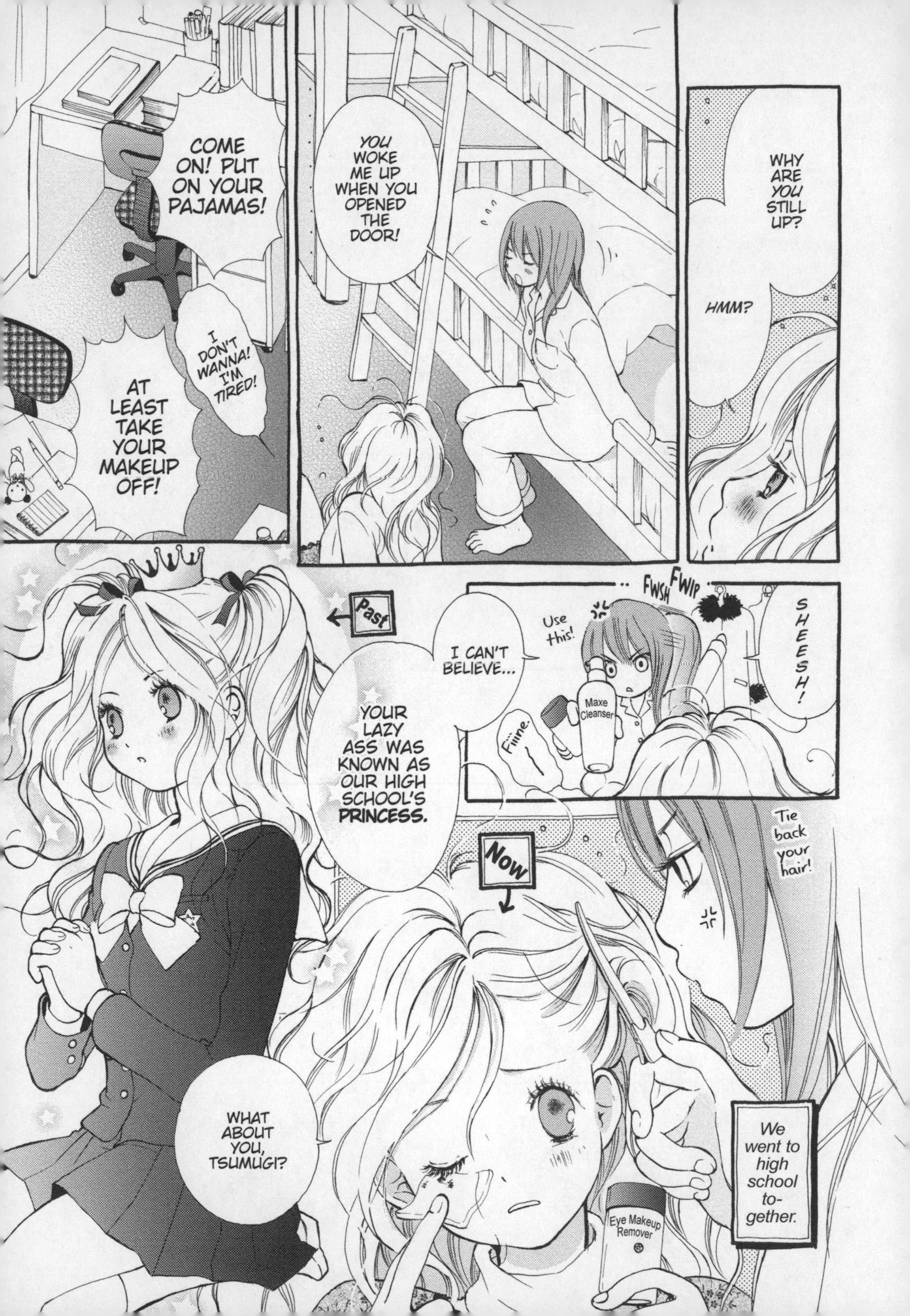
WHY ARE YOU STILL UP?
HMM?
YOU WOKE ME UP WHEN YOU OPENED THE DOOR!
COME ON! PUT ON YOUR PAJAMAS!
I DON'T WANNA! I'M TIRED!
AT LEAST TAKE YOUR MAKEUP OFF!
SHEESH!
FWIP
FWSH
Use this!
Maxe Cleanser
Fiiine.
I CAN'T BELIEVE...
YOUR LAZY ASS WAS KNOWN AS OUR HIGH SCHOOL'S PRINCESS.
Past
Tie back your hair!
Now
We went to high school to-gether.
Eye Makeup Remover
WHAT ABOUT YOU, TSUMUGI?

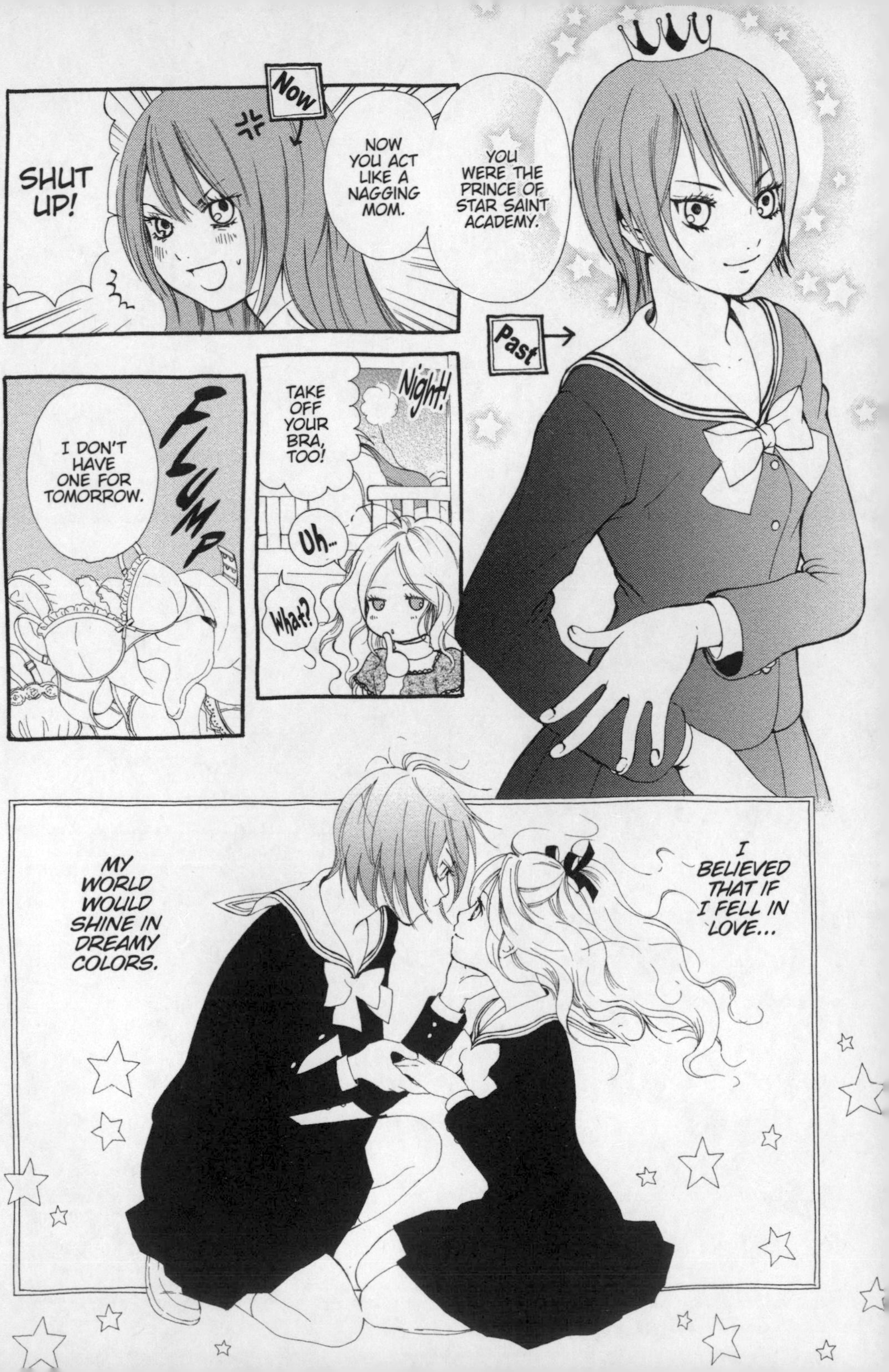
Past
YOU WERE THE PRINCE OF STAR SAINT ACADEMY.
Now
NOW YOU ACT LIKE A NAGGING MOM.
SHUT UP!
Night!
TAKE OFF YOUR BRA, TOO!
Uh...
What?
FLUMP
I DON'T HAVE ONE FOR TOMORROW.
I BELIEVED THAT IF I FELL IN LOVE...
MY WORLD WOULD SHINE IN DREAMY COLORS.

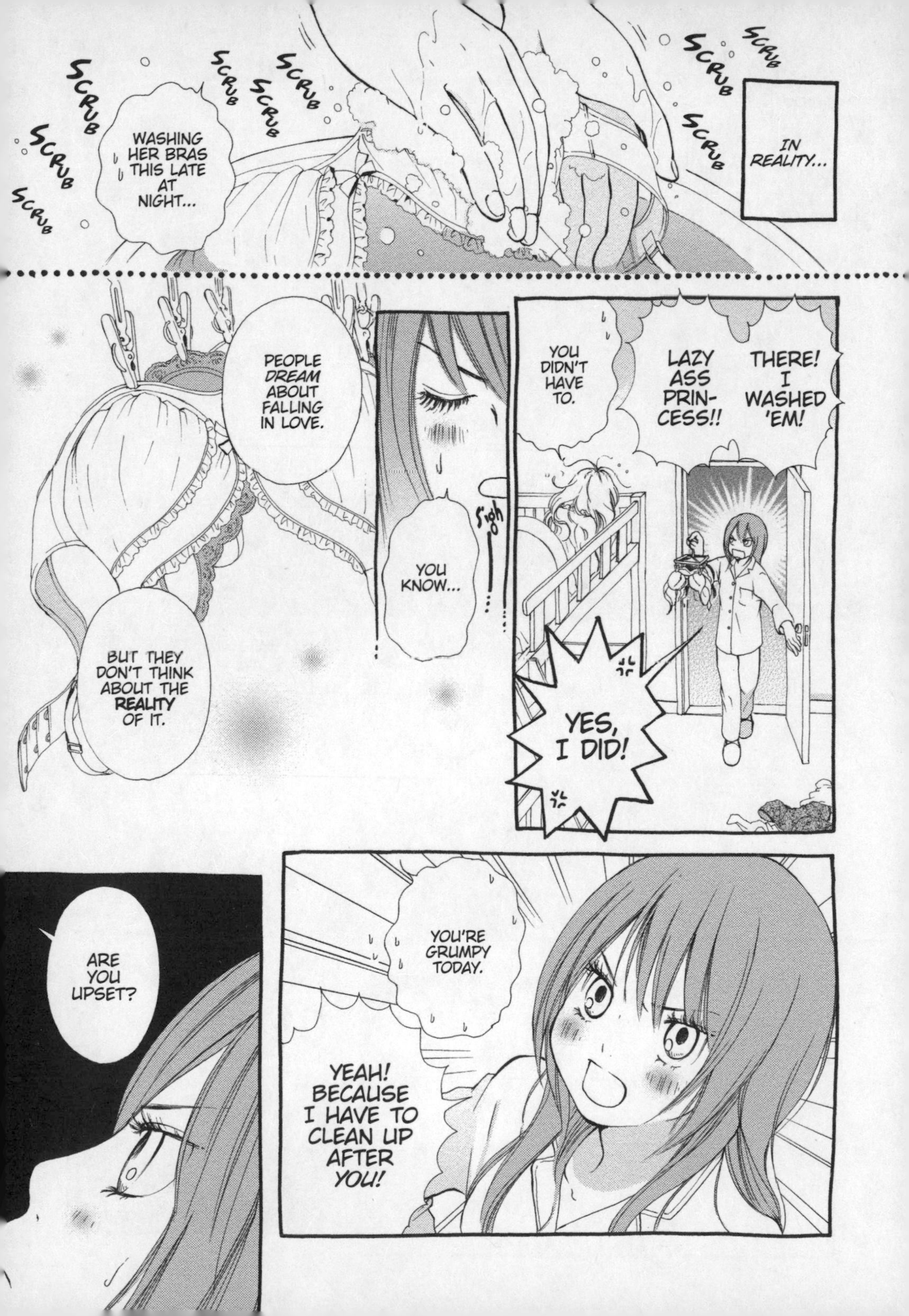
IN REALITY...
SCRUB
SCRUB
SCRUB
SCRUB
SCRUB
SCRUB
SCRUB
SCRUB
WASHING HER BRAS THIS LATE AT NIGHT...
THERE! I WASHED 'EM!
LAZY ASS PRIN-CESS!!
YOU DIDN'T HAVE TO.
YES, I DID!
Sigh
YOU KNOW...
PEOPLE DREAM ABOUT FALLING IN LOVE.
BUT THEY DON'T THINK ABOUT THE REALITY OF IT.
YOU'RE GRUMPY TODAY.
YEAH! BECAUSE I HAVE TO CLEAN UP AFTER YOU!
ARE YOU UPSET?

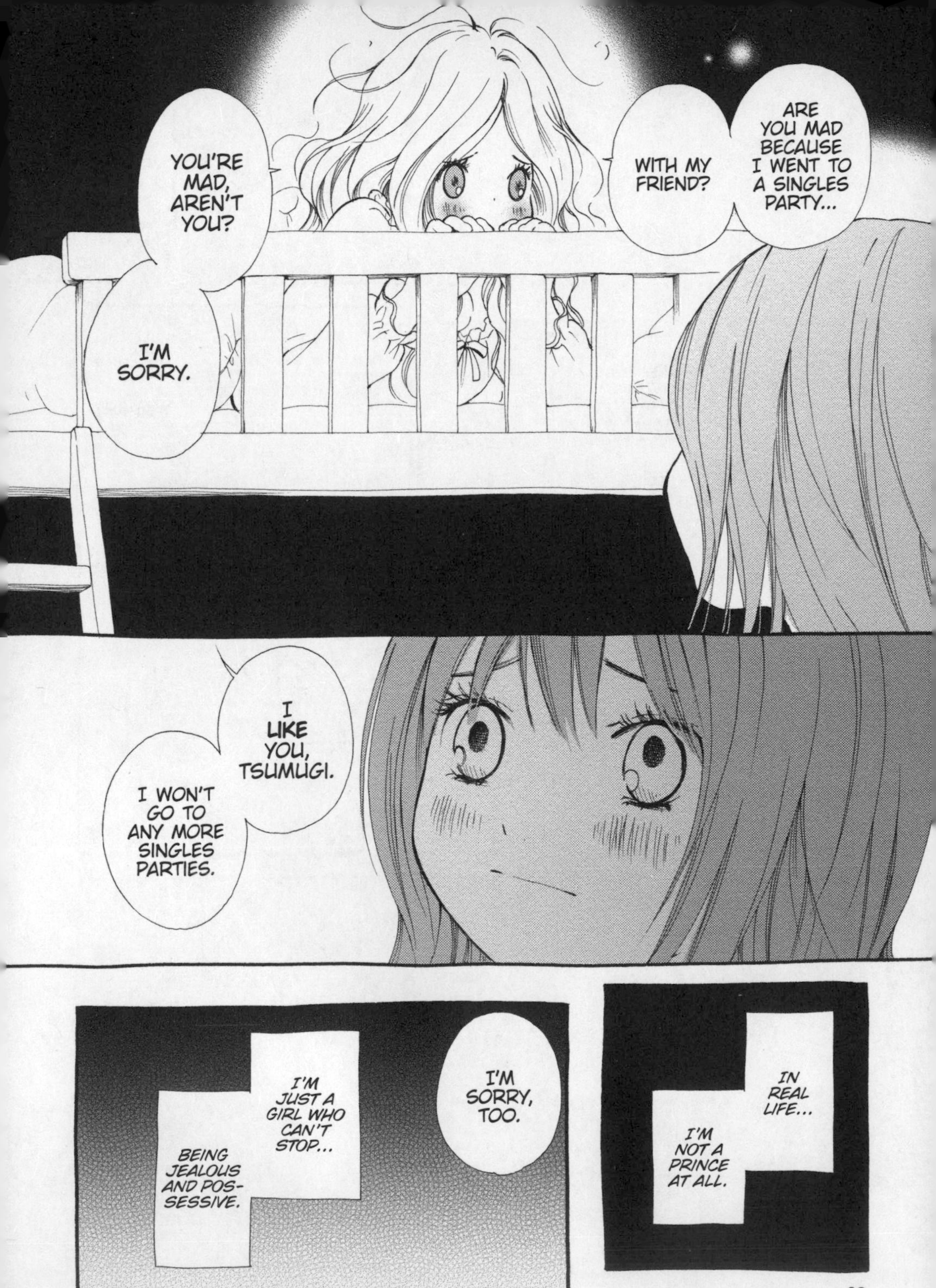
ARE YOU MAD BECAUSE I WENT TO A SINGLES PARTY...
WITH MY FRIEND?
YOU'RE MAD, AREN'T YOU?
I'M SORRY.
I LIKE YOU, TSUMUGI.
I WON'T GO TO ANY MORE SINGLES PARTIES.
IN REAL LIFE...
I'M NOT A PRINCE AT ALL.
I'M SORRY, TOO.
I'M JUST A GIRL WHO CAN'T STOP...
BEING JEALOUS AND POS-SESSIVE.

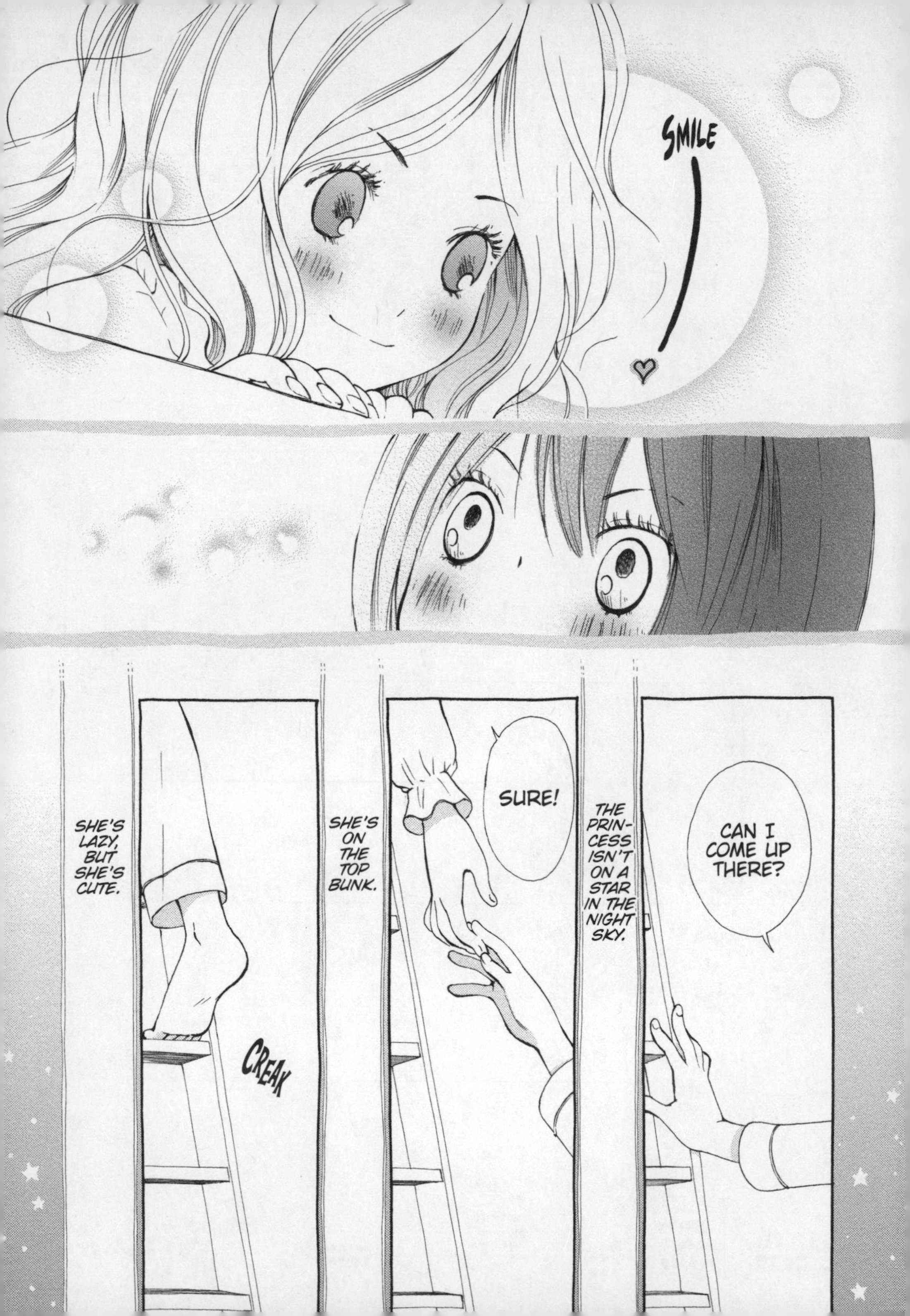
SMILE
CAN I COME UP THERE?
THE PRINCESS ISN'T ON A STAR IN THE NIGHT SKY.
SURE!
SHE'S ON THE TOP BUNK.
CREAK
SHE'S LAZY, BUT SHE'S CUTE.

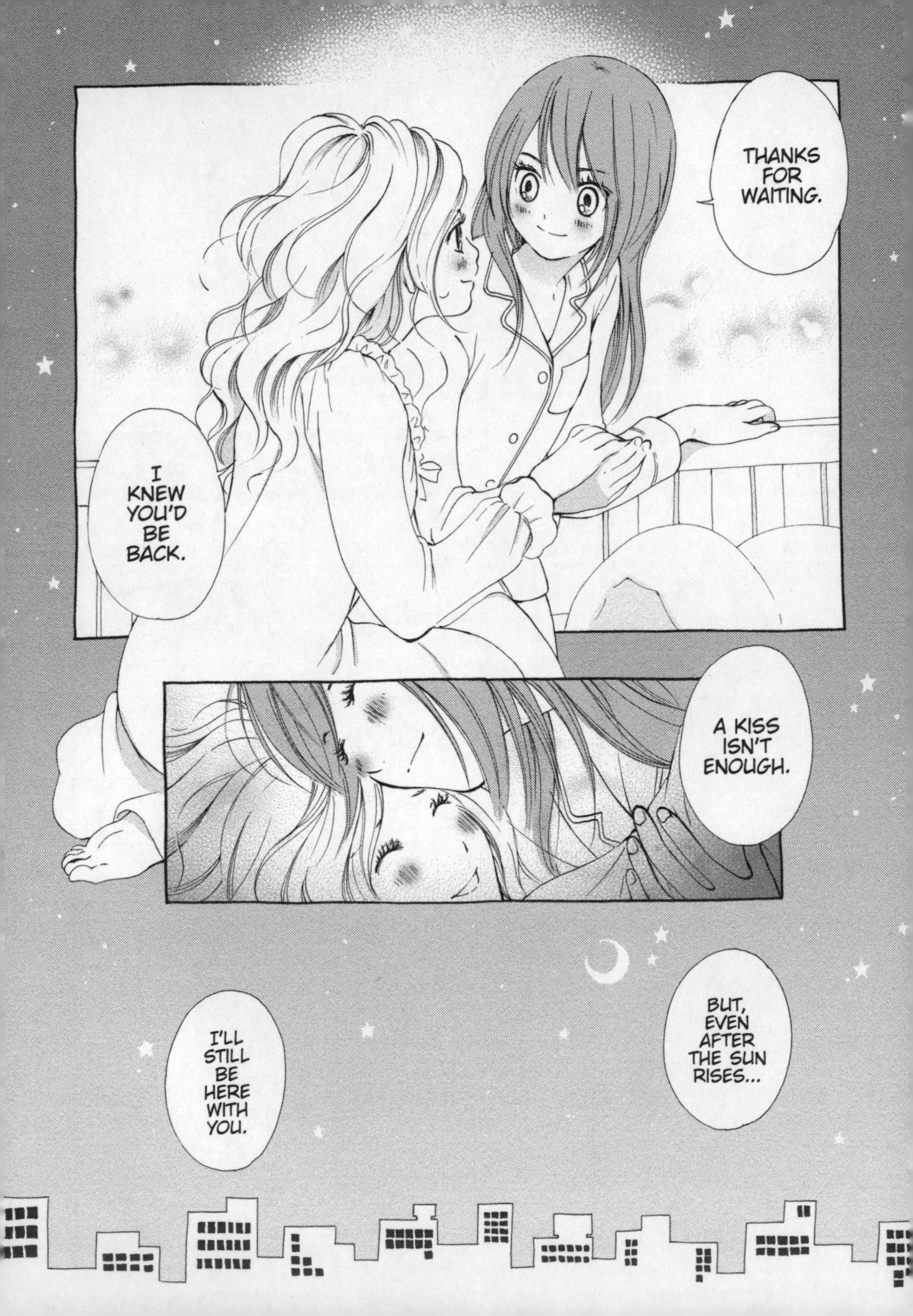
THANKS FOR WAITING.
I KNEW YOU'D BE BACK.
A KISS ISN'T ENOUGH.
BUT, EVEN AFTER THE SUN RISES...
I'LL STILL BE HERE WITH YOU.

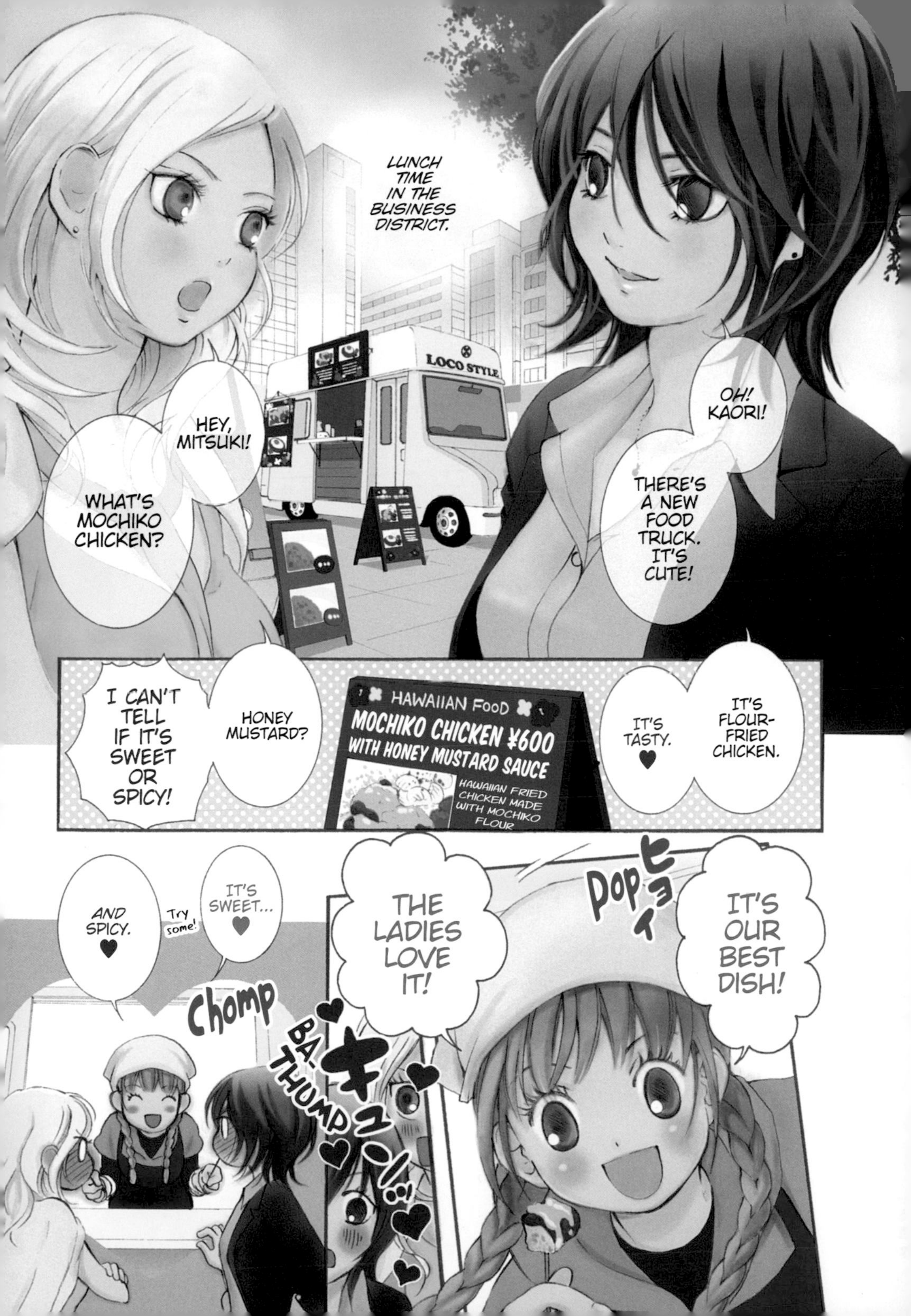
LUNCH TIME IN THE BUSINESS DISTRICT.
LOCO STYLE
OH! KAORI!
THERE'S A NEW FOOD TRUCK. IT'S CUTE!
HEY, MITSUKI!
WHAT'S MOCHIKO CHICKEN?
IT'S FLOUR-FRIED CHICKEN.
IT'S TASTY. ♥
HAWAIIAN FOOD
MOCHIKO CHICKEN ¥600
WITH HONEY MUSTARD SAUCE
HAWAIIAN FRIED CHICKEN MADE WITH MOCHIKO FLOUR
HONEY MUSTARD?
I CAN'T TELL IF IT'S SWEET OR SPICY!
IT'S OUR BEST DISH!
Pop ヒョイ
THE LADIES LOVE IT!
BA-THUMP
IT'S SWEET... ♥
Try some!
AND SPICY. ♥
Chomp

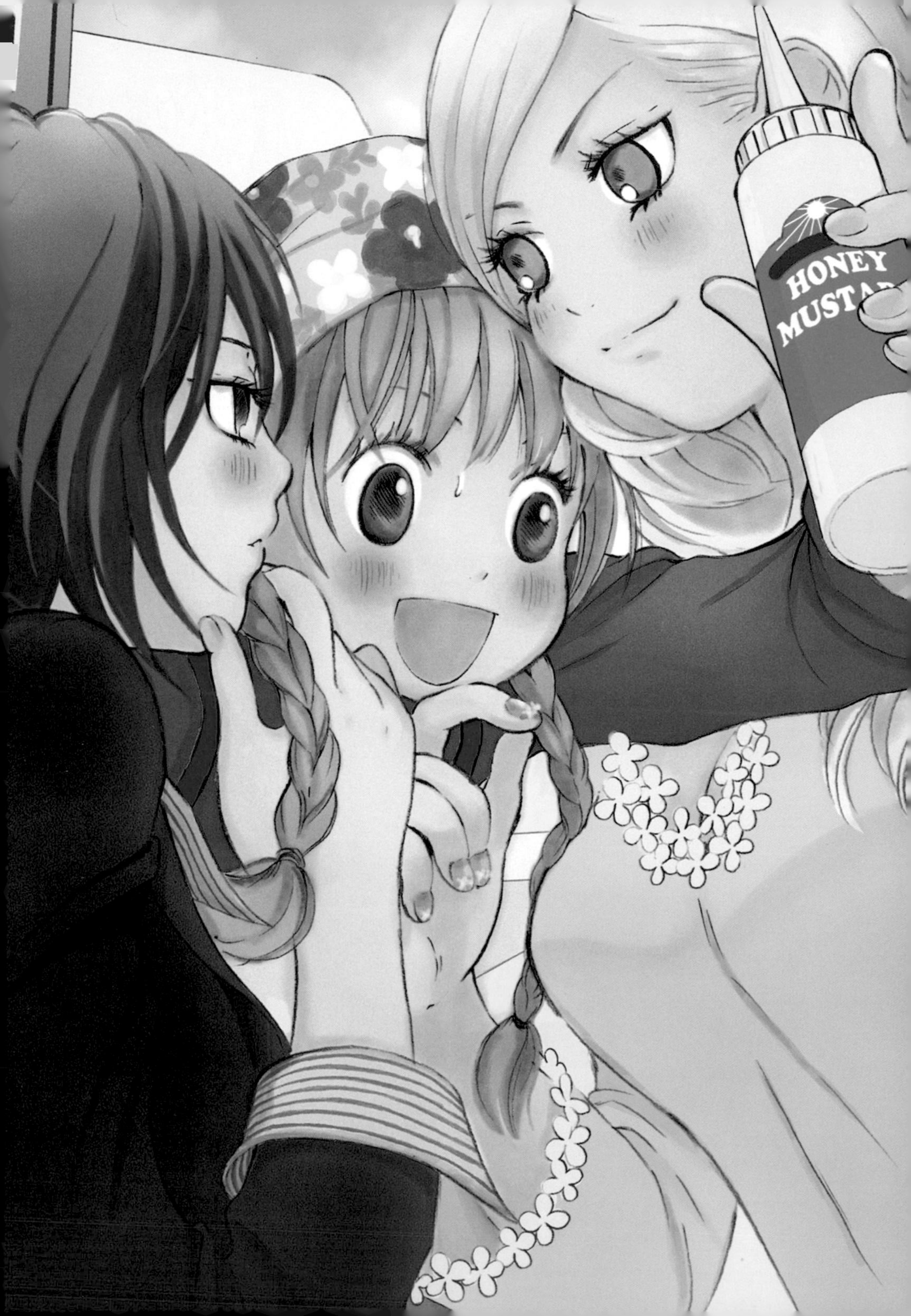
HONEY
MUSTAR

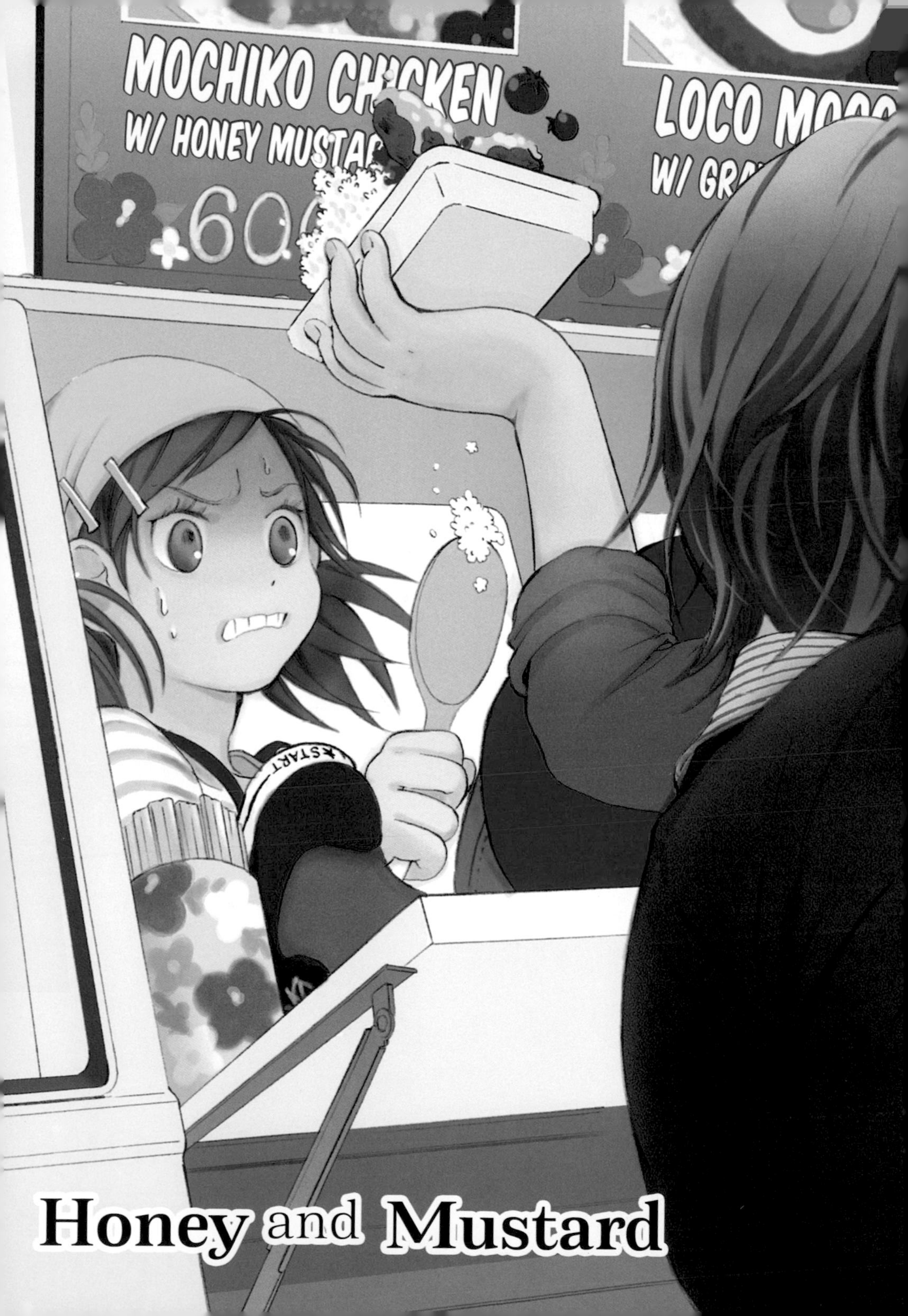
MOCHIKO CHICKEN
W/ HONEY
START

Honey and Mustard

The Conditions
of Paradise
AZURE DREAMS

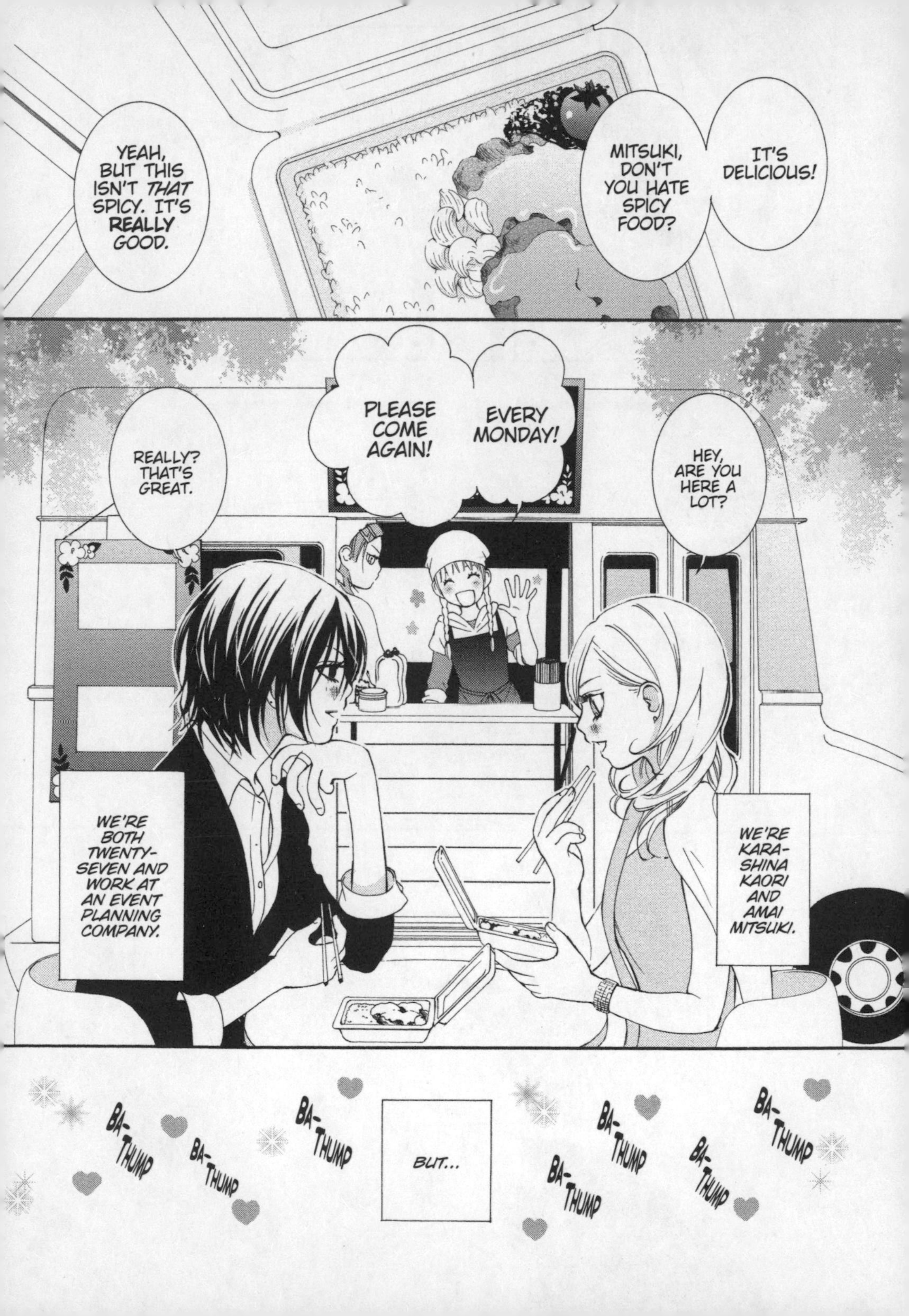
IT'S DELICIOUS!
MITSUKI, DON'T YOU HATE SPICY FOOD?
YEAH, BUT THIS ISN'T *THAT* SPICY. IT'S **REALLY** GOOD.
HEY, ARE YOU HERE A LOT?
EVERY MONDAY!
PLEASE COME AGAIN!
REALLY? THAT'S GREAT.
WE'RE KARA-SHINA KAORI AND AMAI MITSUKI.
WE'RE BOTH TWENTY-SEVEN AND WORK AT AN EVENT PLANNING COMPANY.
BA-THUMP
BA-THUMP
BA-THUMP
BA-THUMP
BUT...
BA-THUMP
BA-THUMP
BA-THUMP
BA-THUMP

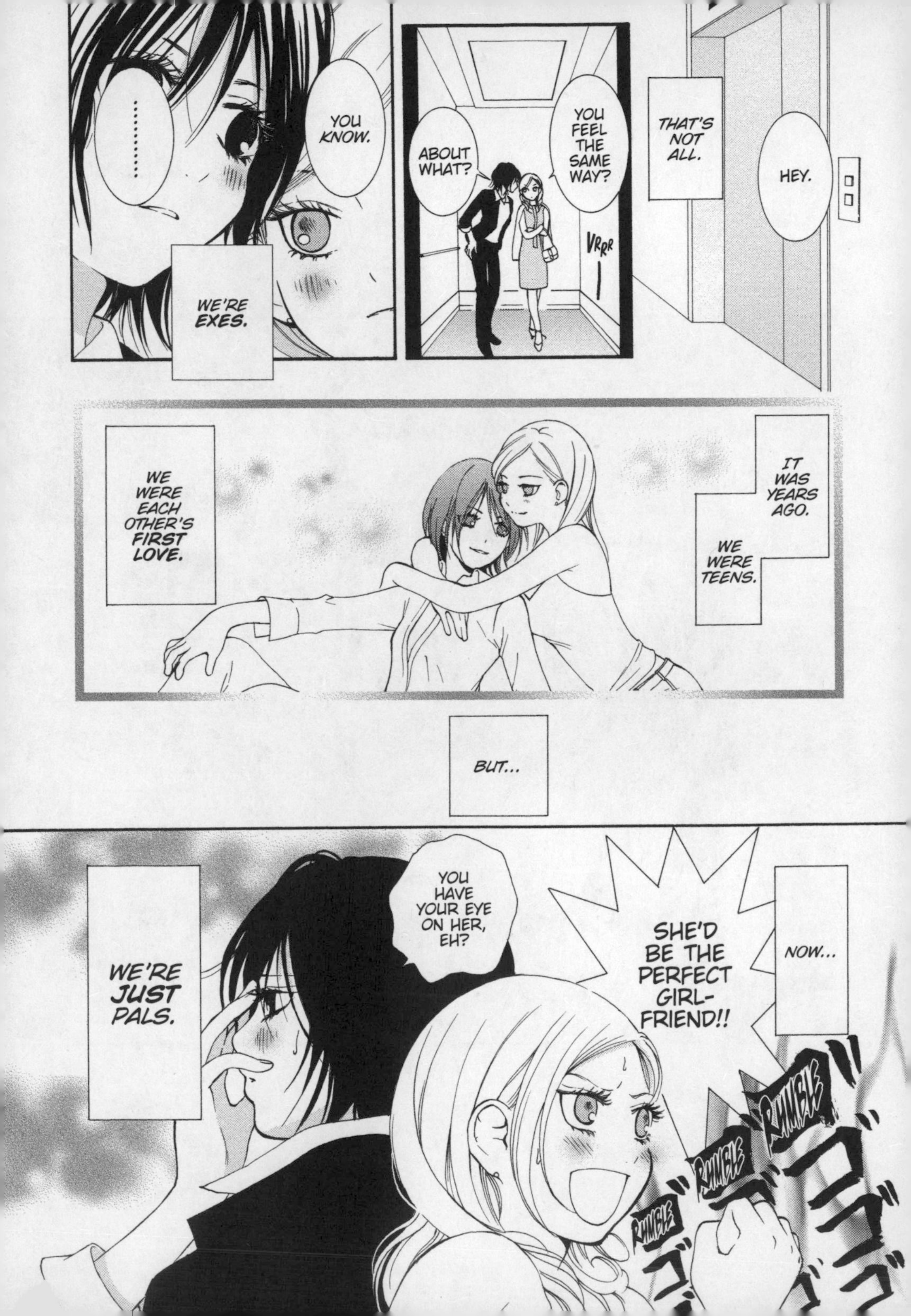
HEY.
THAT'S NOT ALL.
YOU FEEL THE SAME WAY?
ABOUT WHAT?
VRRR
YOU KNOW.
......
WE'RE EXES.
IT WAS YEARS AGO.
WE WERE TEENS.
WE WERE EACH OTHER'S FIRST LOVE.
BUT...
NOW...
SHE'D BE THE PERFECT GIRL-FRIEND!!
YOU HAVE YOUR EYE ON HER, EH?
WE'RE JUST PALS.
RUMBLE
RUMBLE
RUMBLE

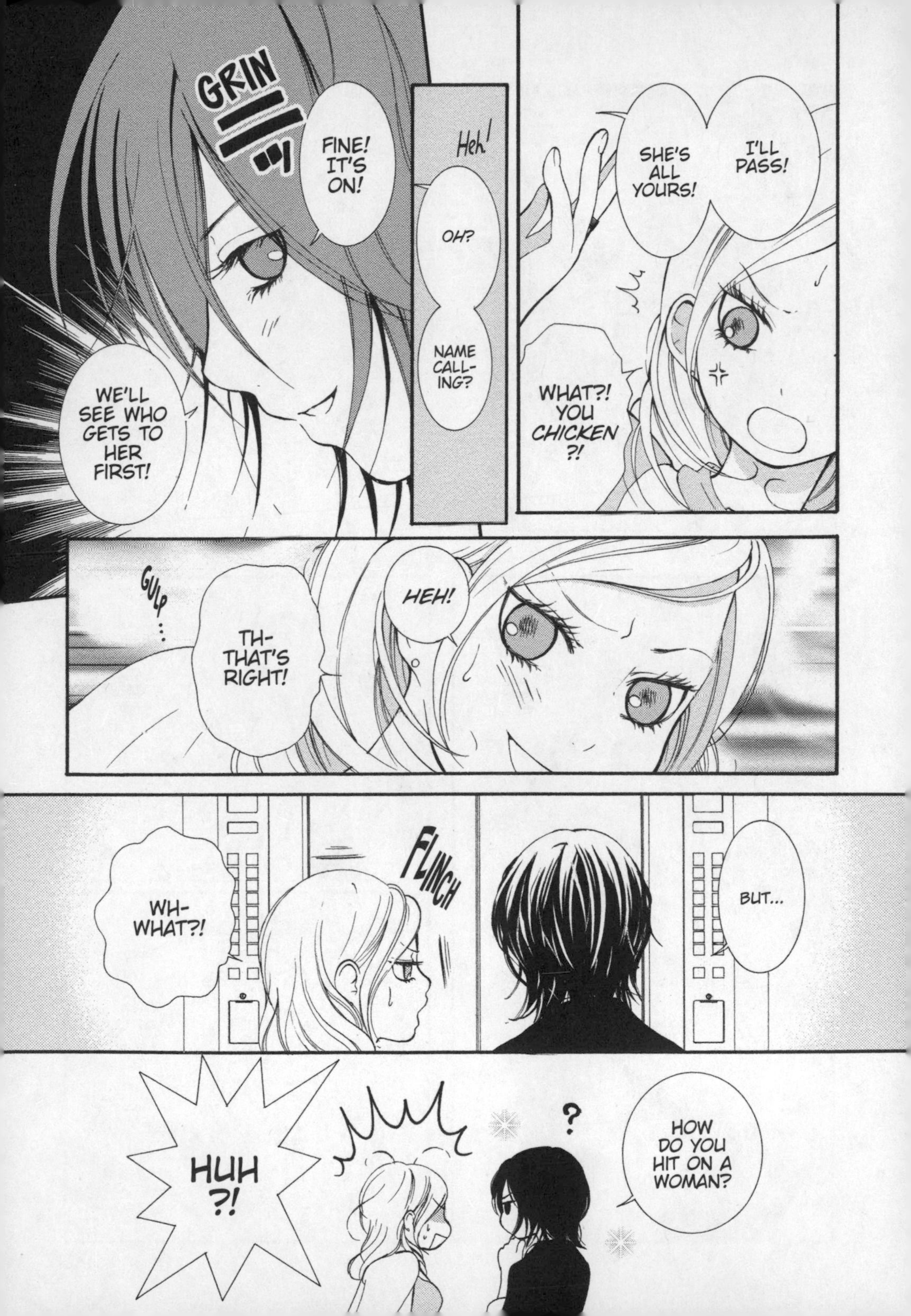
I'LL PASS!
SHE'S ALL YOURS!
WHAT?! YOU CHICKEN?!
Heh!
OH?
NAME CALLING?
GRIN
FINE! IT'S ON!
WE'LL SEE WHO GETS TO HER FIRST!
HEH!
TH-THAT'S RIGHT!
GULP...
BUT...
FLINCH
WH-WHAT?!
HOW DO YOU HIT ON A WOMAN?
?
HUH?!

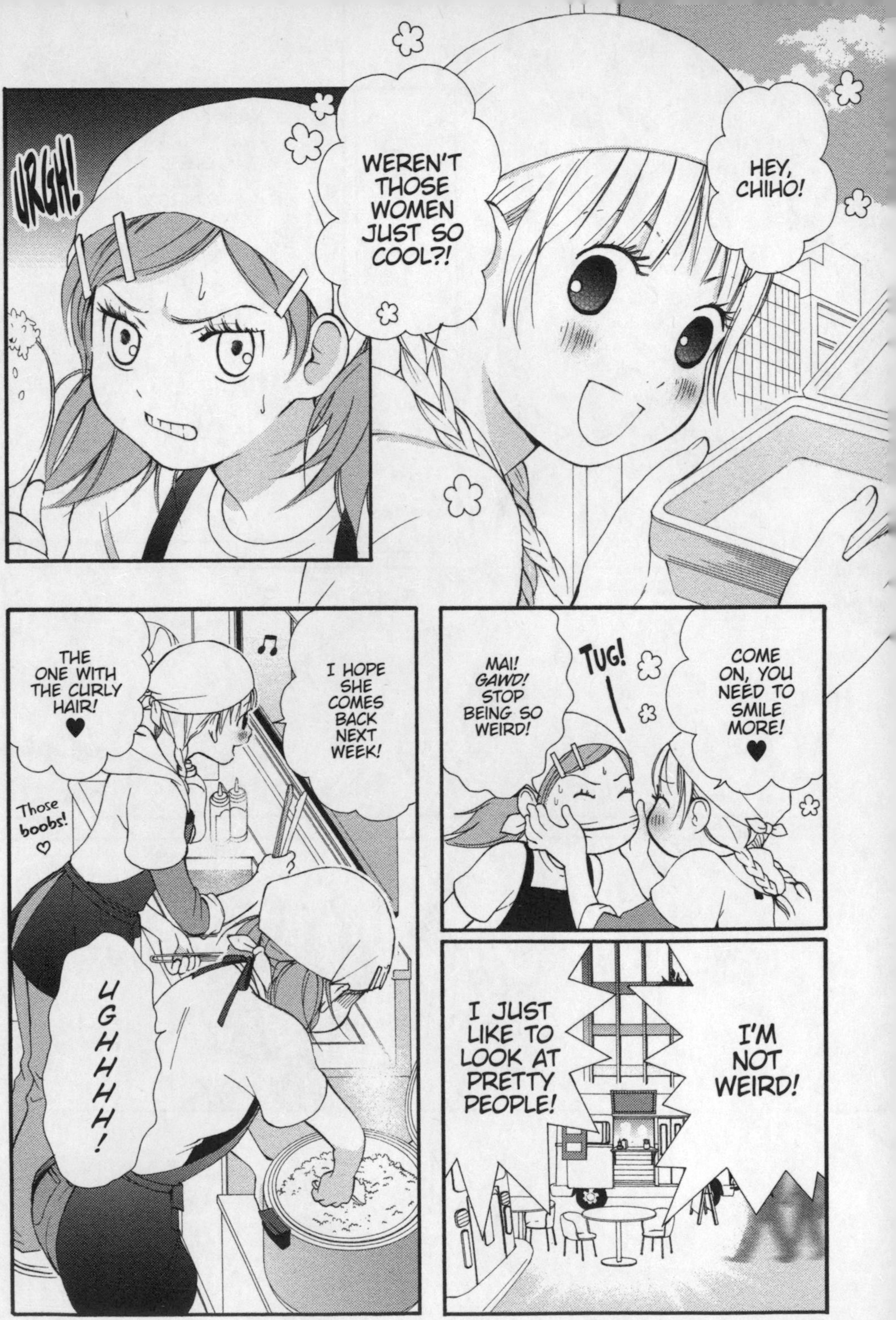
HEY, CHIHO!
WEREN'T THOSE WOMEN JUST SO COOL?!
URGH!
COME ON, YOU NEED TO SMILE MORE! ♥
TUG!
MAI! GAWD! STOP BEING SO WEIRD!
I'M NOT WEIRD!
I JUST LIKE TO LOOK AT PRETTY PEOPLE!
I HOPE SHE COMES BACK NEXT WEEK!
THE ONE WITH THE CURLY HAIR! ♥
Those boobs! ♡
UGHHHHH!

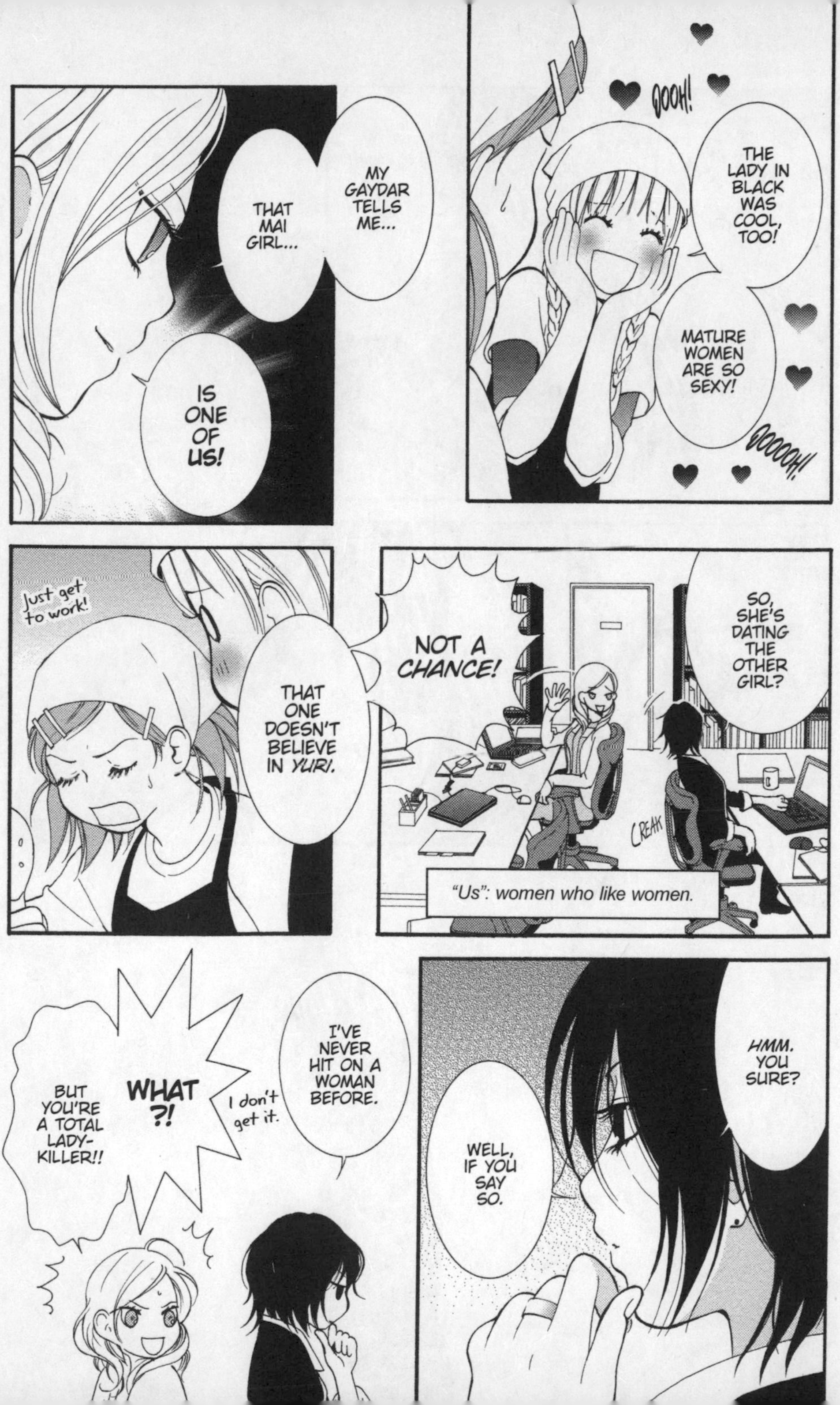
OOOH!
THE LADY IN BLACK WAS COOL, TOO!
MATURE WOMEN ARE SO SEXY!
OOOOH!
MY GAYDAR TELLS ME...
THAT MAI GIRL...
IS ONE OF US!
SO, SHE'S DATING THE OTHER GIRL?
NOT A CHANCE!
CREAK
"Us": women who like women.
THAT ONE DOESN'T BELIEVE IN YURI.
Just get to work!
HMM. YOU SURE?
WELL, IF YOU SAY SO.
I'VE NEVER HIT ON A WOMAN BEFORE.
I don't get it.
WHAT?!
BUT YOU'RE A TOTAL LADY-KILLER!!

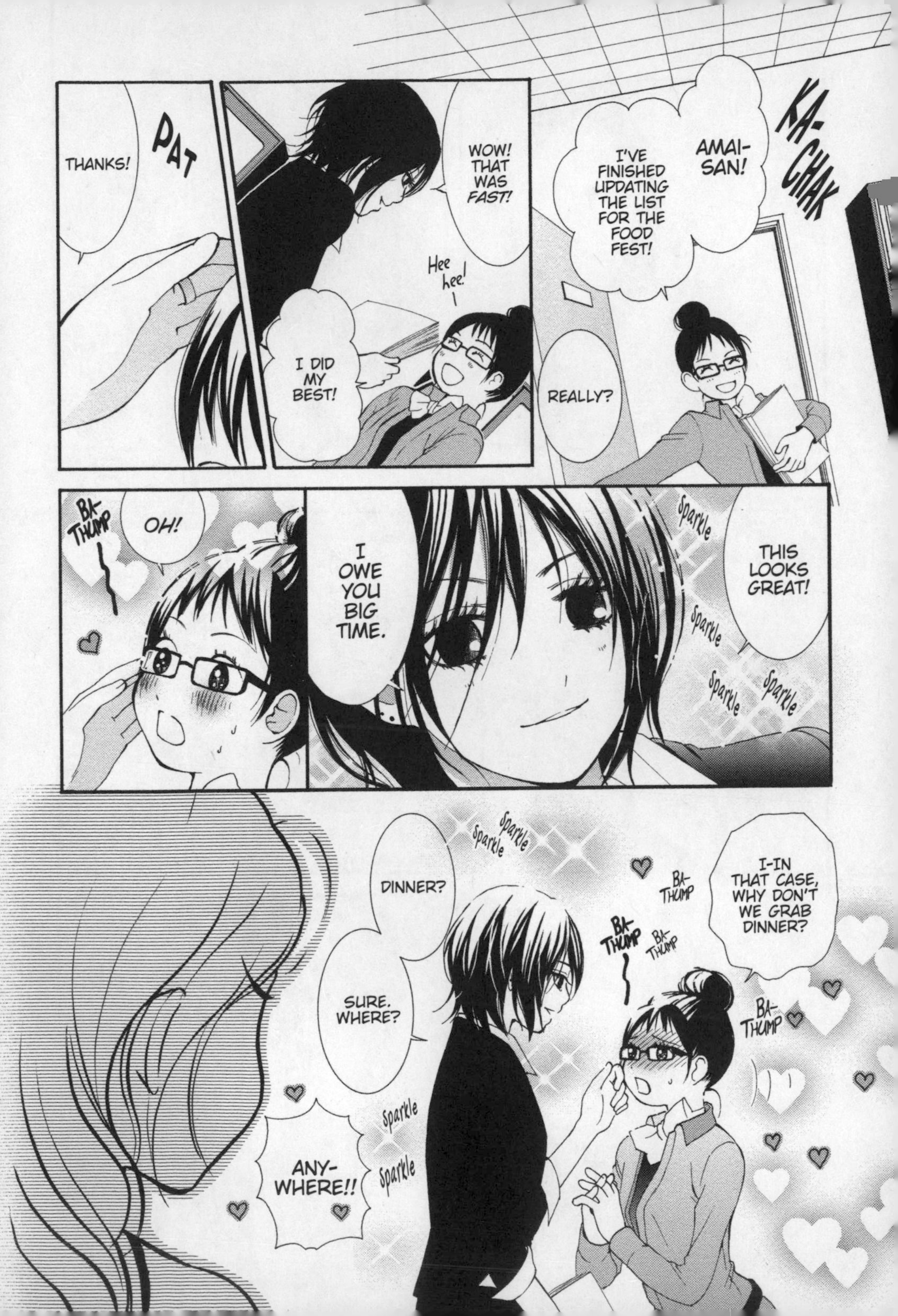
KA-CHAK
AMAI-SAN!
I'VE FINISHED UPDATING THE LIST FOR THE FOOD FEST!
REALLY?
WOW! THAT WAS FAST!
Hee hee!
I DID MY BEST!
PAT
THANKS!
THIS LOOKS GREAT!
Sparkle
Sparkle
Sparkle
Sparkle
I OWE YOU BIG TIME.
BA-THUMP
OH!
I-IN THAT CASE, WHY DON'T WE GRAB DINNER?
BA-THUMP
BA-THUMP
BA-THUMP
BA-THUMP
Sparkle
Sparkle
DINNER?
SURE. WHERE?
ANY-WHERE!!
Sparkle
Sparkle

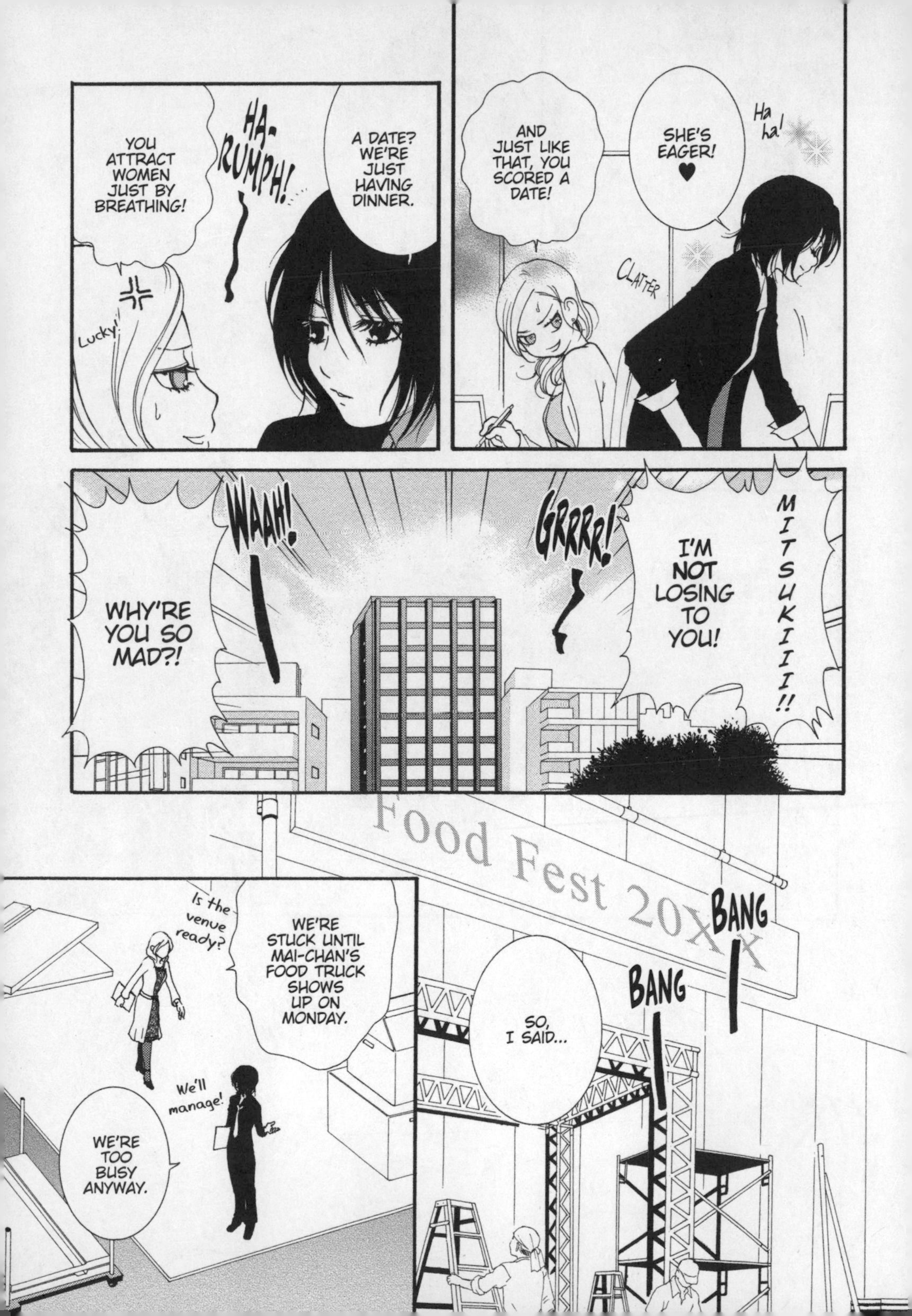
Ha ha!
SHE'S EAGER! ♥
AND JUST LIKE THAT, YOU SCORED A DATE!
CLATTER
A DATE? WE'RE JUST HAVING DINNER.
HA-RUMPH!
YOU ATTRACT WOMEN JUST BY BREATHING!
Lucky!
MITSUKIIII!!
I'M NOT LOSING TO YOU!
GRRRR!
WAAH!
WHY'RE YOU SO MAD?!
Food Fest 20XX
BANG
BANG
SO, I SAID...
WE'RE STUCK UNTIL MAI-CHAN'S FOOD TRUCK SHOWS UP ON MONDAY.
Is the venue ready?
We'll manage!
WE'RE TOO BUSY ANYWAY.

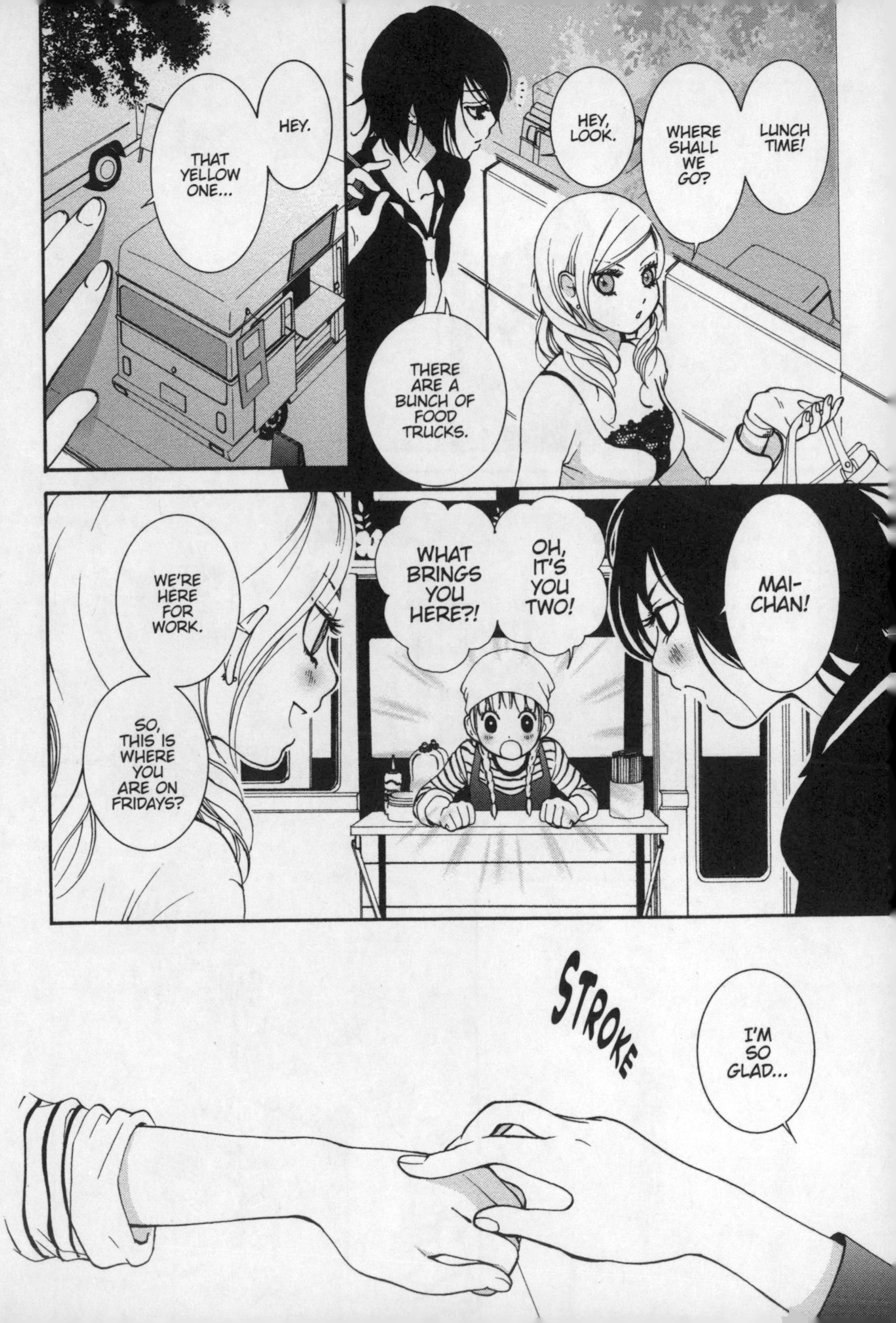
LUNCH TIME!
WHERE SHALL WE GO?
HEY, LOOK.
THERE ARE A BUNCH OF FOOD TRUCKS.
HEY.
THAT YELLOW ONE...
MAI-CHAN!
OH, IT'S YOU TWO!
WHAT BRINGS YOU HERE?!
WE'RE HERE FOR WORK.
SO, THIS IS WHERE YOU ARE ON FRIDAYS?
I'M SO GLAD...
STROKE

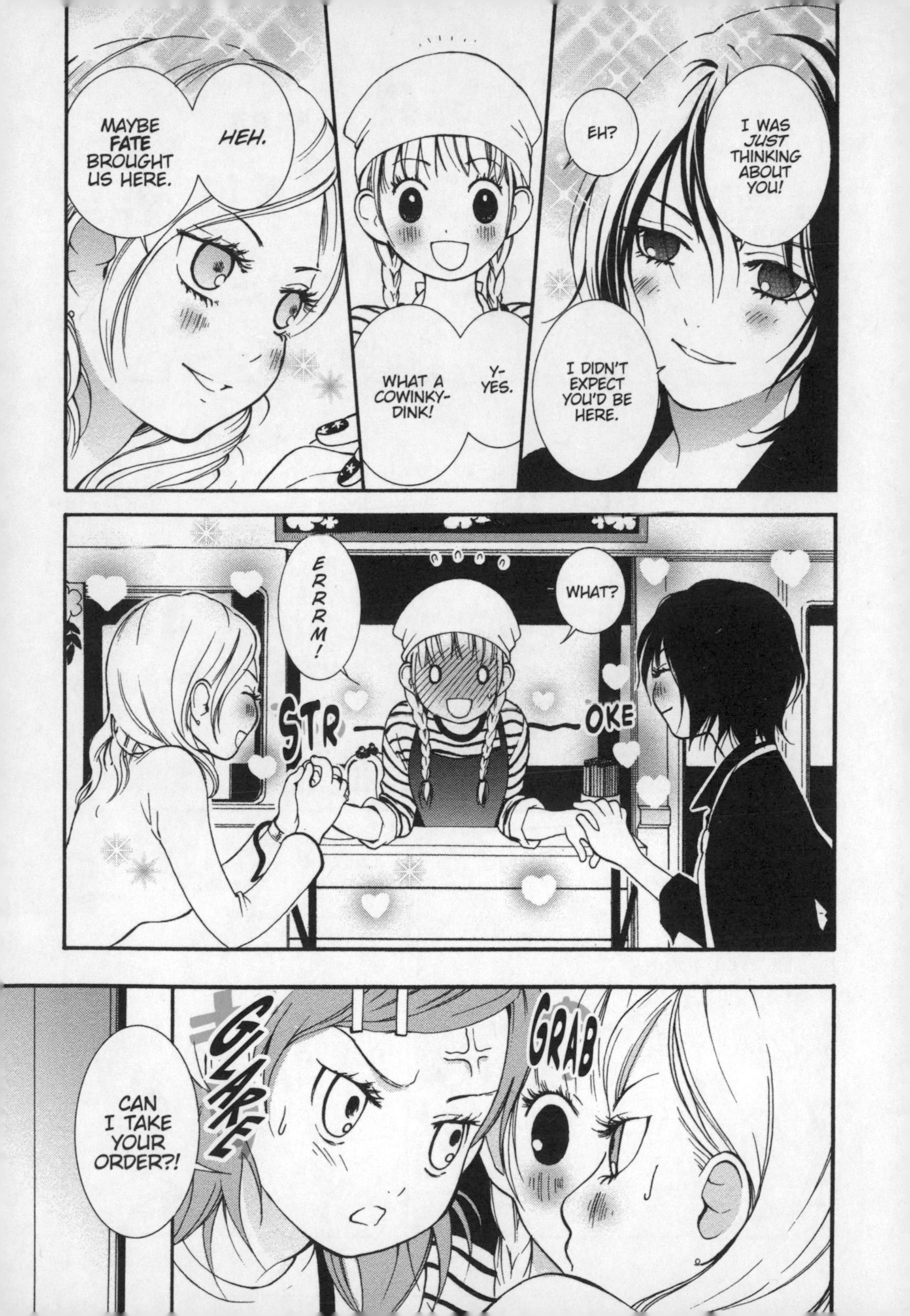
I WAS JUST THINKING ABOUT YOU!
EH?
I DIDN'T EXPECT YOU'D BE HERE.
Y-YES.
WHAT A COWINKY-DINK!
HEH.
MAYBE FATE BROUGHT US HERE.
WHAT?
ERRRM!
STR—OKE
GRAB
GLARE
CAN I TAKE YOUR ORDER?!

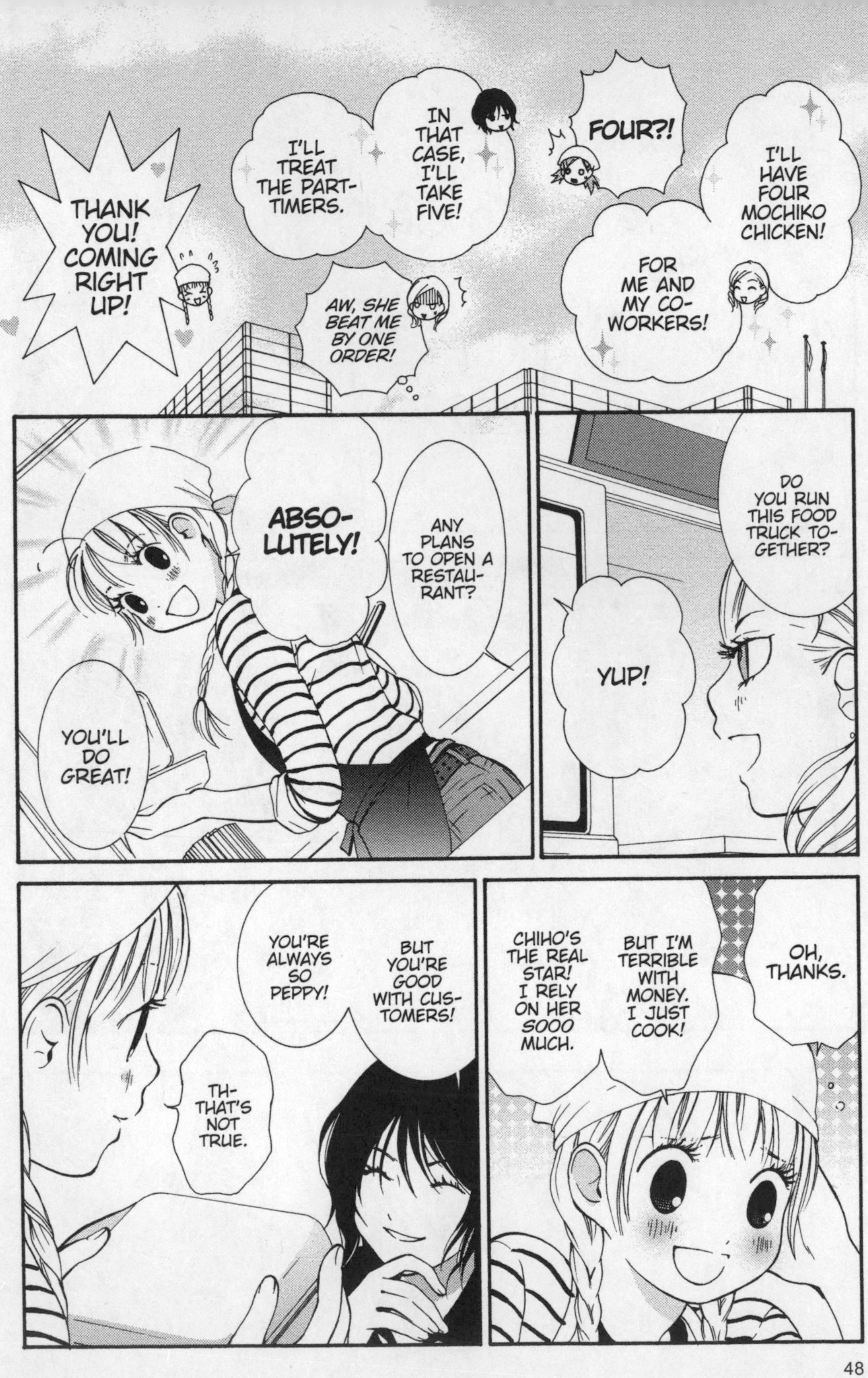
I'LL HAVE FOUR MOCHIKO CHICKEN!
FOR ME AND MY CO-WORKERS!
FOUR?!
IN THAT CASE, I'LL TAKE FIVE!
I'LL TREAT THE PART-TIMERS.
AW, SHE BEAT ME BY ONE ORDER!
THANK YOU! COMING RIGHT UP!
DO YOU RUN THIS FOOD TRUCK TOGETHER?
YUP!
ANY PLANS TO OPEN A RESTAURANT?
ABSOLUTELY!
YOU'LL DO GREAT!
OH, THANKS.
BUT I'M TERRIBLE WITH MONEY. I JUST COOK!
CHIHO'S THE REAL STAR! I RELY ON HER SOOO MUCH.
BUT YOU'RE GOOD WITH CUSTOMERS!
YOU'RE ALWAYS SO PEPPY!
TH-THAT'S NOT TRUE.

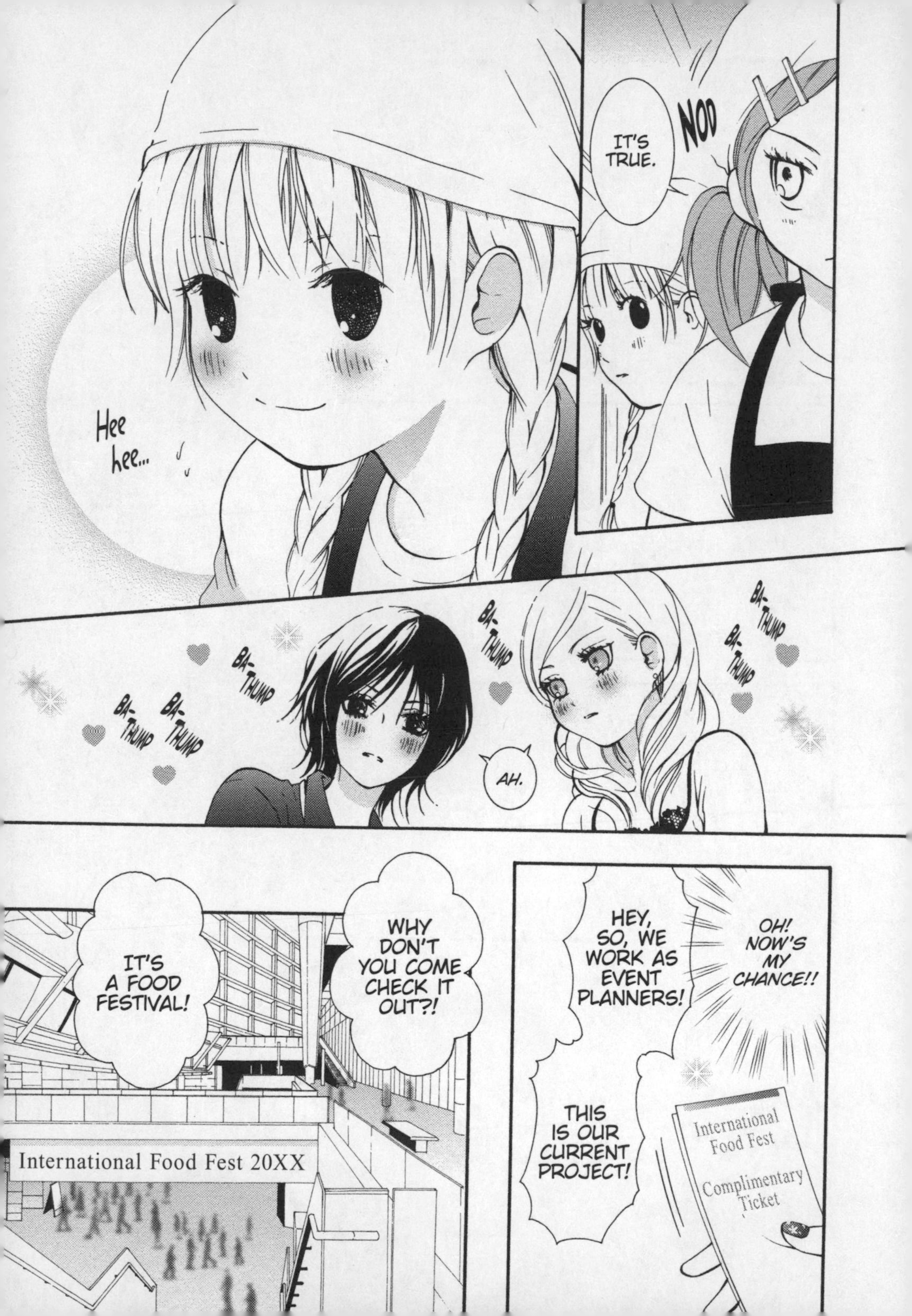

IT'S TRUE.
NOD
Hee hee...
BA-THUMP
BA-THUMP
BA-THUMP
BA-THUMP
BA-THUMP
BA-THUMP
AH.
OH! NOW'S MY CHANCE!!
HEY, SO, WE WORK AS EVENT PLANNERS!
THIS IS OUR CURRENT PROJECT!
International Food Fest
Complimentary Ticket
WHY DON'T YOU COME CHECK IT OUT?!
IT'S A FOOD FESTIVAL!
International Food Fest 20XX

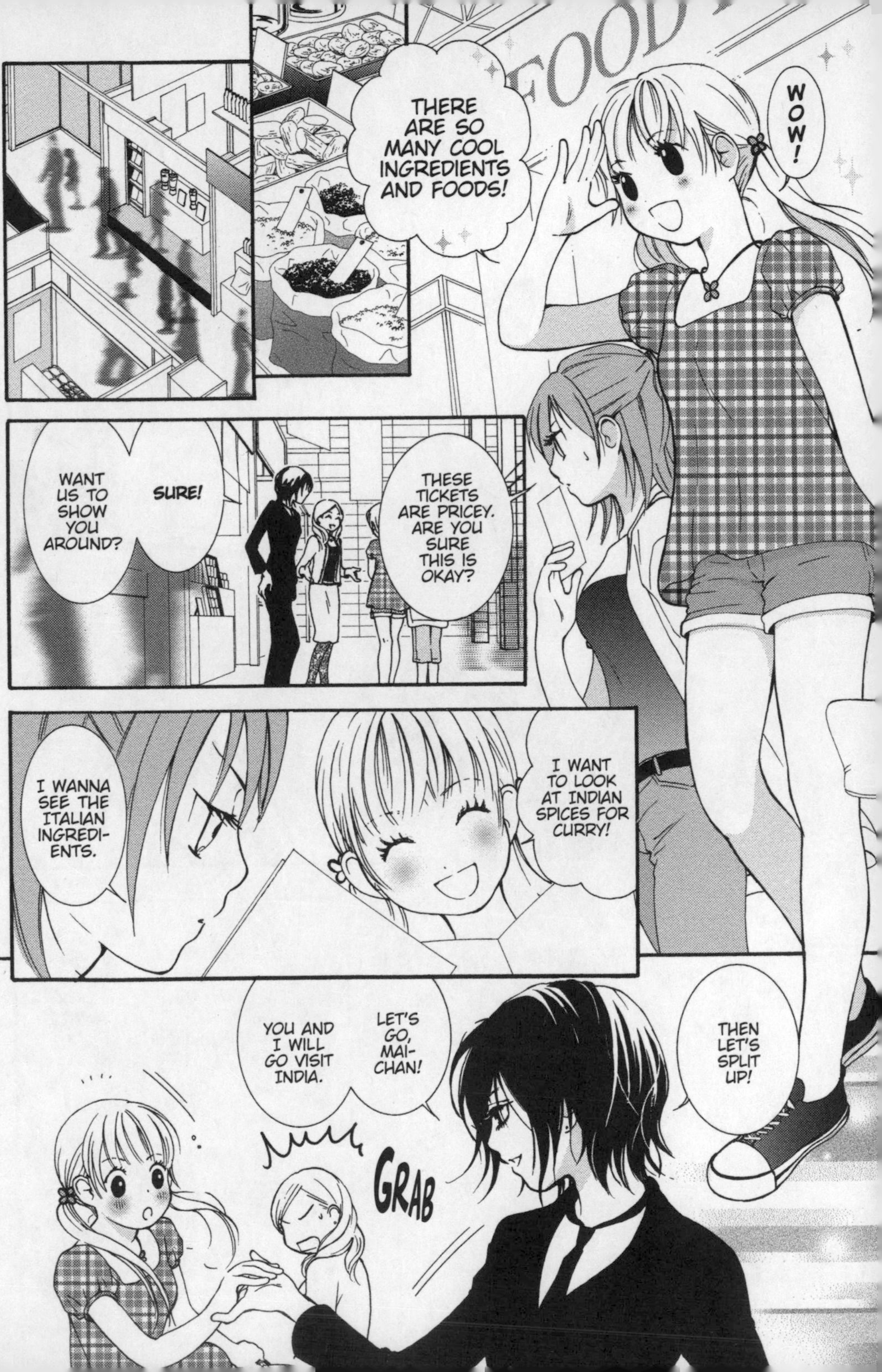
WOW!
THERE ARE SO MANY COOL INGREDIENTS AND FOODS!
FOOD
THESE TICKETS ARE PRICEY. ARE YOU SURE THIS IS OKAY?
SURE!
WANT US TO SHOW YOU AROUND?
I WANT TO LOOK AT INDIAN SPICES FOR CURRY!
I WANNA SEE THE ITALIAN INGREDI-ENTS.
THEN LET'S SPLIT UP!
LET'S GO, MAI-CHAN!
YOU AND I WILL GO VISIT INDIA.
GRAB

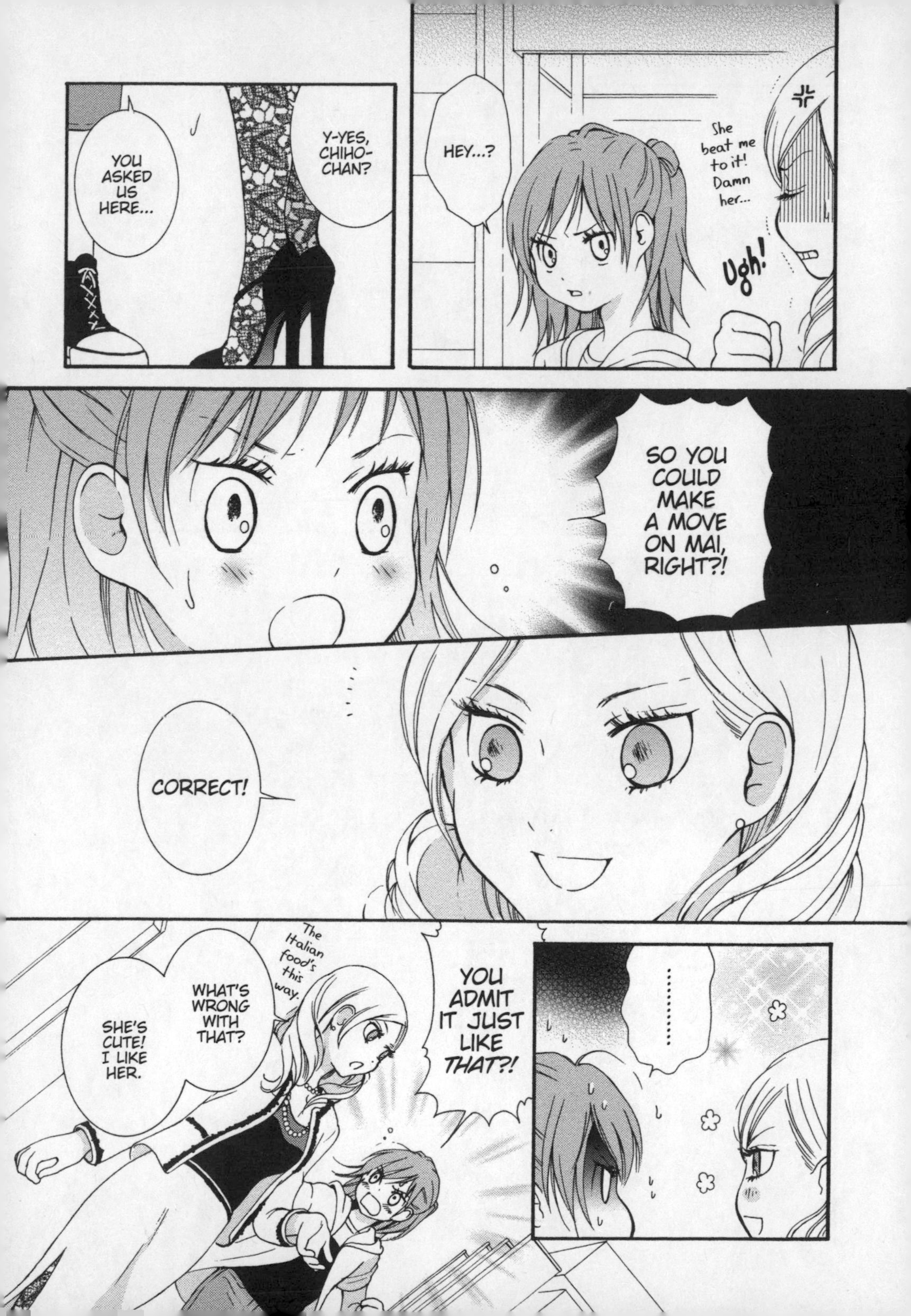
HEY...?
She beat me to it! Damn her...
Ugh!
Y-YES, CHIHO-CHAN?
YOU ASKED US HERE...
SO YOU COULD MAKE A MOVE ON MAI, RIGHT?!
CORRECT!
......
YOU ADMIT IT JUST LIKE *THAT*?!
The Italian food's this way.
WHAT'S WRONG WITH THAT?
SHE'S CUTE! I LIKE HER.

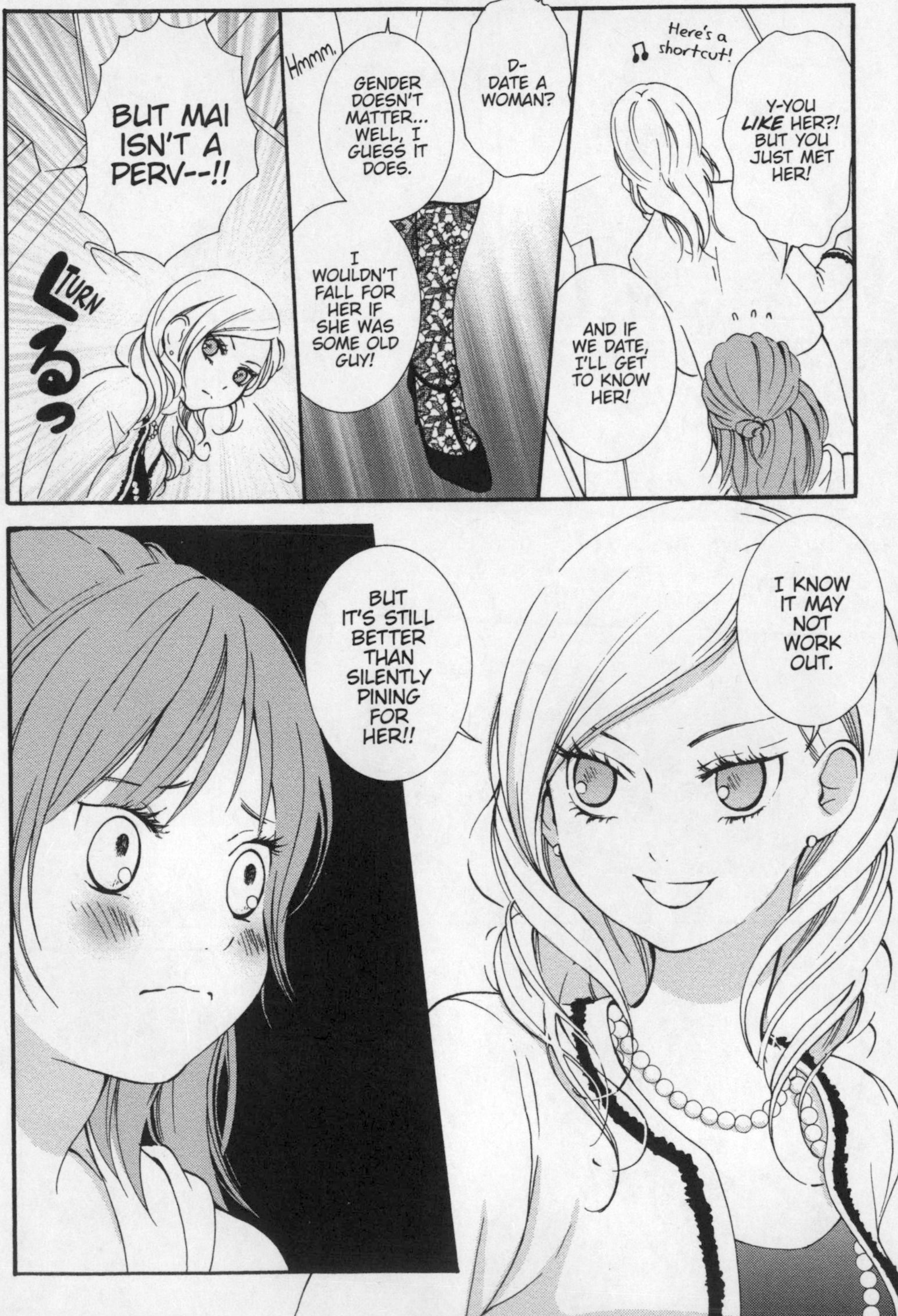
Here's a shortcut!
Y-YOU LIKE HER?! BUT YOU JUST MET HER!
AND IF WE DATE, I'LL GET TO KNOW HER!
D- DATE A WOMAN?
Hmmm.
GENDER DOESN'T MATTER... WELL, I GUESS IT DOES.
I WOULDN'T FALL FOR HER IF SHE WAS SOME OLD GUY!
BUT MAI ISN'T A PERV--!!
TURN
I KNOW IT MAY NOT WORK OUT.
BUT IT'S STILL BETTER THAN SILENTLY PINING FOR HER!!

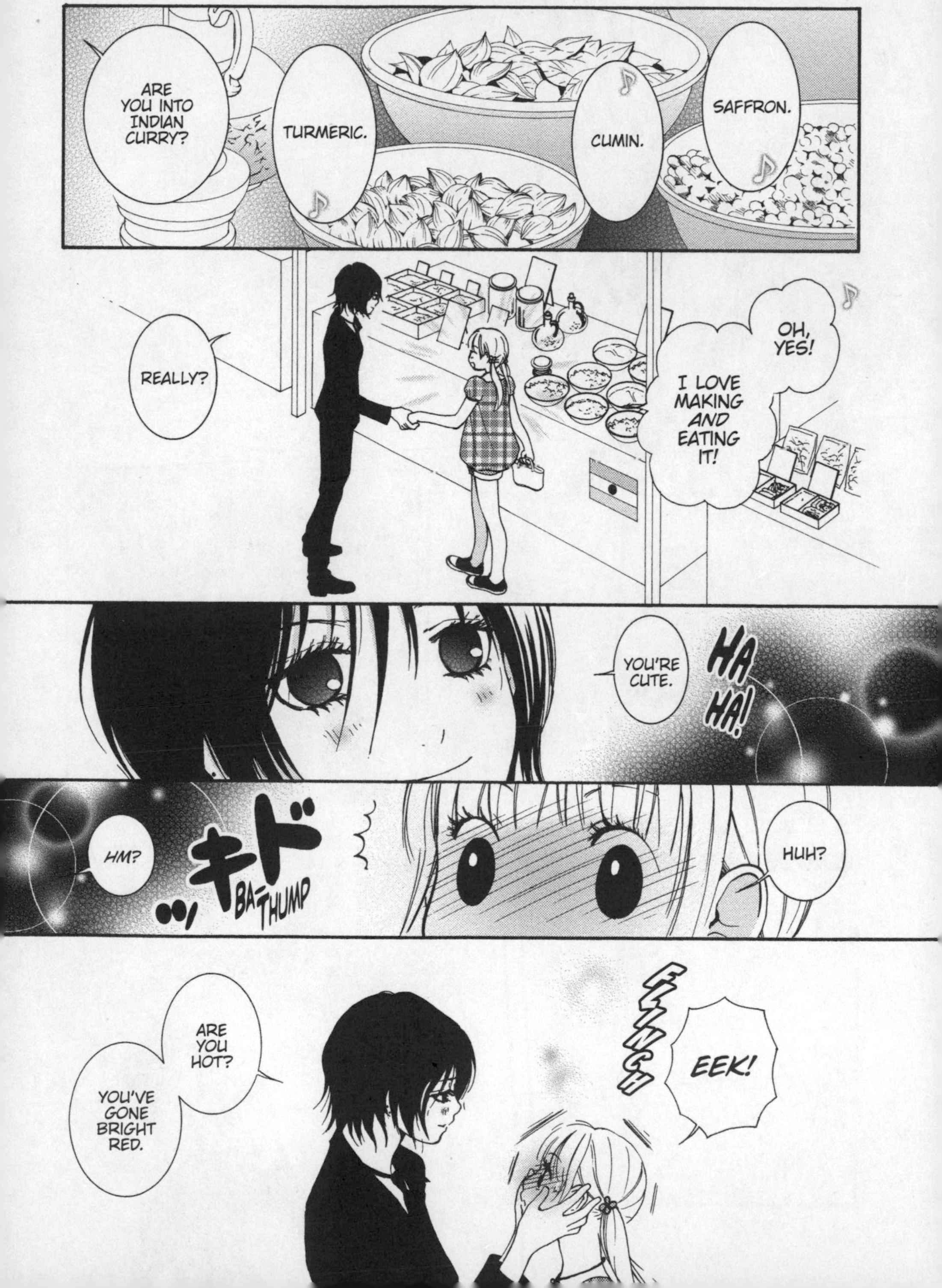
SAFFRON.
CUMIN.
TURMERIC.
ARE YOU INTO INDIAN CURRY?
OH, YES! I LOVE MAKING AND EATING IT!
REALLY?
HA HA!
YOU'RE CUTE.
HUH?
キド BA-THUMP
HM?
EEK!
FLINCH
ARE YOU HOT?
YOU'VE GONE BRIGHT RED.

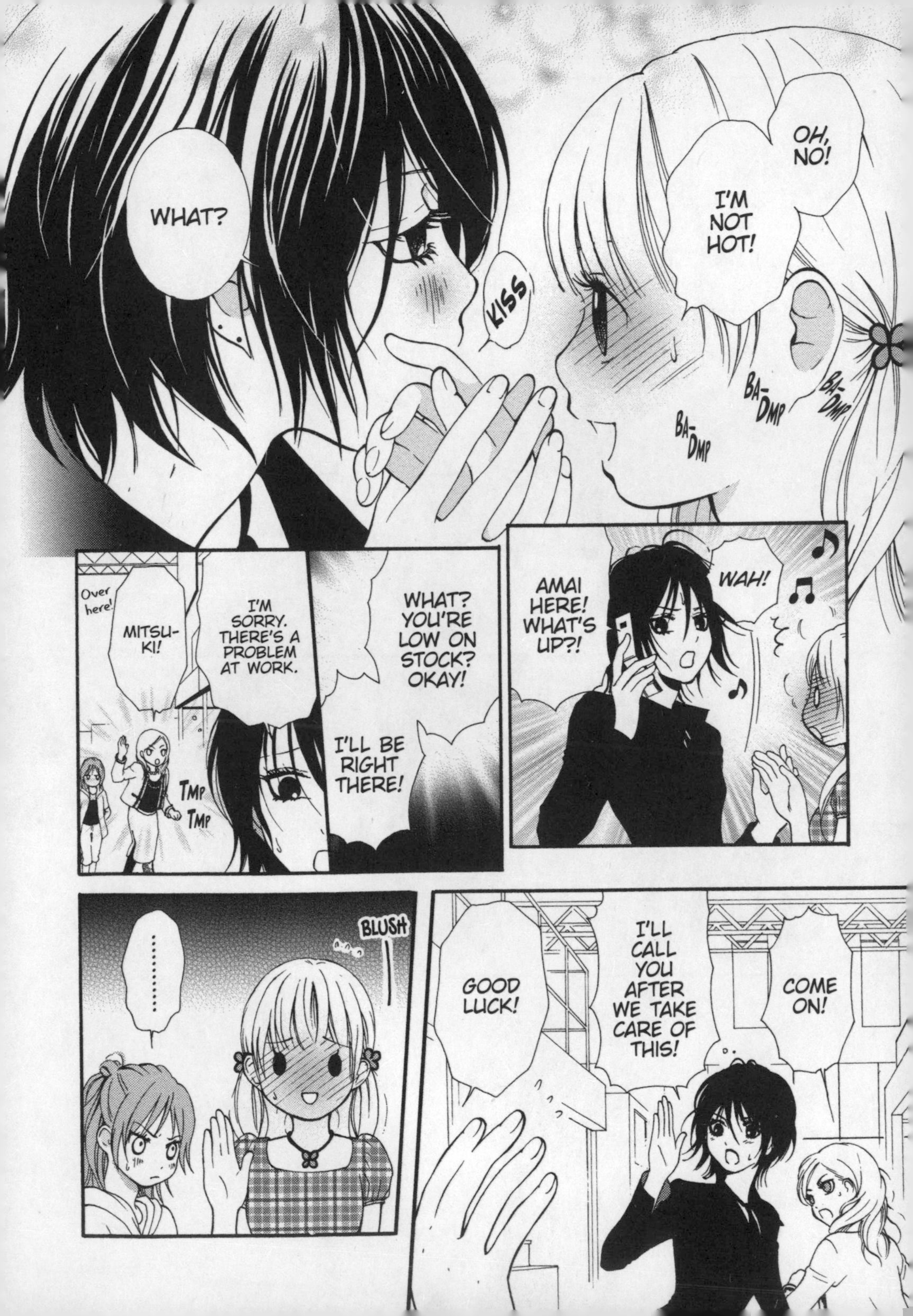
OH, NO!
I'M NOT HOT!
BA-DMP
BA-DMP
BA-DMP
KISS
WHAT?
WAH!
AMAI HERE! WHAT'S UP?!
WHAT? YOU'RE LOW ON STOCK? OKAY!
I'LL BE RIGHT THERE!
I'M SORRY. THERE'S A PROBLEM AT WORK.
MITSU-KI!
Over here!
TMP
TMP
COME ON!
I'LL CALL YOU AFTER WE TAKE CARE OF THIS!
GOOD LUCK!
BLUSH
....

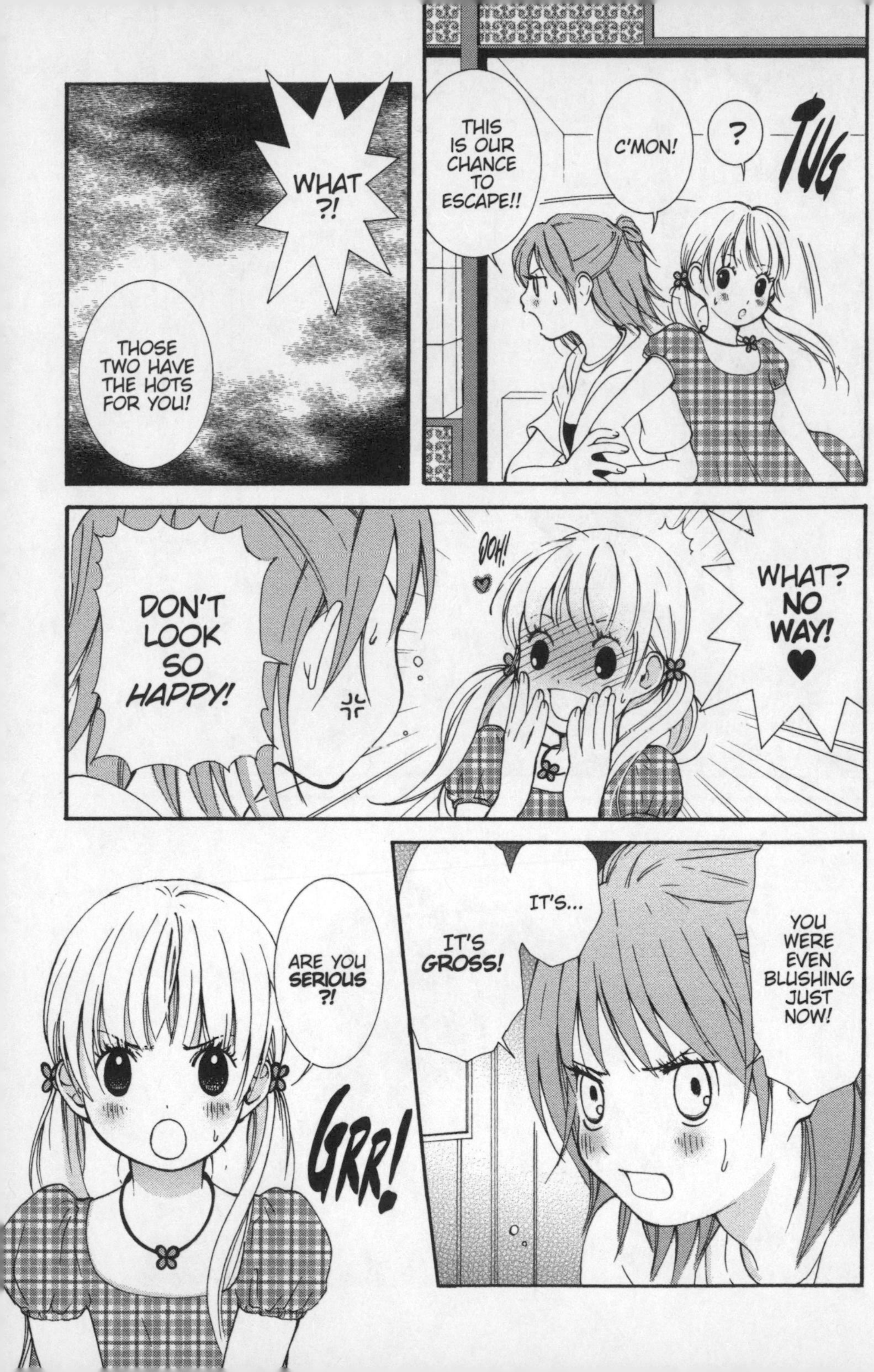
TUG
?
C'MON!
THIS IS OUR CHANCE TO ESCAPE!!
WHAT?!
THOSE TWO HAVE THE HOTS FOR YOU!
WHAT? NO WAY! ♥
OOH! ♥
DON'T LOOK SO HAPPY!
YOU WERE EVEN BLUSHING JUST NOW!
IT'S...
IT'S GROSS!
ARE YOU SERIOUS?!
GRR!

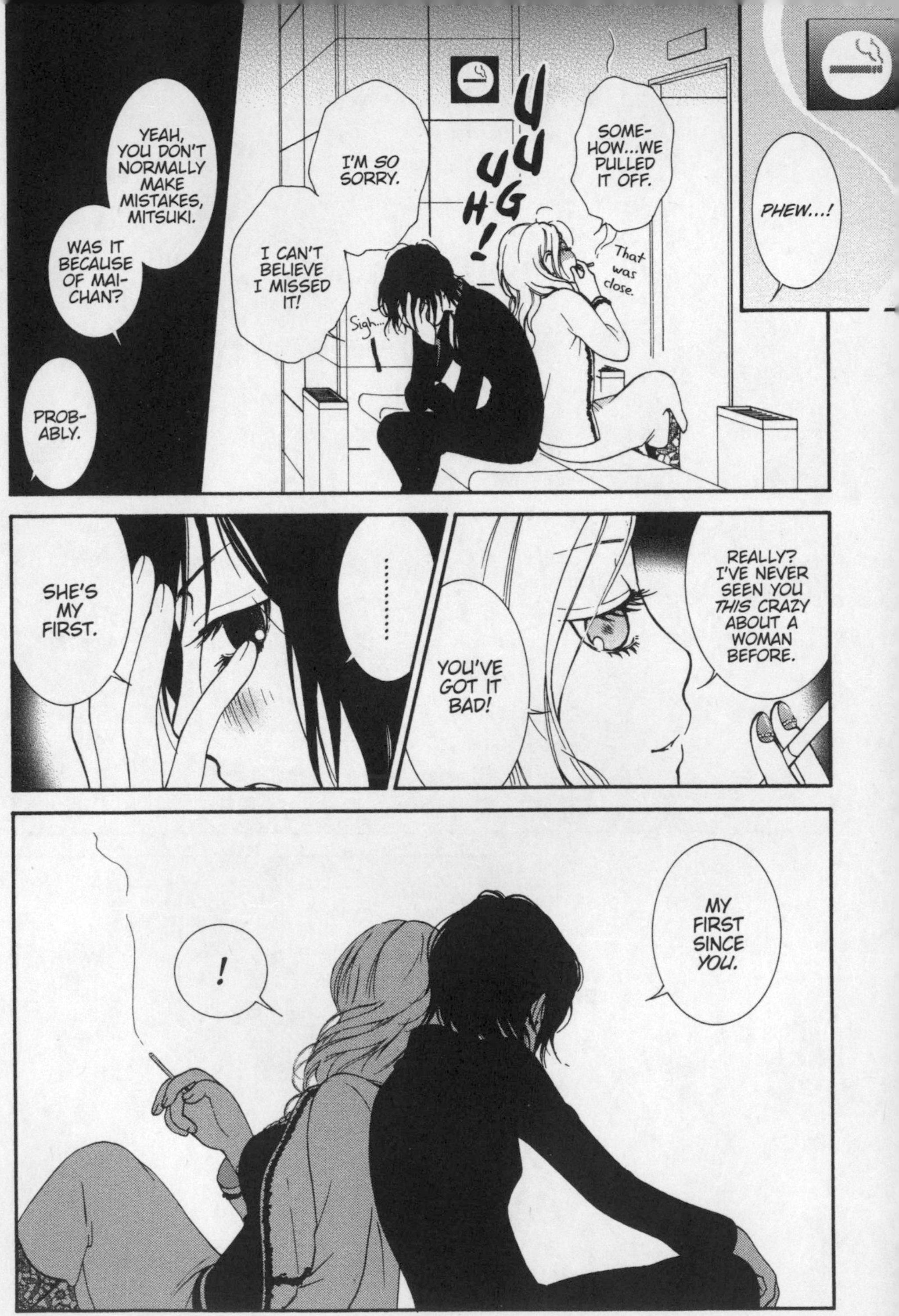
PHEW...!
SOME-HOW...WE PULLED IT OFF.
That was close.
UUGH!
I'M SO SORRY.
I CAN'T BELIEVE I MISSED IT!
Sigh...
YEAH, YOU DON'T NORMALLY MAKE MISTAKES, MITSUKI.
WAS IT BECAUSE OF MAI-CHAN?
PROBABLY.
REALLY? I'VE NEVER SEEN YOU *THIS* CRAZY ABOUT A WOMAN BEFORE.
YOU'VE GOT IT BAD!
......
SHE'S MY FIRST.
MY FIRST SINCE *YOU*.
!

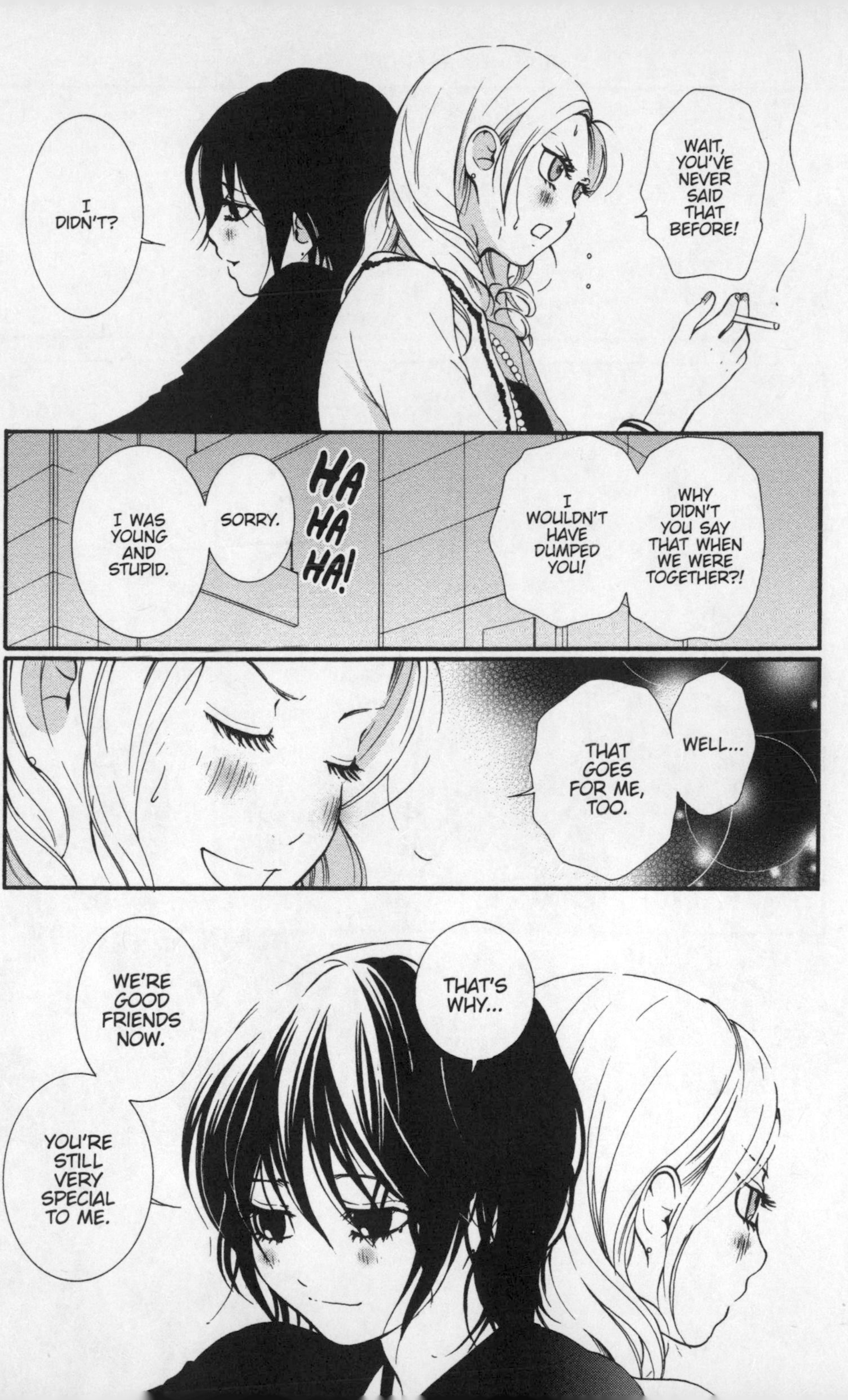
WAIT, YOU'VE NEVER SAID THAT BEFORE!
I DIDN'T?
WHY DIDN'T YOU SAY THAT WHEN WE WERE TOGETHER?!
I WOULDN'T HAVE DUMPED YOU!
HA HA HA!
SORRY.
I WAS YOUNG AND STUPID.
WELL...
THAT GOES FOR ME, TOO.
THAT'S WHY...
WE'RE GOOD FRIENDS NOW.
YOU'RE STILL VERY SPECIAL TO ME.

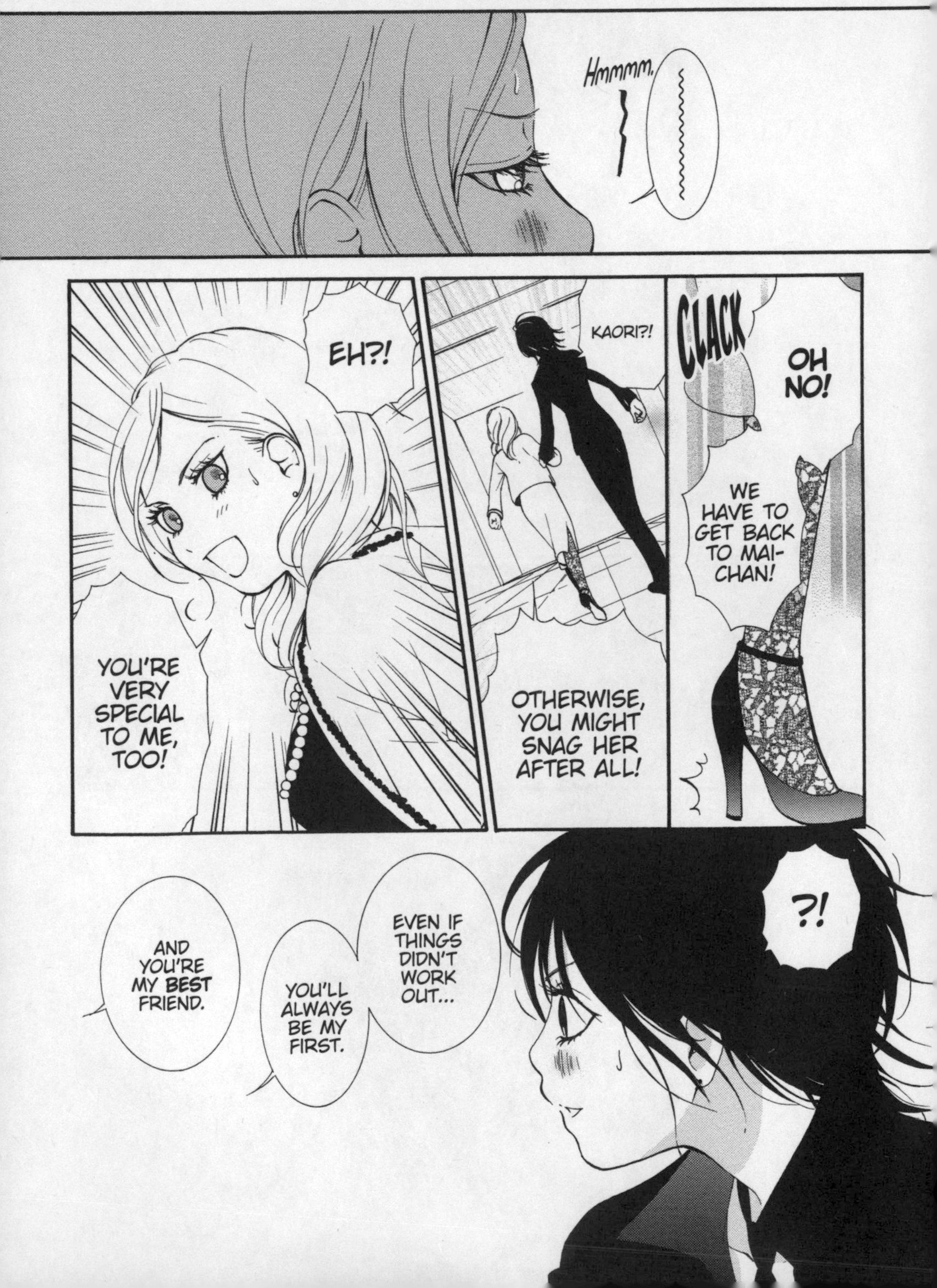
Hmmmm.
CLACK
OH NO!
WE HAVE TO GET BACK TO MAI-CHAN!
KAORI?!
OTHERWISE, YOU MIGHT SNAG HER AFTER ALL!
EH?!
YOU'RE VERY SPECIAL TO ME, TOO!
?!
EVEN IF THINGS DIDN'T WORK OUT...
YOU'LL ALWAYS BE MY FIRST.
AND YOU'RE MY BEST FRIEND.

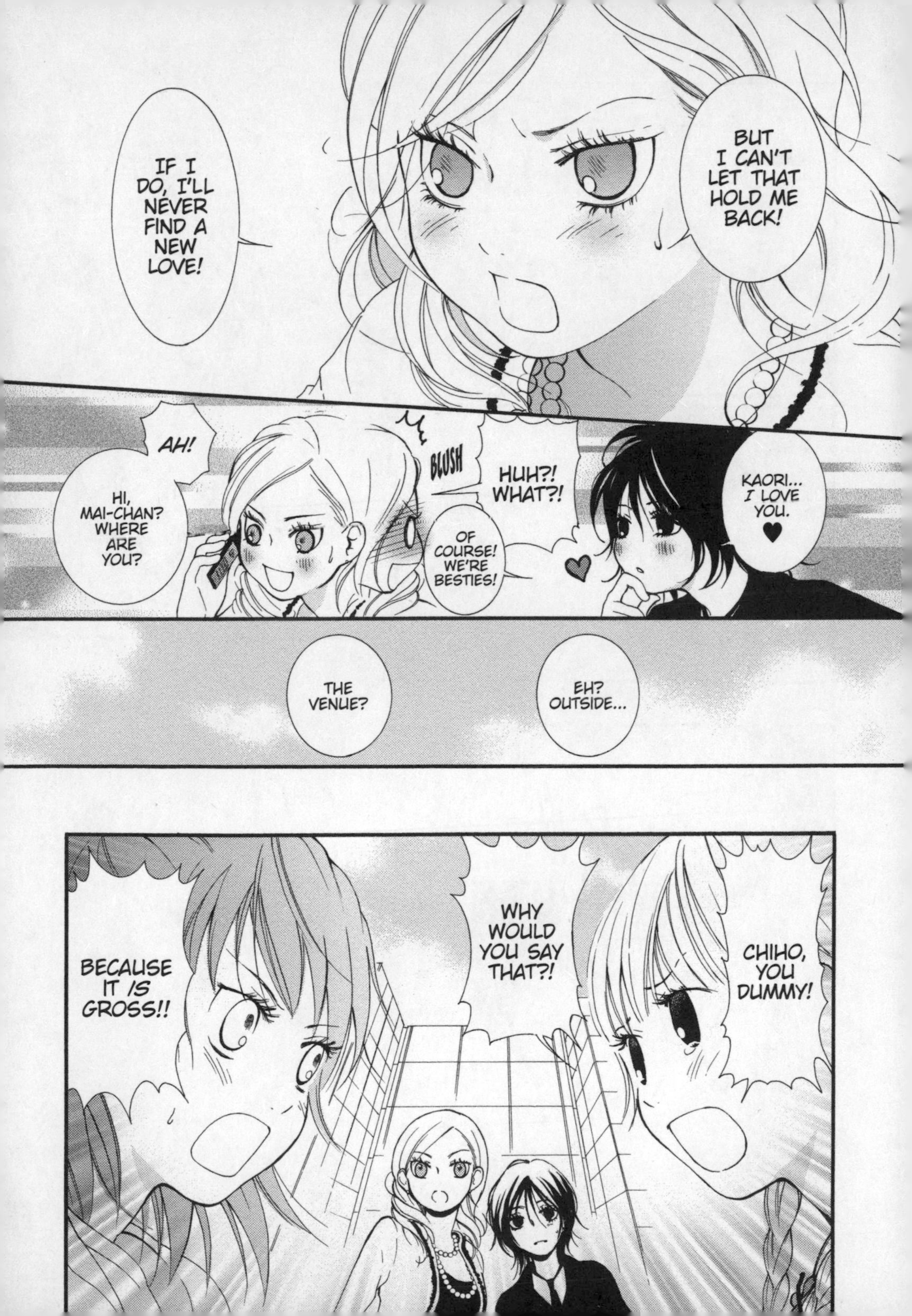
BUT I CAN'T LET THAT HOLD ME BACK!
IF I DO, I'LL NEVER FIND A NEW LOVE!
KAORI... I LOVE YOU. ♥
HUH?! WHAT?!
BLUSH
OF COURSE! WE'RE BESTIES!
AH!
HI, MAI-CHAN? WHERE ARE YOU?
EH? OUTSIDE...
THE VENUE?
CHIHO, YOU DUMMY!
WHY WOULD YOU SAY THAT?!
BECAUSE IT *IS* GROSS!!

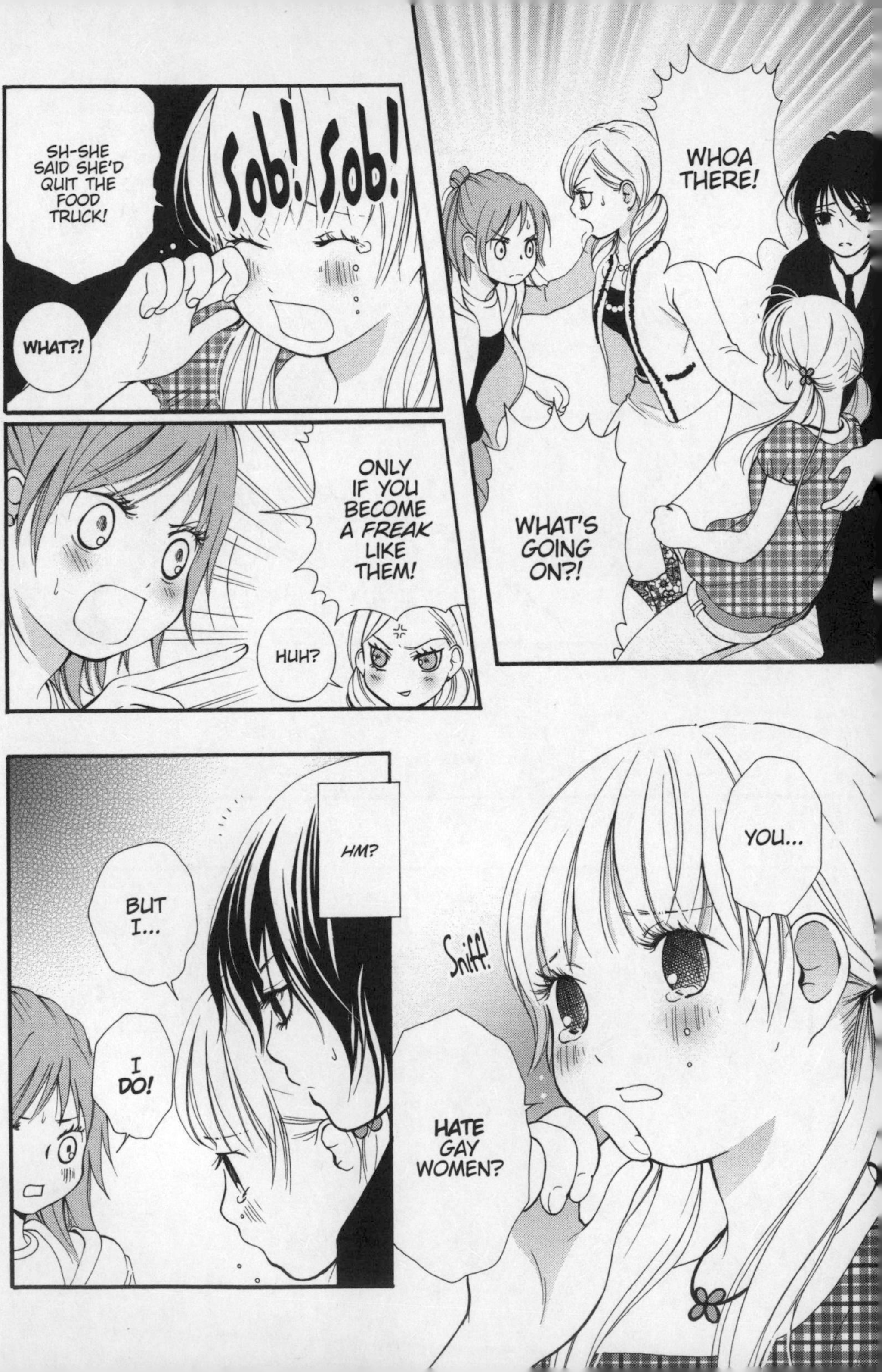
WHOA THERE!
WHAT'S GOING ON?!
SH-SHE SAID SHE'D QUIT THE FOOD TRUCK!
Sob! Sob!
WHAT?!
ONLY IF YOU BECOME A *FREAK* LIKE THEM!
HUH?
YOU...
Sniff!
HATE GAY WOMEN?
HM?
BUT I...
I DO!

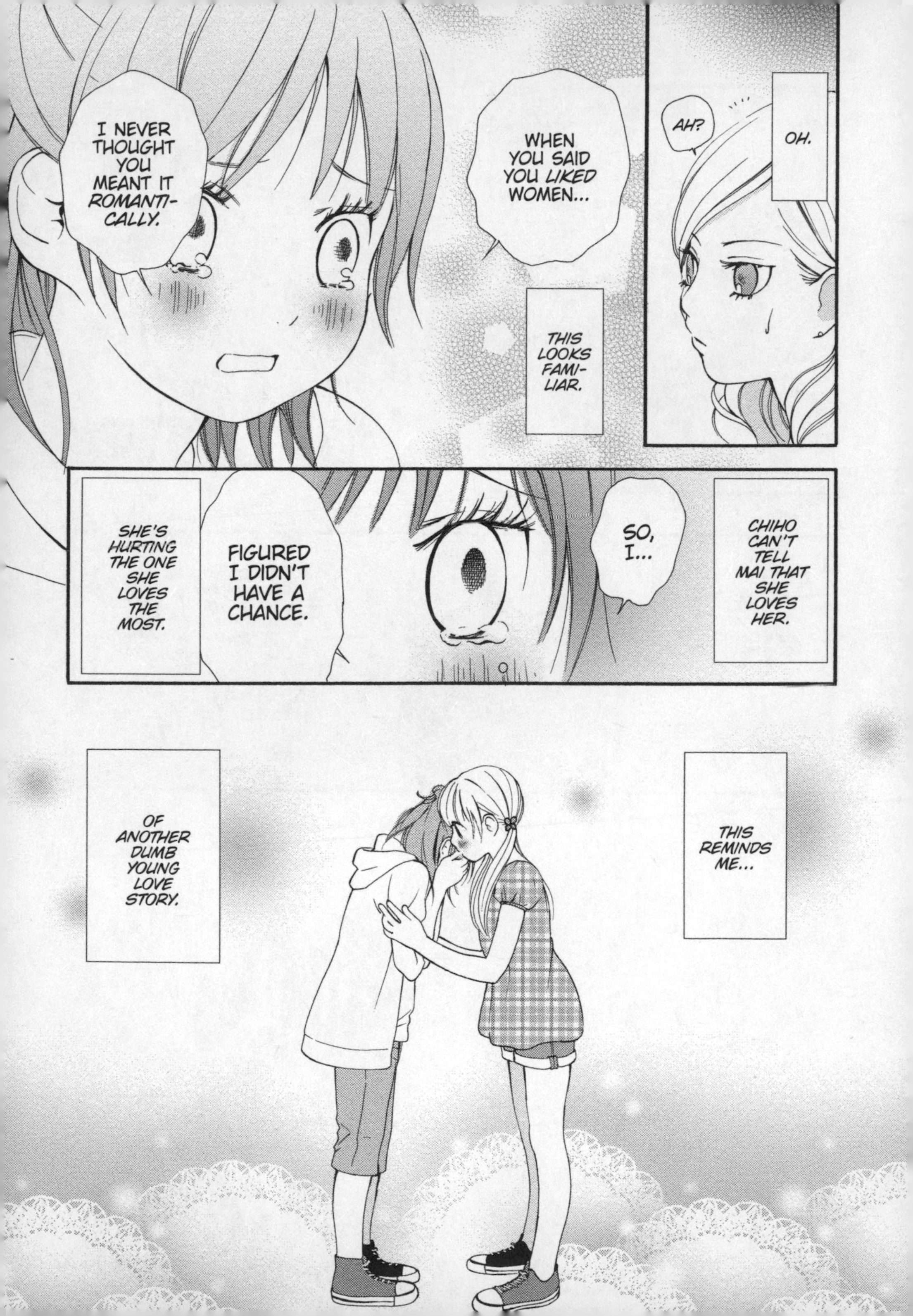
OH.
AH?
WHEN YOU SAID YOU LIKED WOMEN...
I NEVER THOUGHT YOU MEANT IT ROMANTICALLY.
THIS LOOKS FAMILIAR.
CHIHO CAN'T TELL MAI THAT SHE LOVES HER.
SO, I...
FIGURED I DIDN'T HAVE A CHANCE.
SHE'S HURTING THE ONE SHE LOVES THE MOST.
THIS REMINDS ME...
OF ANOTHER DUMB YOUNG LOVE STORY.

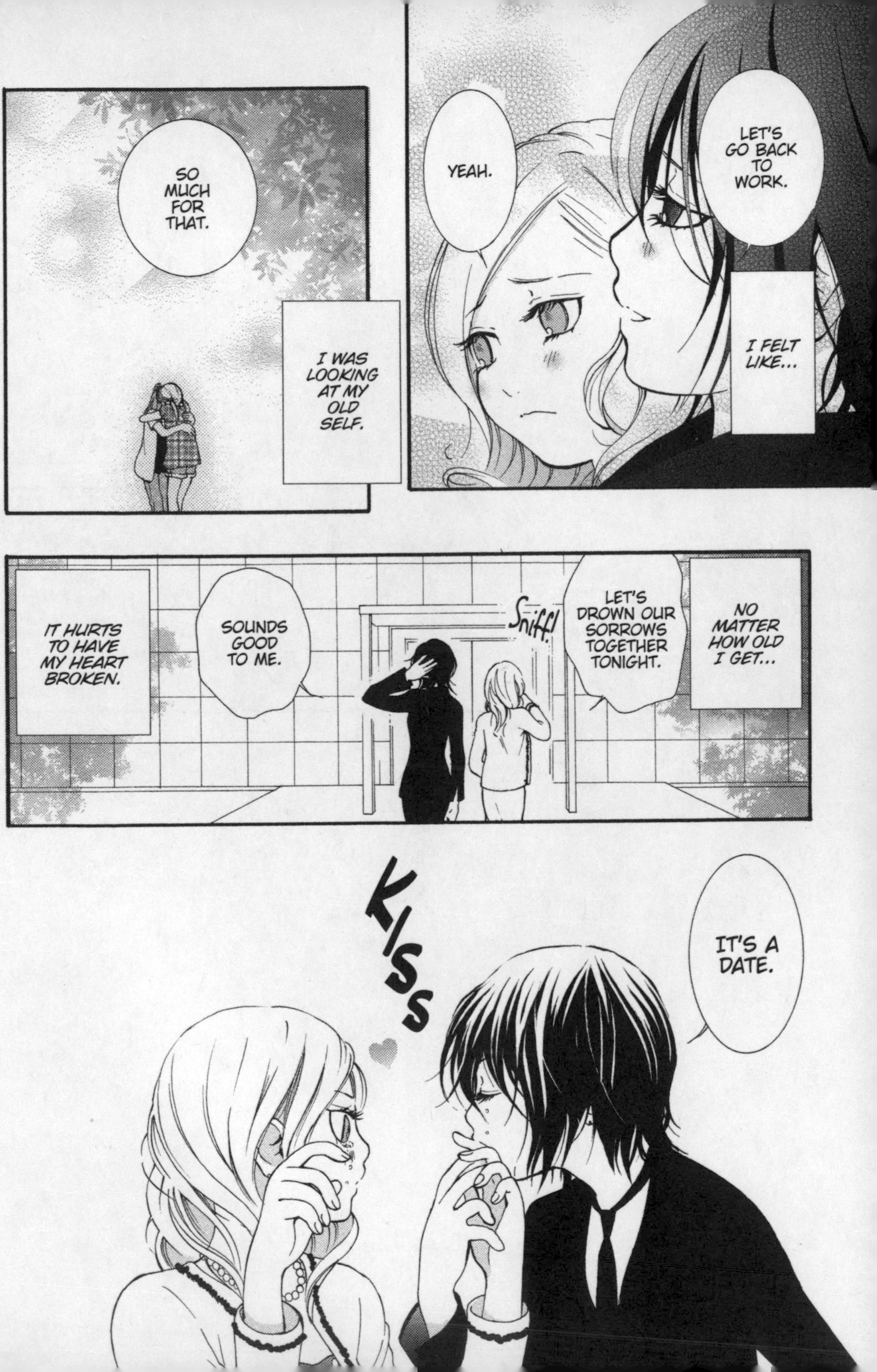
LET'S GO BACK TO WORK.
YEAH.
I FELT LIKE...
I WAS LOOKING AT MY OLD SELF.
SO MUCH FOR THAT.
NO MATTER HOW OLD I GET...
LET'S DROWN OUR SORROWS TOGETHER TONIGHT.
Sniff!
SOUNDS GOOD TO ME.
IT HURTS TO HAVE MY HEART BROKEN.
IT'S A DATE.
KISS

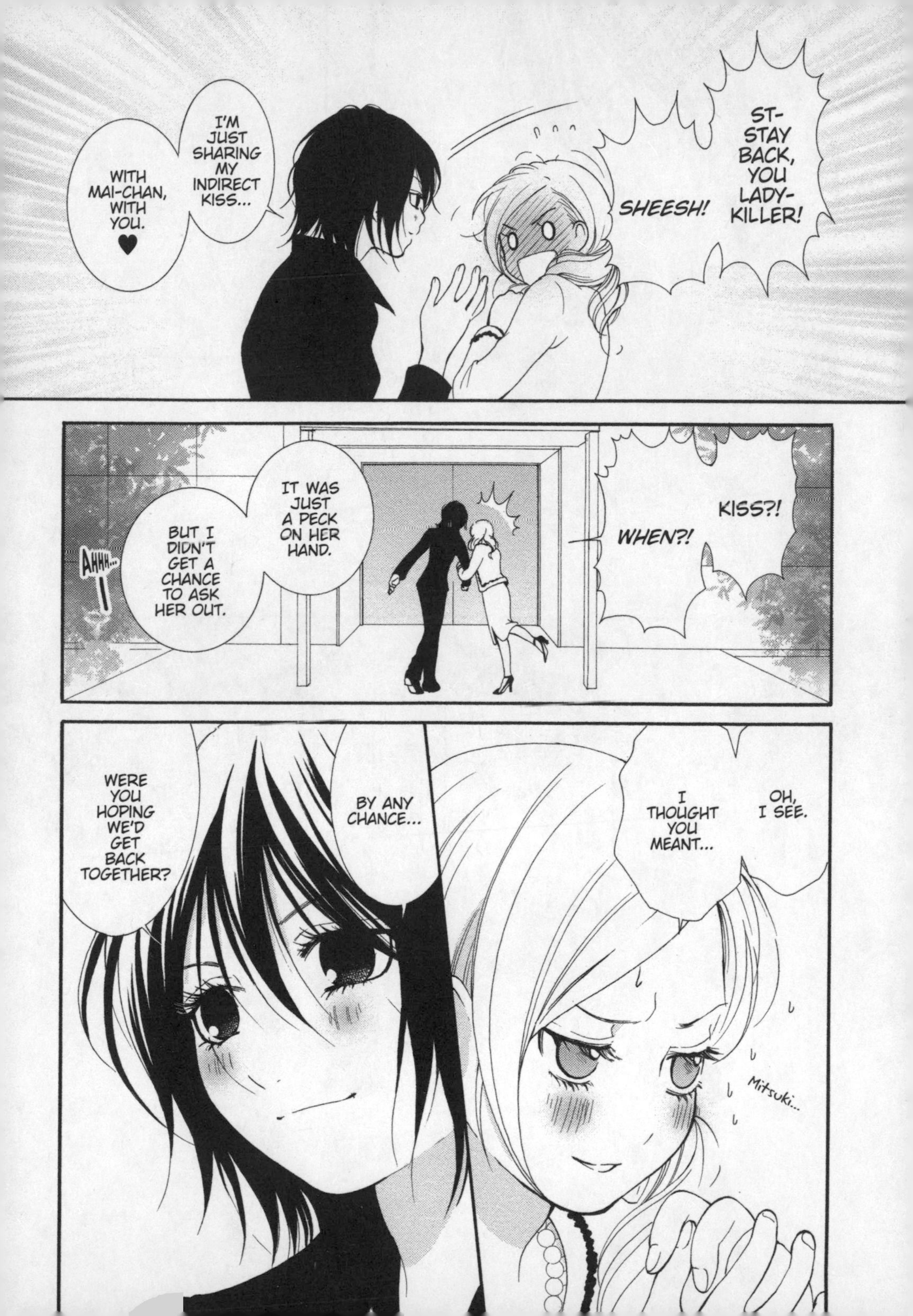
ST-STAY BACK, YOU LADY-KILLER!
SHEESH!
I'M JUST SHARING MY INDIRECT KISS...
WITH MAI-CHAN, WITH YOU. ♥
KISS?!
WHEN?!
IT WAS JUST A PECK ON HER HAND.
BUT I DIDN'T GET A CHANCE TO ASK HER OUT.
AHHH...
OH, I SEE.
I THOUGHT YOU MEANT...
Mitsuki...
BY ANY CHANCE...
WERE YOU HOPING WE'D GET BACK TOGETHER?

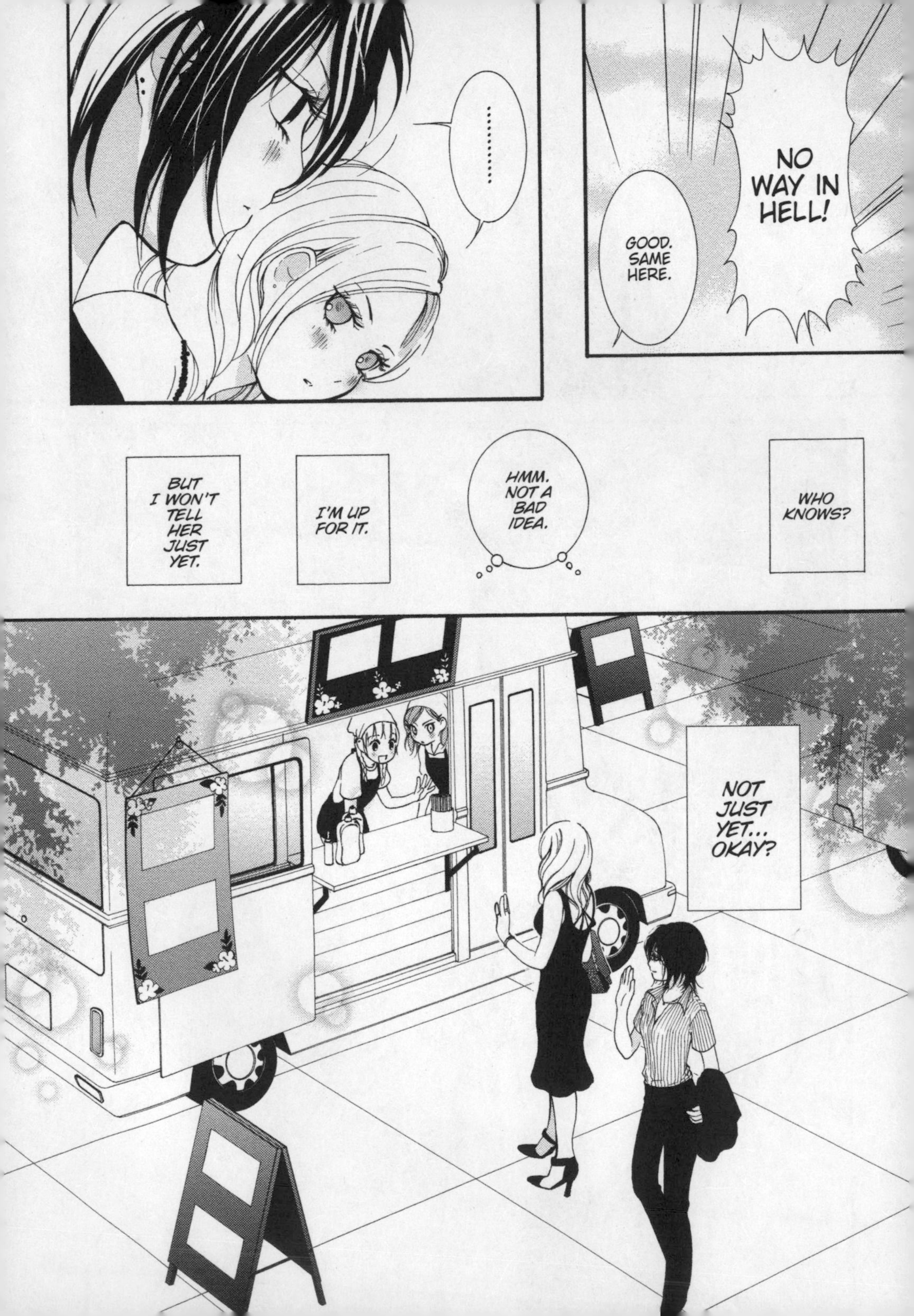
NO WAY IN HELL!
GOOD. SAME HERE.
......
WHO KNOWS?
HMM. NOT A BAD IDEA.
I'M UP FOR IT.
BUT I WON'T TELL HER JUST YET.
NOT JUST YET... OKAY?

The Conditions
of Paradise

AZURE DREAMS

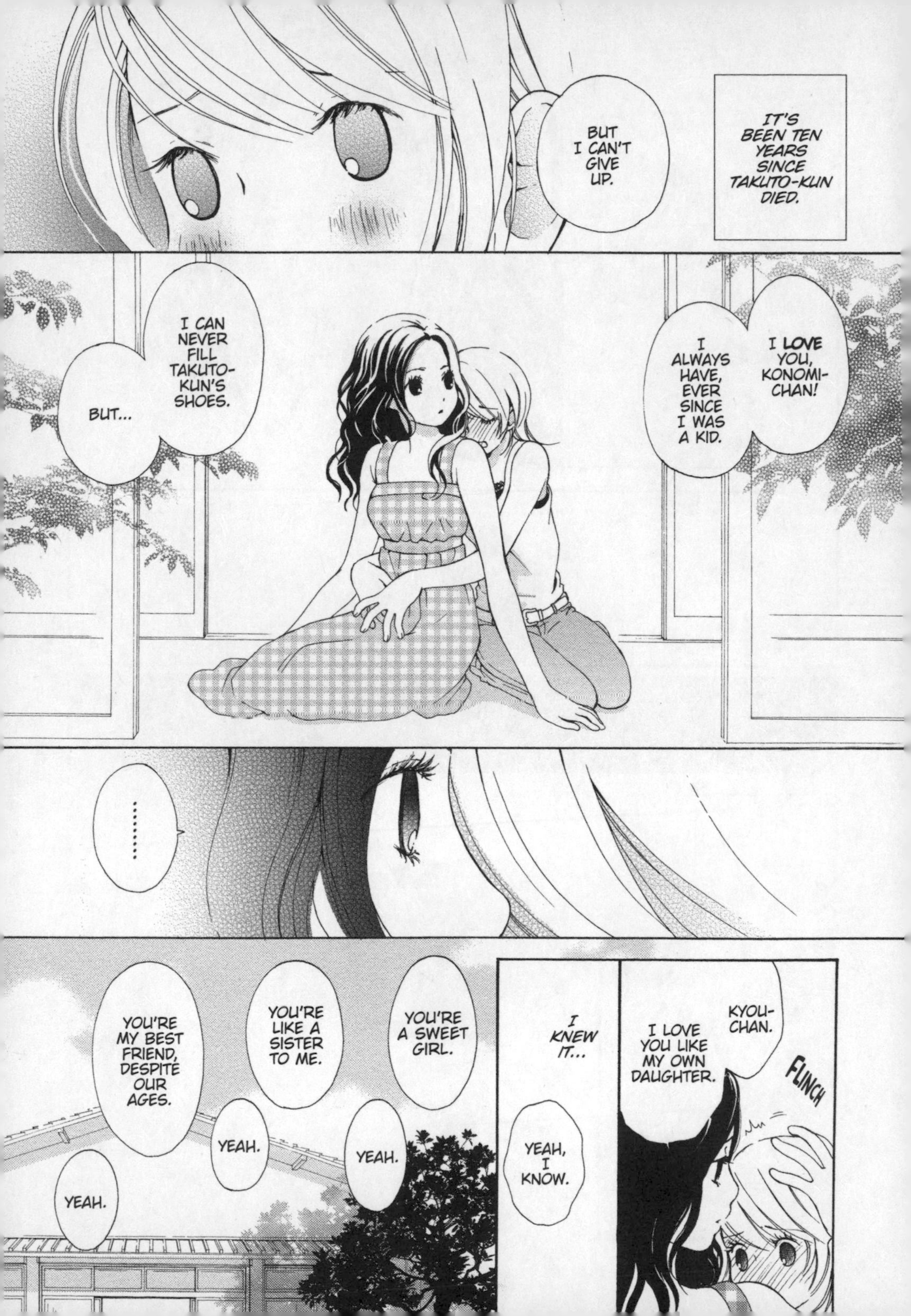
IT'S BEEN TEN YEARS SINCE TAKUTO-KUN DIED.
BUT I CAN'T GIVE UP.
I LOVE YOU, KONOMI-CHAN!
I ALWAYS HAVE, EVER SINCE I WAS A KID.
I CAN NEVER FILL TAKUTO-KUN'S SHOES.
BUT...
......
KYOU-CHAN.
I LOVE YOU LIKE MY OWN DAUGHTER.
FLINCH
I KNEW IT...
YEAH, I KNOW.
YOU'RE A SWEET GIRL.
YEAH.
YOU'RE LIKE A SISTER TO ME.
YEAH.
YOU'RE MY BEST FRIEND, DESPITE OUR AGES.
YEAH.

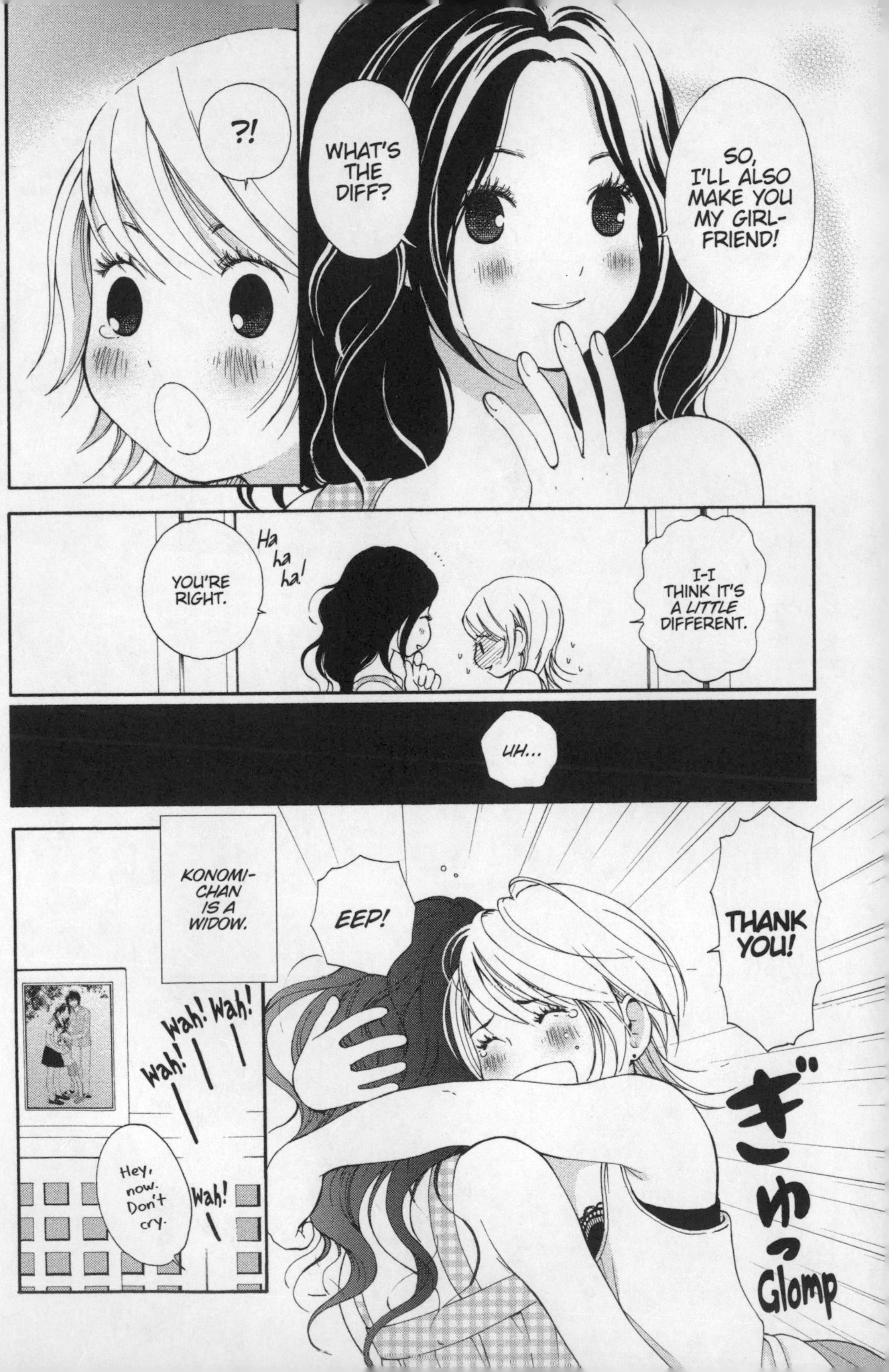
SO, I'LL ALSO MAKE YOU MY GIRL-FRIEND!
WHAT'S THE DIFF?
?!
I-I THINK IT'S A *LITTLE* DIFFERENT.
Ha ha ha!
YOU'RE RIGHT.
UH...
THANK YOU!
ぎゅっ
Glomp
EEP!
KONOMI-CHAN IS A WIDOW.
Wah! Wah!
Wah!
Hey, now. Don't cry.
Wah!

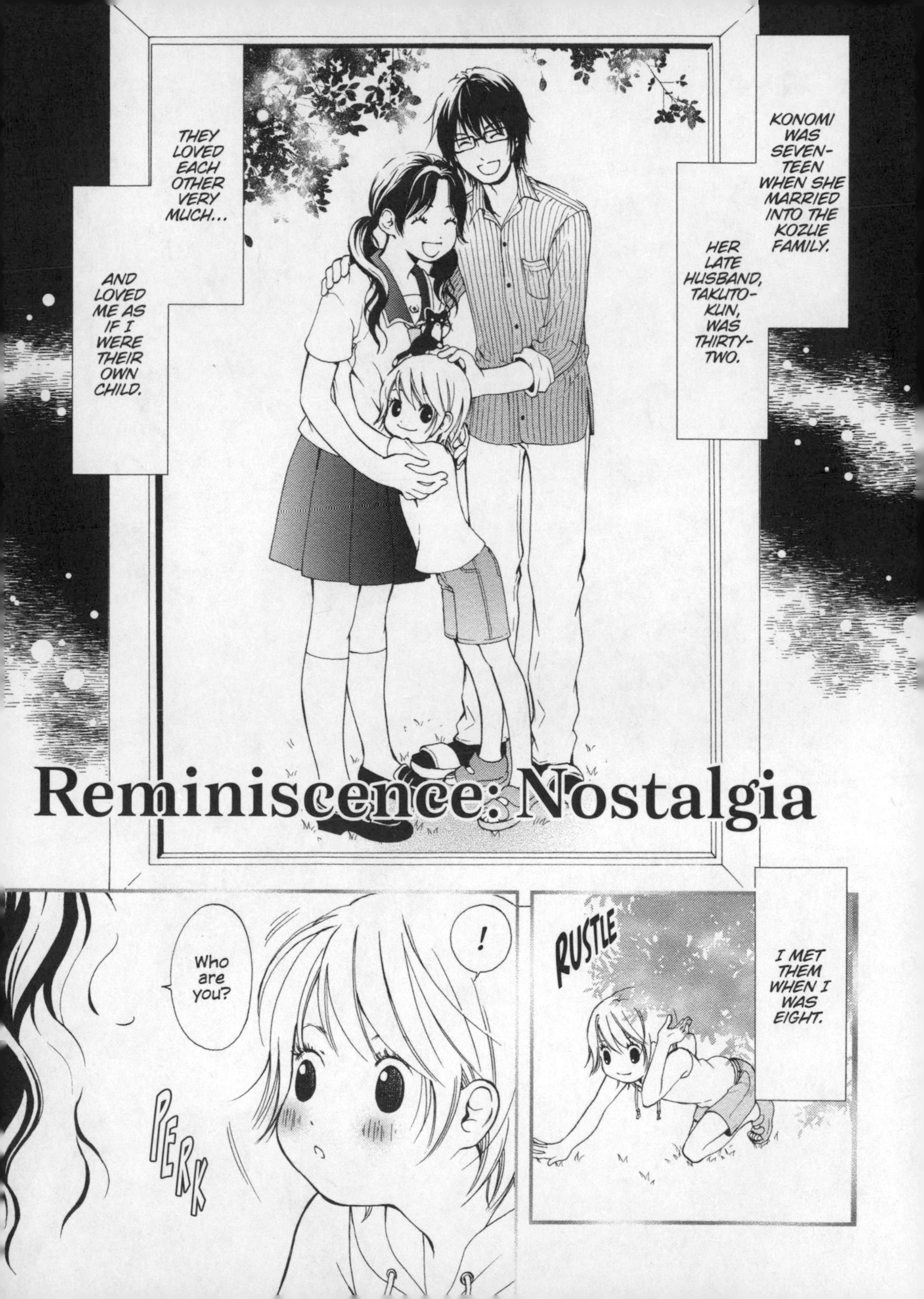
KONOMI WAS SEVENTEEN WHEN SHE MARRIED INTO THE KOZUE FAMILY.
HER LATE HUSBAND, TAKUTO-KUN, WAS THIRTY-TWO.
THEY LOVED EACH OTHER VERY MUCH...
AND LOVED ME AS IF I WERE THEIR OWN CHILD.
Reminiscence: Nostalgia
I MET THEM WHEN I WAS EIGHT.
RUSTLE
!
Who are you?
PERK

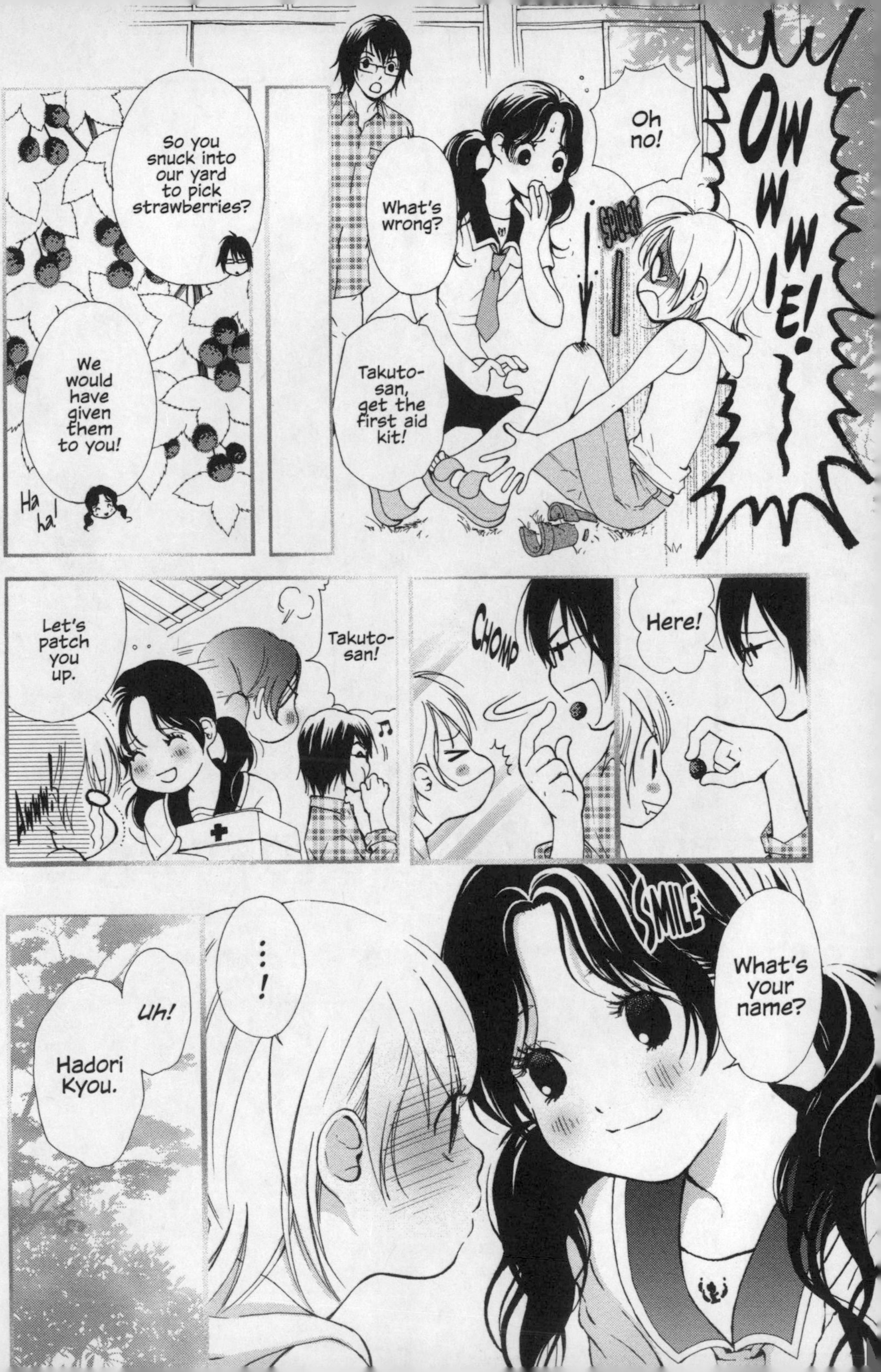
OWWWWIE!
Oh no!
What's wrong?
Takuto-san, get the first aid kit!
So you snuck into our yard to pick strawberries?
We would have given them to you!
Ha ha!
Here!
CHOMP
Takuto-san!
Let's patch you up.
SMILE
What's your name?
...!
Uh!
Hadori Kyou.

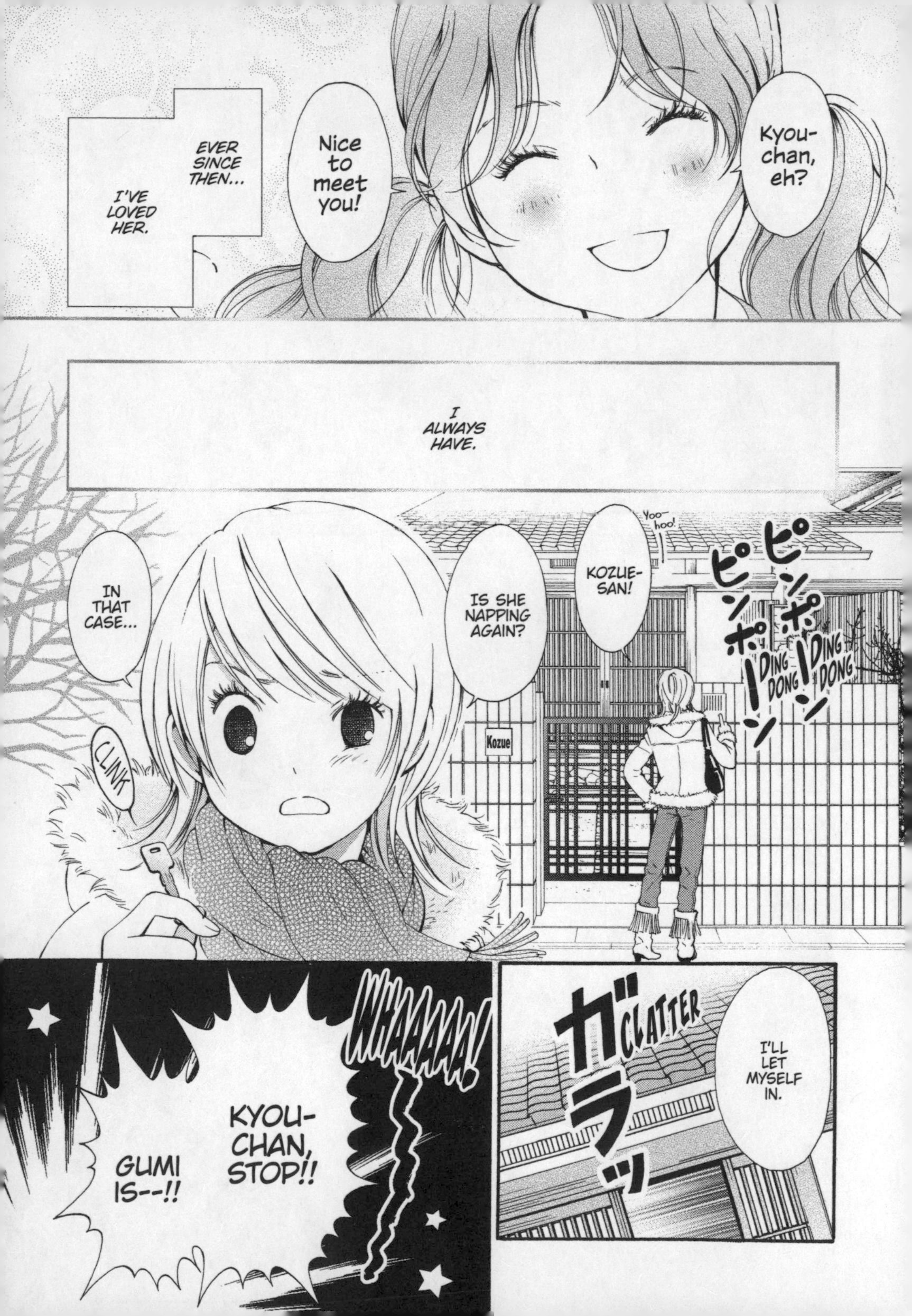
Kyou-chan, eh?
Nice to meet you!
EVER SINCE THEN... I'VE LOVED HER.
I ALWAYS HAVE.
ピンポーン
DING DONG
ピンポーン
DING DONG
Yoo-hoo!
KOZUE-SAN!
IS SHE NAPPING AGAIN?
Kozue
IN THAT CASE...
CLINK
ガラッ
CLATTER
I'LL LET MYSELF IN.
WHAAAAA!
KYOU-CHAN, STOP!!
GUMI IS--!!

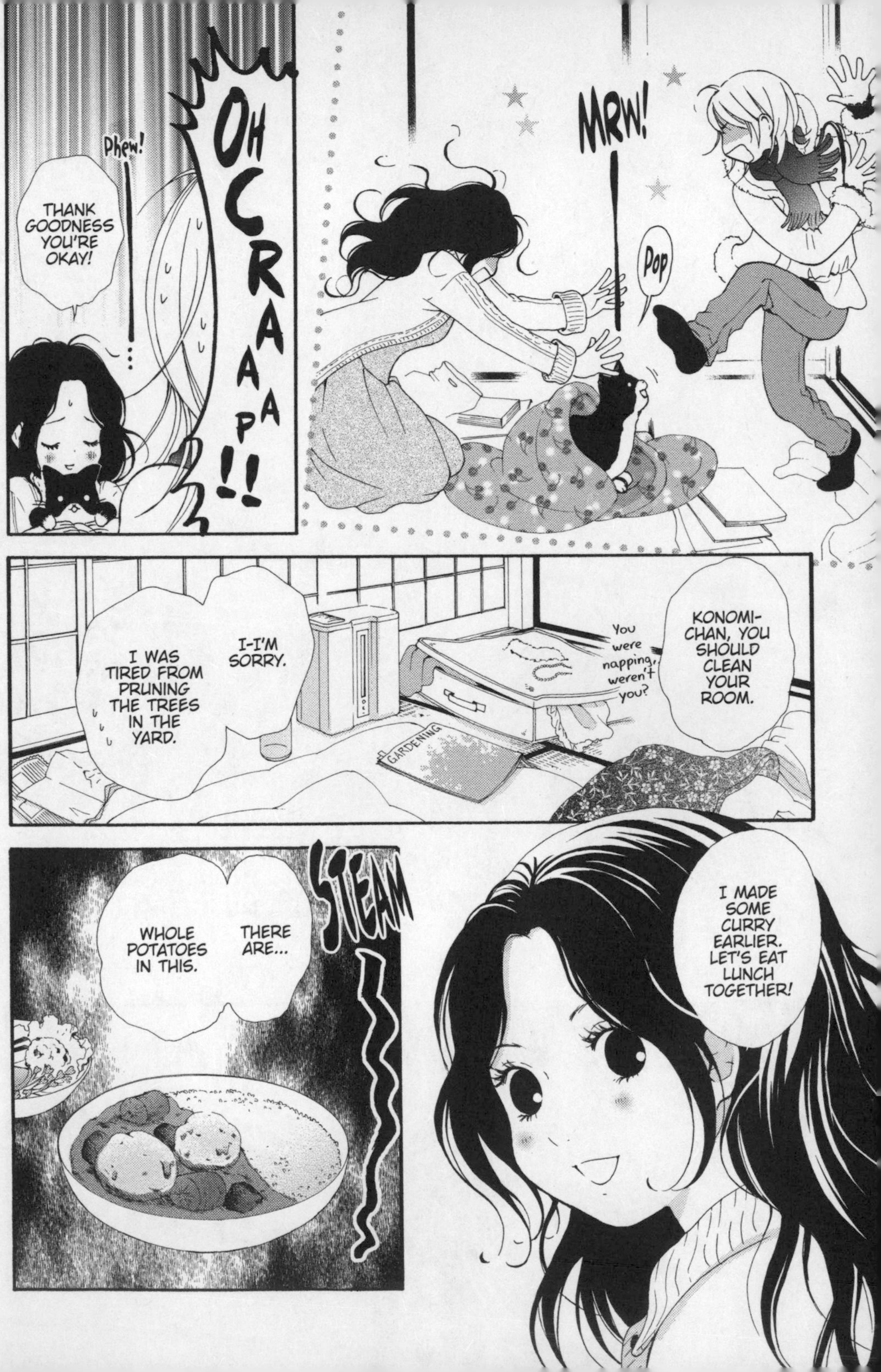
MRW!
Pop
OH CRAAAAP!!
Phew!
THANK GOODNESS YOU'RE OKAY!
KONOMI-CHAN, YOU SHOULD CLEAN YOUR ROOM.
You were napping, weren't you?
I-I'M SORRY.
I WAS TIRED FROM PRUNING THE TREES IN THE YARD.
GARDENING
I MADE SOME CURRY EARLIER. LET'S EAT LUNCH TOGETHER!
STEAM
THERE ARE...
WHOLE POTATOES IN THIS.

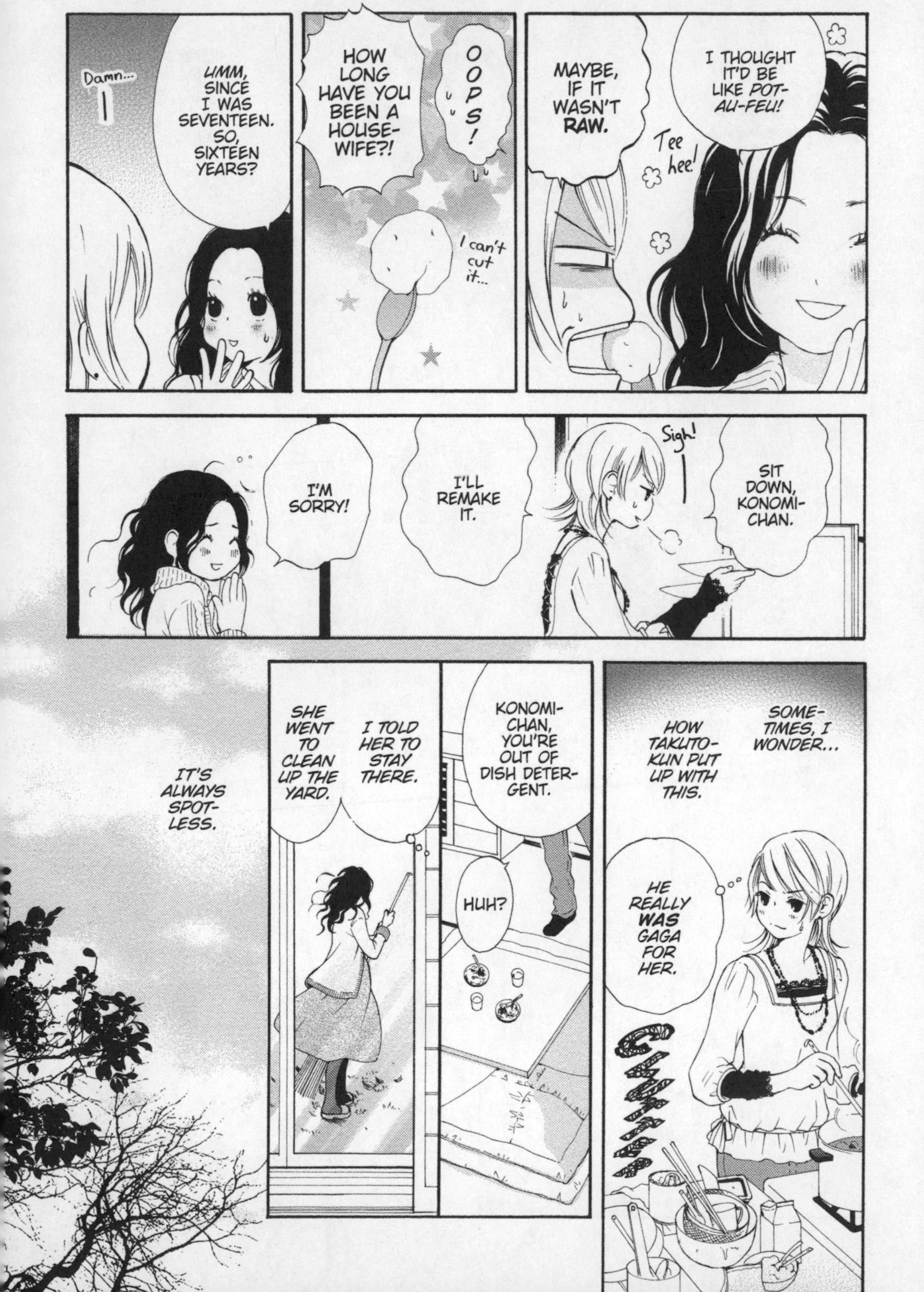
I THOUGHT IT'D BE LIKE POT-AU-FEU!
Tee hee!
MAYBE, IF IT WASN'T RAW.
OOPS!
HOW LONG HAVE YOU BEEN A HOUSE-WIFE?!
I can't cut it...
Damn...
UMM, SINCE I WAS SEVENTEEN. SO, SIXTEEN YEARS?
SIT DOWN, KONOMI-CHAN.
Sigh!
I'LL REMAKE IT.
I'M SORRY!
SOME-TIMES, I WONDER...
HOW TAKUTO-KUN PUT UP WITH THIS.
HE REALLY WAS GAGA FOR HER.
KONOMI-CHAN, YOU'RE OUT OF DISH DETER-GENT.
HUH?
I TOLD HER TO STAY THERE.
SHE WENT TO CLEAN UP THE YARD.
IT'S ALWAYS SPOT-LESS.

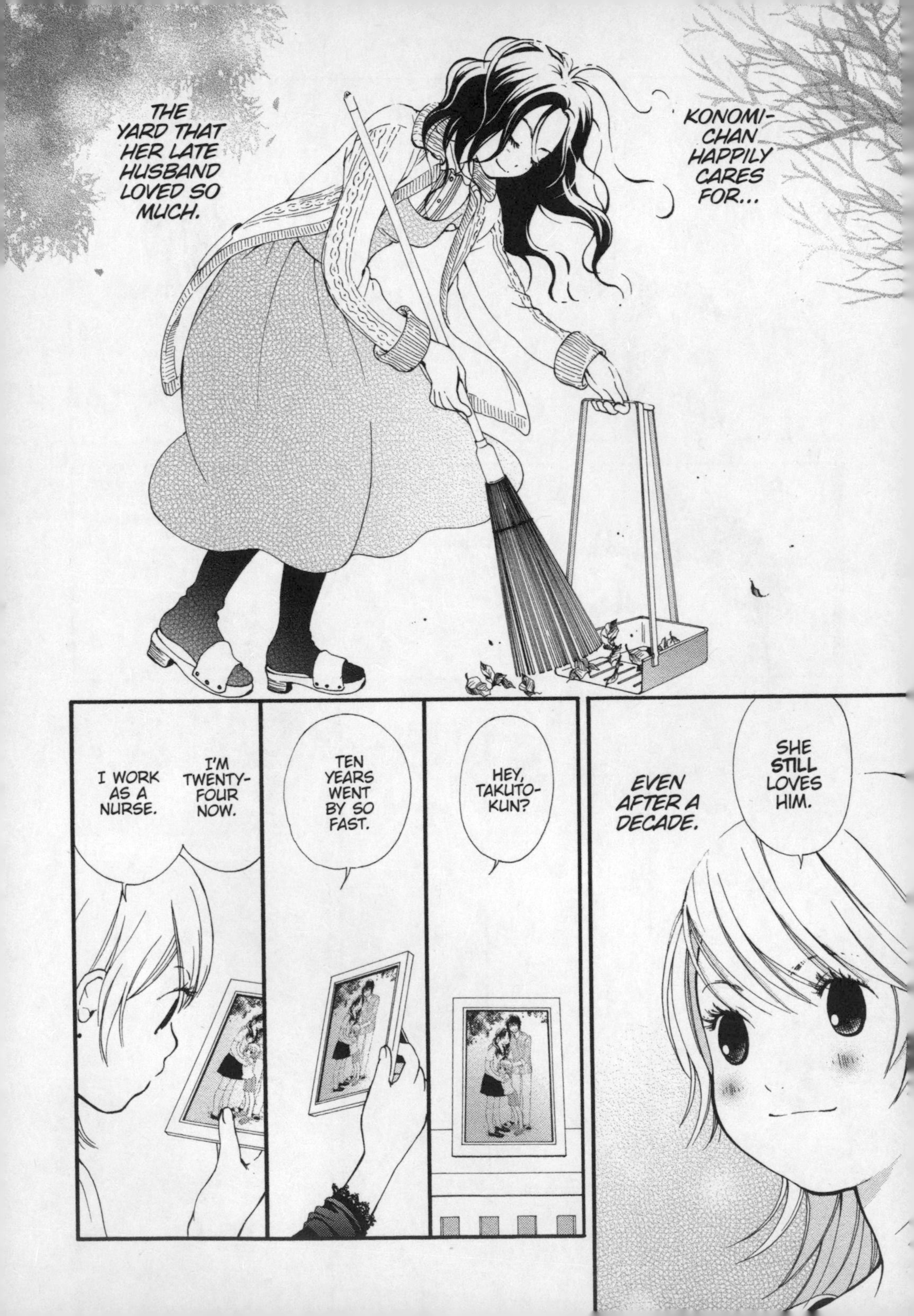
KONOMI-CHAN HAPPILY CARES FOR...
THE YARD THAT HER LATE HUSBAND LOVED SO MUCH.
SHE STILL LOVES HIM.
EVEN AFTER A DECADE.
HEY, TAKUTO-KUN?
TEN YEARS WENT BY SO FAST.
I'M TWENTY-FOUR NOW.
I WORK AS A NURSE.

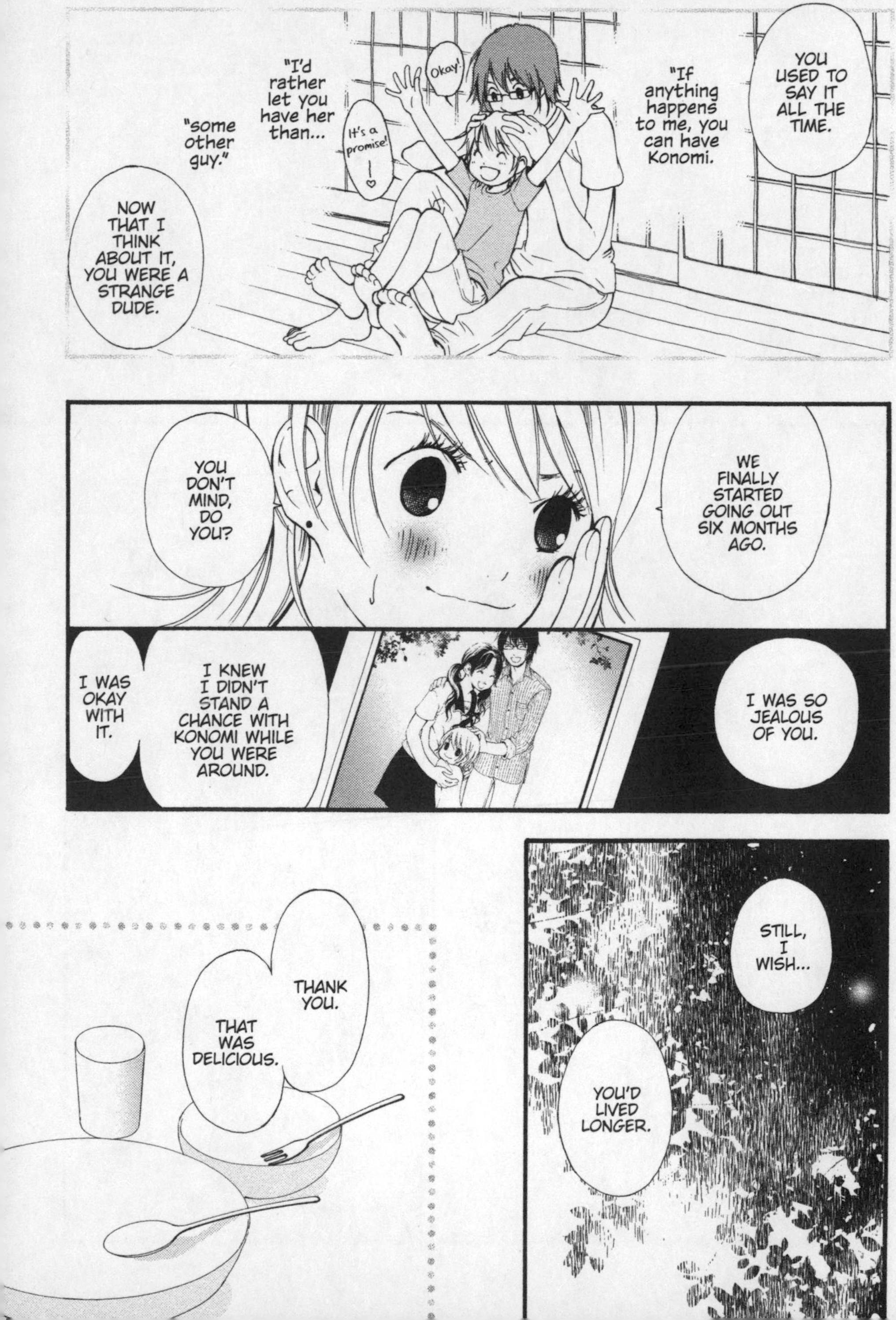
YOU USED TO SAY IT ALL THE TIME.
"If anything happens to me, you can have Konomi.
Okay!
"I'd rather let you have her than...
It's a promise! ♡
"some other guy."
NOW THAT I THINK ABOUT IT, YOU WERE A STRANGE DUDE.
WE FINALLY STARTED GOING OUT SIX MONTHS AGO.
YOU DON'T MIND, DO YOU?
I WAS SO JEALOUS OF YOU.
I KNEW I DIDN'T STAND A CHANCE WITH KONOMI WHILE YOU WERE AROUND.
I WAS OKAY WITH IT.
STILL, I WISH...
YOU'D LIVED LONGER.
THANK YOU.
THAT WAS DELICIOUS.

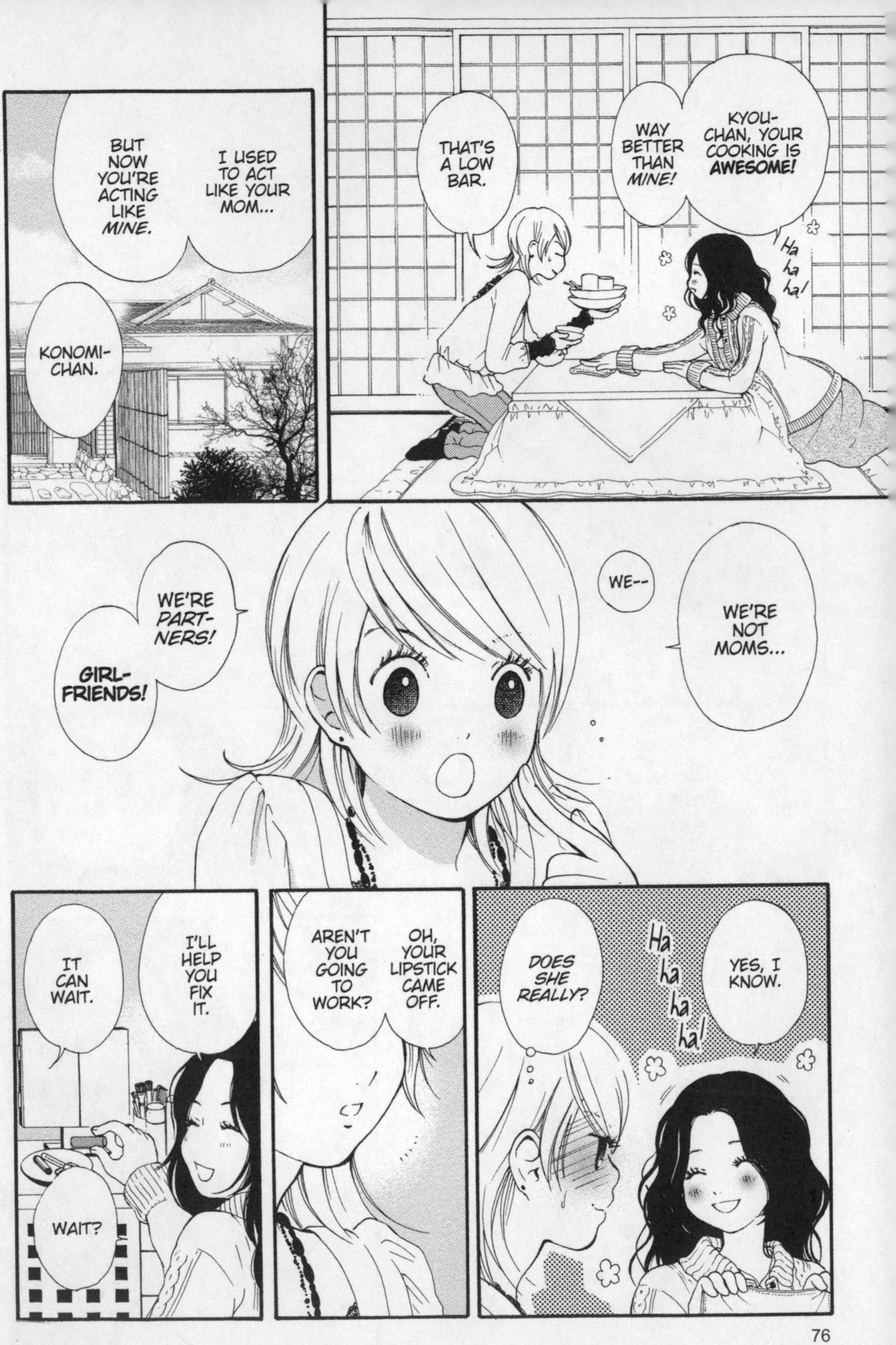
KYOU-CHAN, YOUR COOKING IS AWESOME!
WAY BETTER THAN MINE!
THAT'S A LOW BAR.
Ha ha ha!
I USED TO ACT LIKE YOUR MOM...
BUT NOW YOU'RE ACTING LIKE MINE.
KONOMI-CHAN.
WE--
WE'RE NOT MOMS...
WE'RE PARTNERS!
GIRLFRIENDS!
YES, I KNOW.
Ha ha ha ha!
DOES SHE REALLY?
OH, YOUR LIPSTICK CAME OFF.
AREN'T YOU GOING TO WORK?
I'LL HELP YOU FIX IT.
IT CAN WAIT.
WAIT?

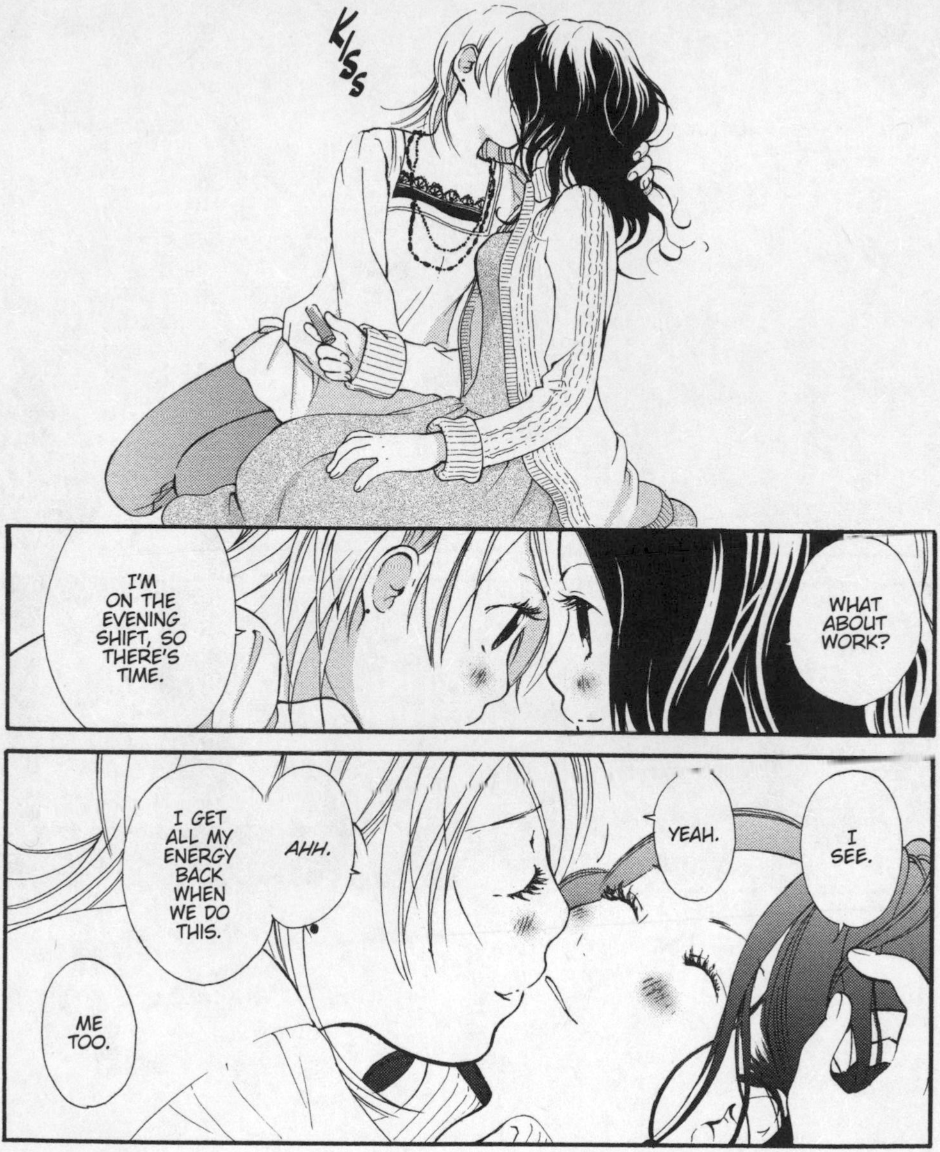
KISS
WHAT ABOUT WORK?
I'M ON THE EVENING SHIFT, SO THERE'S TIME.
I SEE.
YEAH.
AHH.
I GET ALL MY ENERGY BACK WHEN WE DO THIS.
ME TOO.
CAN I UNBUTTON YOUR SHIRT?
WE'RE IN A RELATION-SHIP.

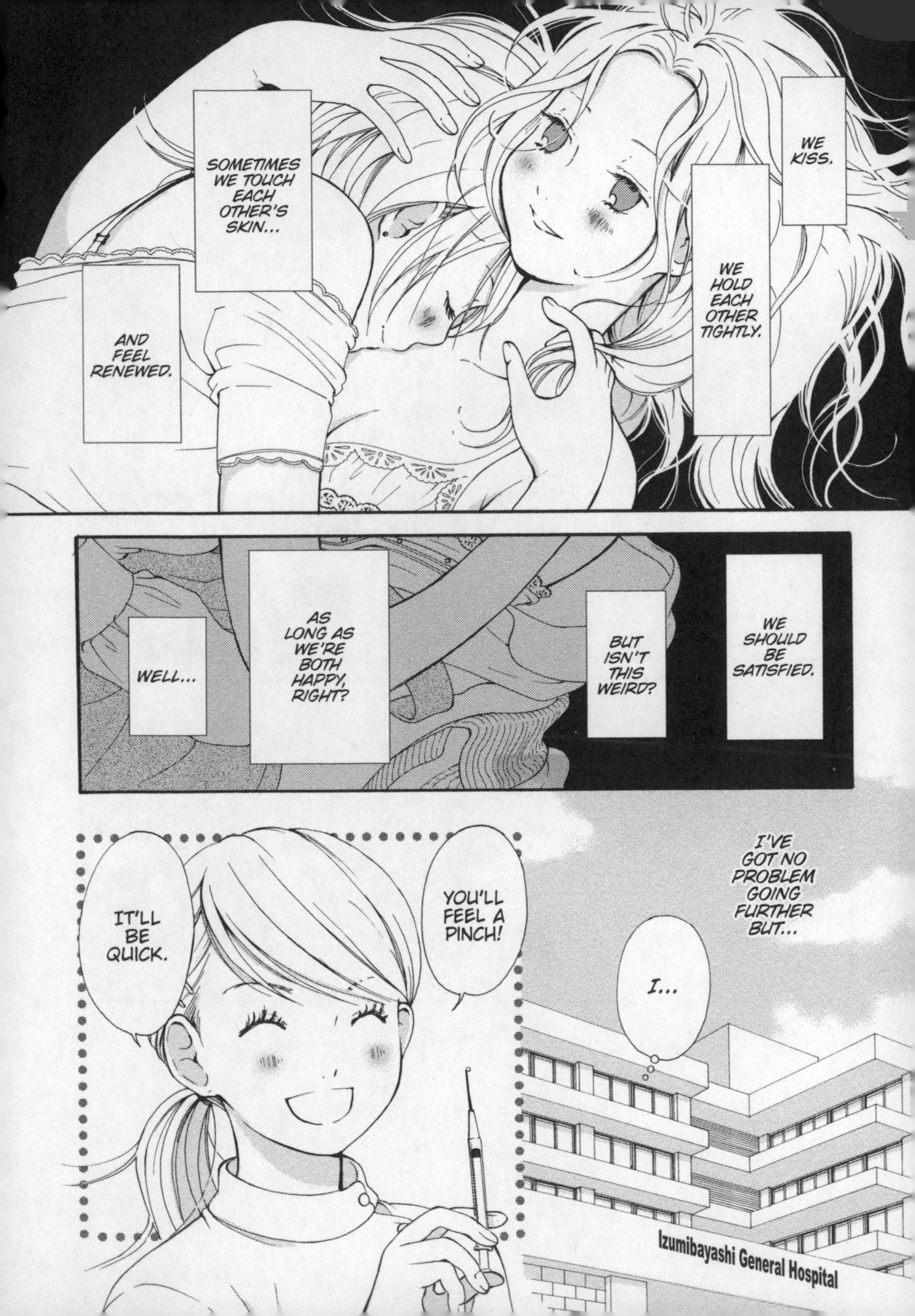
WE KISS.
WE HOLD EACH OTHER TIGHTLY.
SOMETIMES WE TOUCH EACH OTHER'S SKIN...
AND FEEL RENEWED.
WE SHOULD BE SATISFIED.
BUT ISN'T THIS WEIRD?
AS LONG AS WE'RE BOTH HAPPY, RIGHT?
WELL...
I'VE GOT NO PROBLEM GOING FURTHER BUT...
I...
Izumibayashi General Hospital
YOU'LL FEEL A PINCH!
IT'LL BE QUICK.

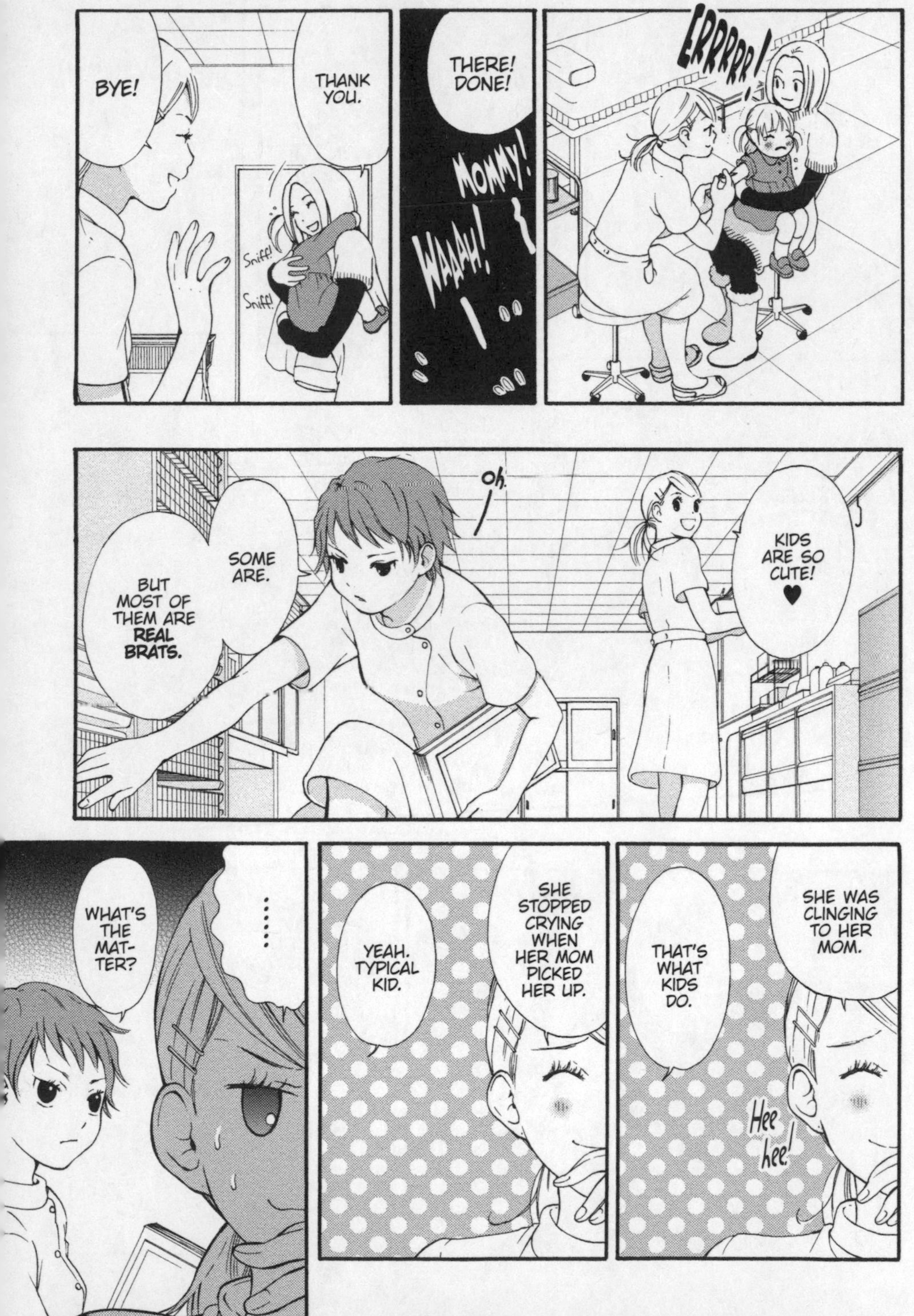
ERRRRR!
THERE! DONE!
MOMMY!
WAAAH!
THANK YOU.
BYE!
Sniff!
Sniff!
KIDS ARE SO CUTE! ♥
Oh.
SOME ARE.
BUT MOST OF THEM ARE REAL BRATS.
SHE WAS CLINGING TO HER MOM.
THAT'S WHAT KIDS DO.
Hee hee!
SHE STOPPED CRYING WHEN HER MOM PICKED HER UP.
YEAH. TYPICAL KID.
......
WHAT'S THE MAT-TER?

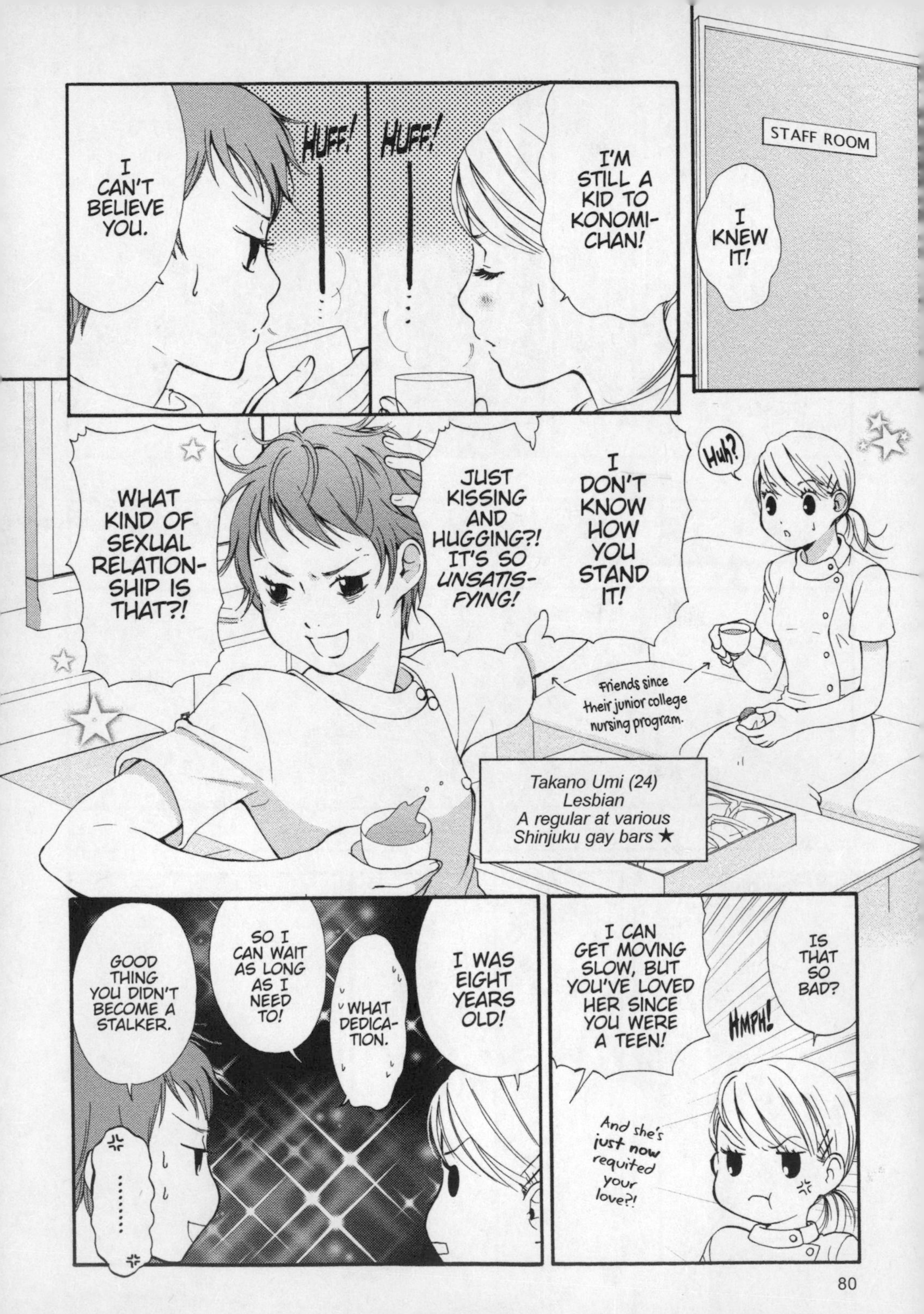
STAFF ROOM
I KNEW IT!
HUFF!
I'M STILL A KID TO KONOMI-CHAN!
HUFF!
I CAN'T BELIEVE YOU.
Huh?
I DON'T KNOW HOW YOU STAND IT!
JUST KISSING AND HUGGING?! IT'S SO UNSATISFYING!
WHAT KIND OF SEXUAL RELATIONSHIP IS THAT?!
Friends since their junior college nursing program.
Takano Umi (24) Lesbian A regular at various Shinjuku gay bars ★
IS THAT SO BAD?
I CAN GET MOVING SLOW, BUT YOU'VE LOVED HER SINCE YOU WERE A TEEN!
HMPH!
And she's just now requited your love?!
I WAS EIGHT YEARS OLD!
WHAT DEDICATION.
SO I CAN WAIT AS LONG AS I NEED TO!
GOOD THING YOU DIDN'T BECOME A STALKER.
....

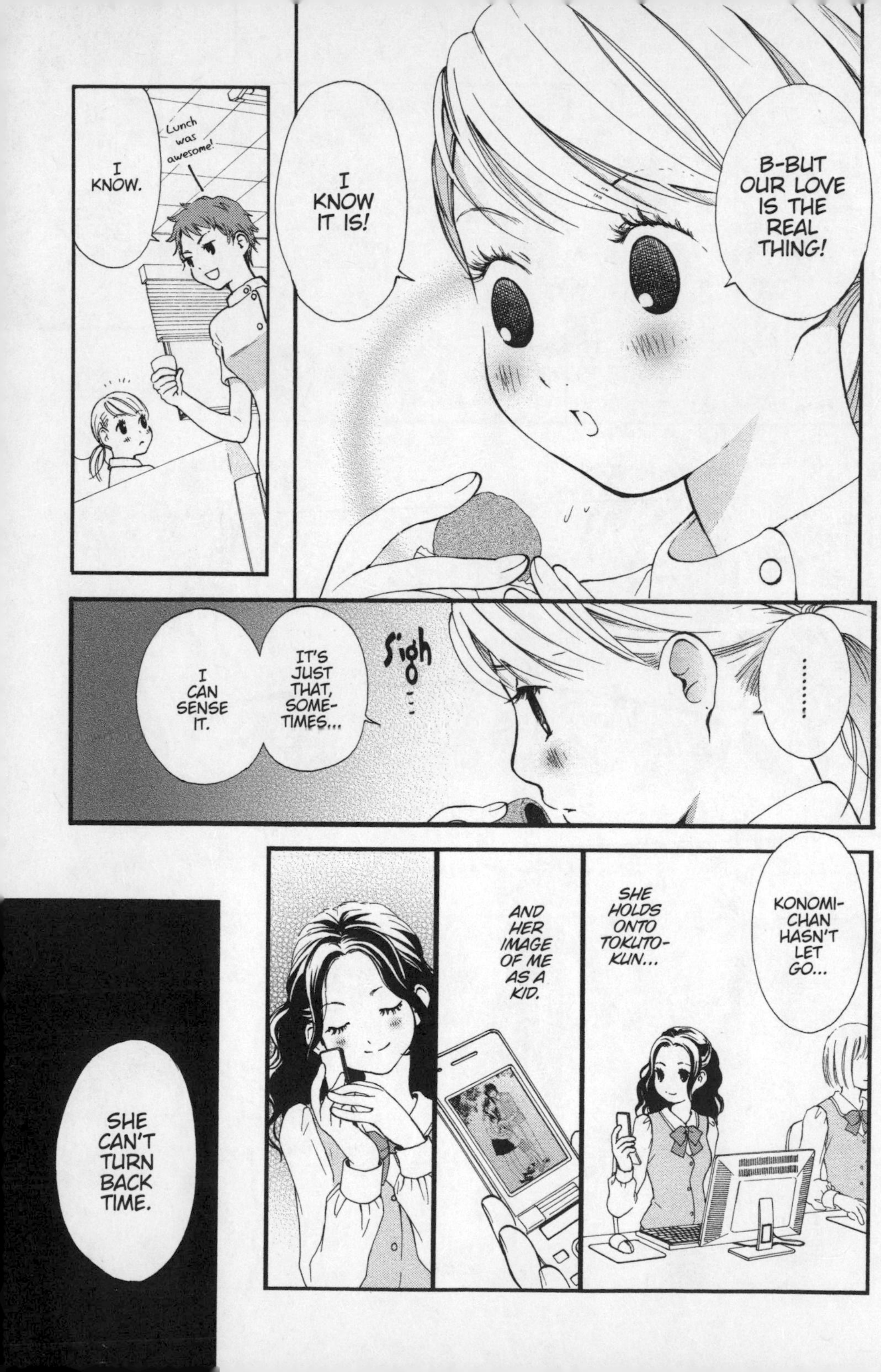
B-BUT OUR LOVE IS THE REAL THING!
I KNOW IT IS!
Lunch was awesome!
I KNOW.
......
Sigh...
IT'S JUST THAT, SOME-TIMES...
I CAN SENSE IT.
KONOMI-CHAN HASN'T LET GO...
SHE HOLDS ONTO TOKUTO-KUN...
AND HER IMAGE OF ME AS A KID.
SHE CAN'T TURN BACK TIME.

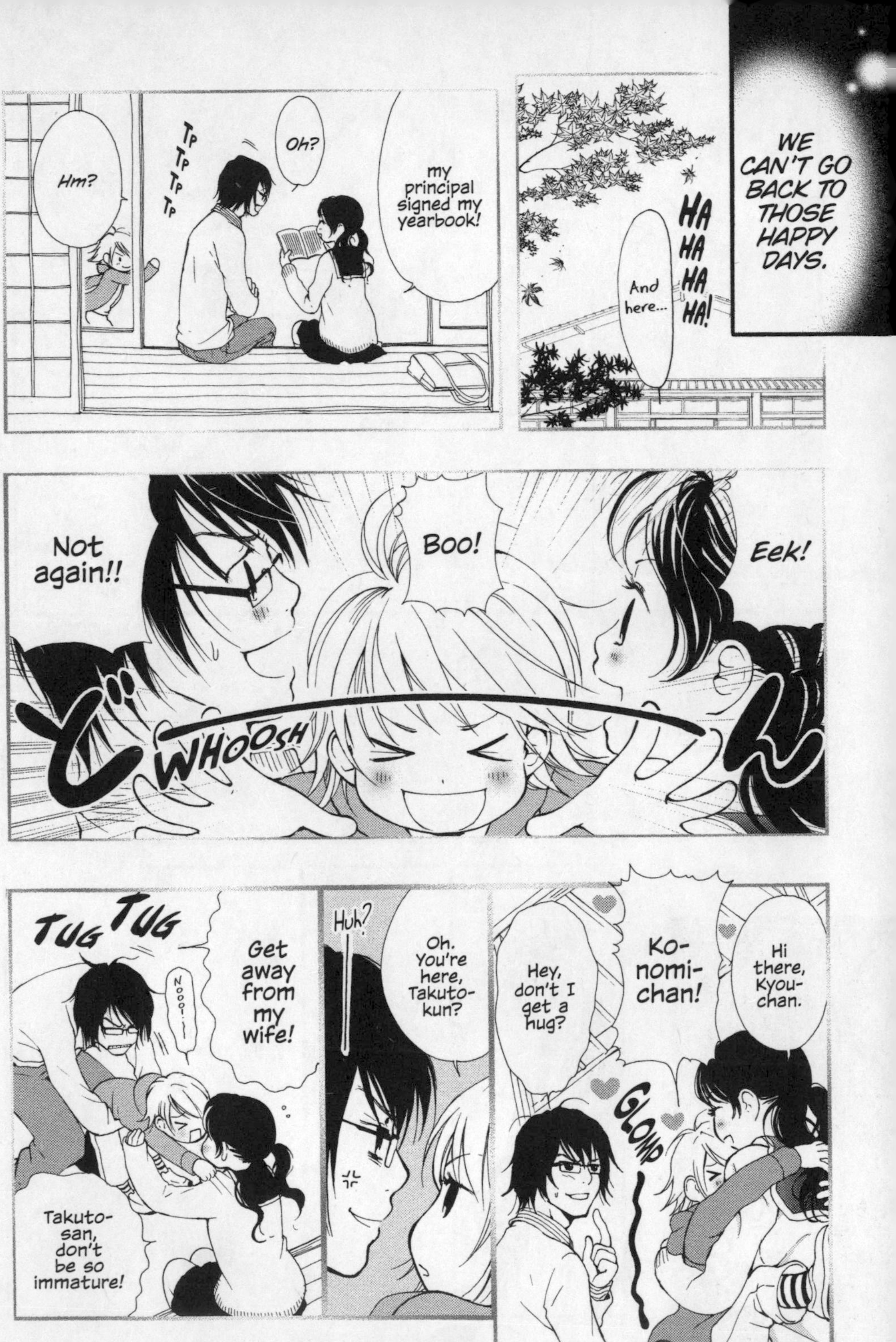
WE CAN'T GO BACK TO THOSE HAPPY DAYS.
HA HA HA HA!
And here...
my principal signed my yearbook!
Oh?
Tp Tp Tp Tp
Hm?
Eek!
Boo!
Not again!!
WHOOSH
Hi there, Kyou-chan.
Ko-nomi-chan!
Hey, don't I get a hug?
GLOMP
Oh. You're here, Takuto-kun?
Huh?
Get away from my wife!
TUG TUG
Nooo!...
Takuto-san, don't be so immature!

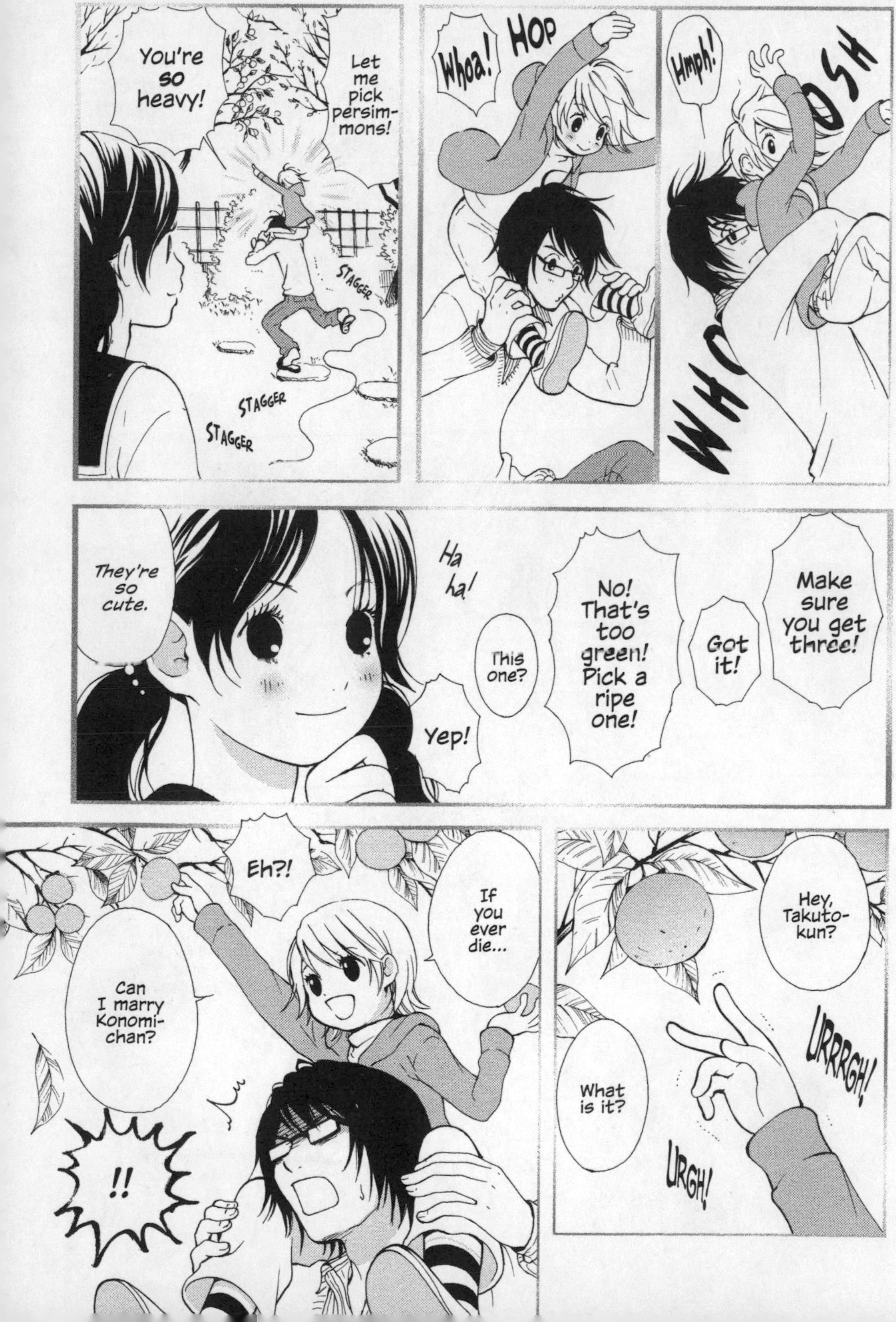
Hmph!
WHOOSH
HOP
Whoa!
Let me pick persimmons!
You're so heavy!
STAGGER
STAGGER
STAGGER
Make sure you get three!
Got it!
No! That's too green! Pick a ripe one!
This one?
Yep!
Ha ha!
They're so cute.
Hey, Takuto-kun?
URRRGH!
What is it?
URGH!
If you ever die...
Eh?!
Can I marry Konomi-chan?
!!

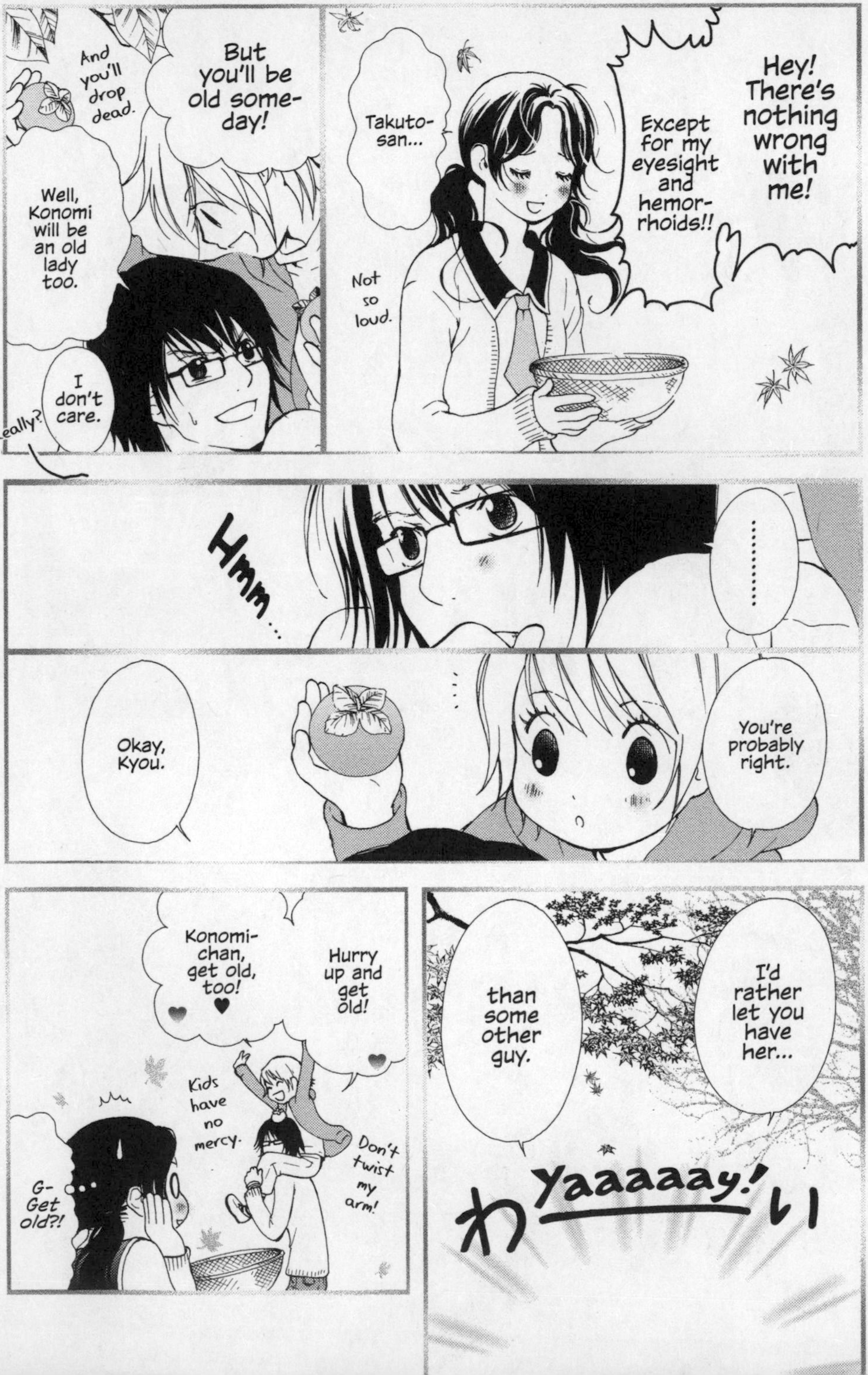
Hey! There's nothing wrong with me!
Except for my eyesight and hemorrhoids!!
Takuto-san...
Not so loud.
But you'll be old someday!
And you'll drop dead.
Well, Konomi will be an old lady too.
I don't care.
Really?
......
Hmm...
You're probably right.
...
Okay, Kyou.
I'd rather let you have her...
than some other guy.
わ Yaaaaay! い
Hurry up and get old!
Konomi-chan, get old, too!
Don't twist my arm!
Kids have no mercy.
G-Get old?!

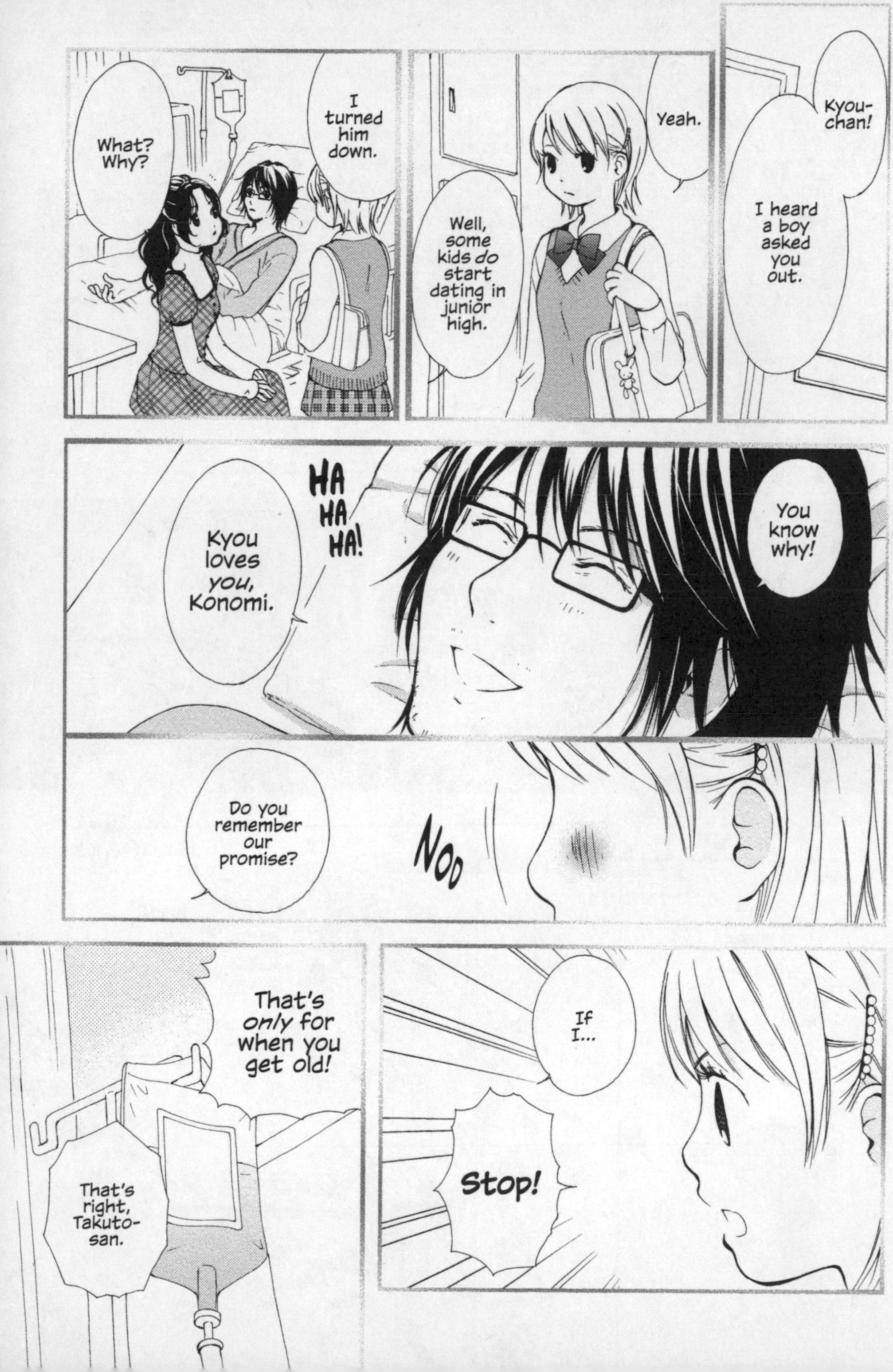
Kyou-chan!
I heard a boy asked you out.
Yeah.
Well, some kids *do* start dating in junior high.
I turned him down.
What? Why?
You know why!
HA HA HA!
Kyou loves *you*, Konomi.
NOD
Do you remember our promise?
If I...
Stop!
That's *only* for when you get old!
That's right, Takuto-san.

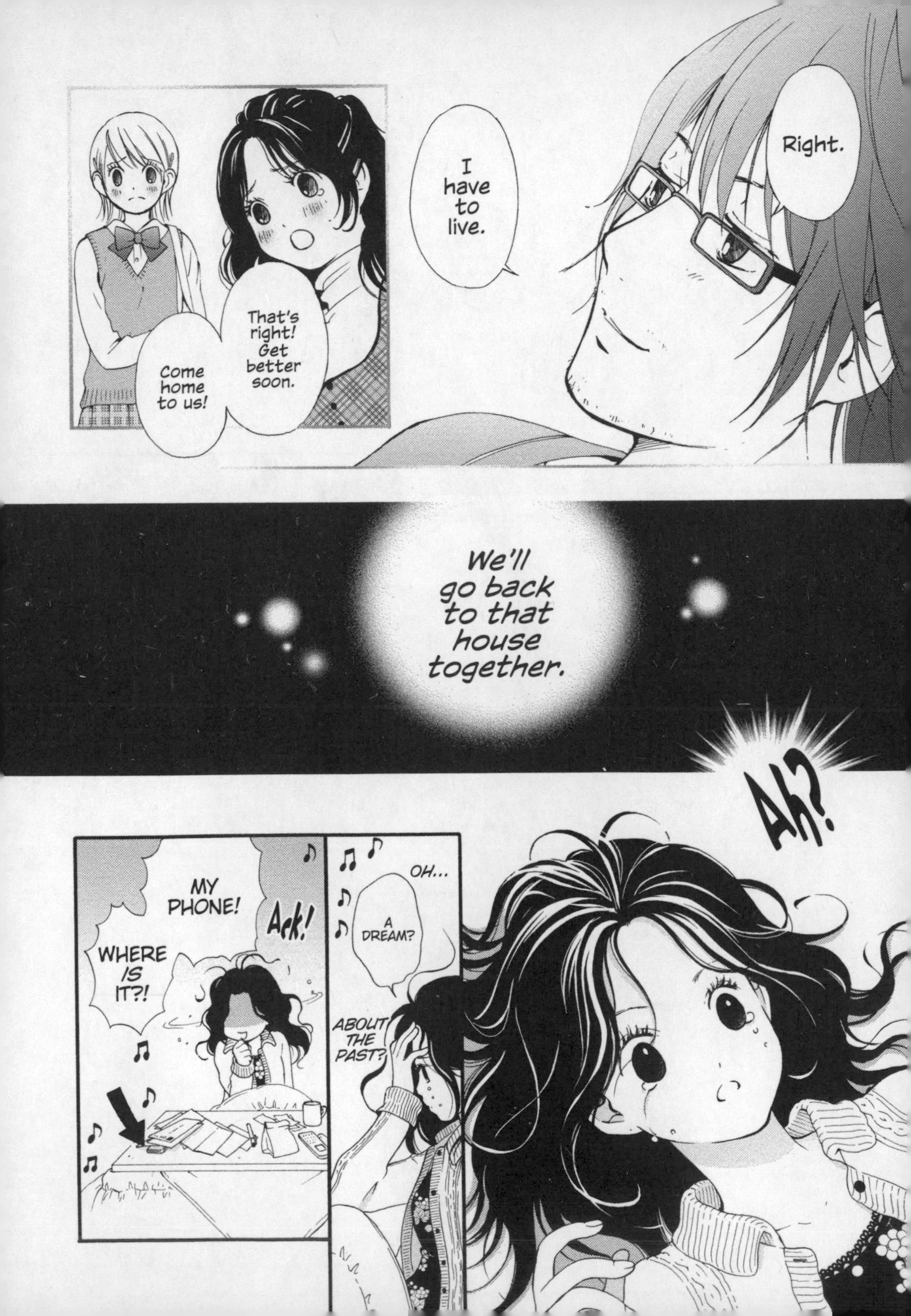
Right.
I have to live.
That's right! Get better soon.
Come home to us!
We'll go back to that house together.
Ah?
OH...
A DREAM?
ABOUT THE PAST?
Ack!
MY PHONE!
WHERE IS IT?!

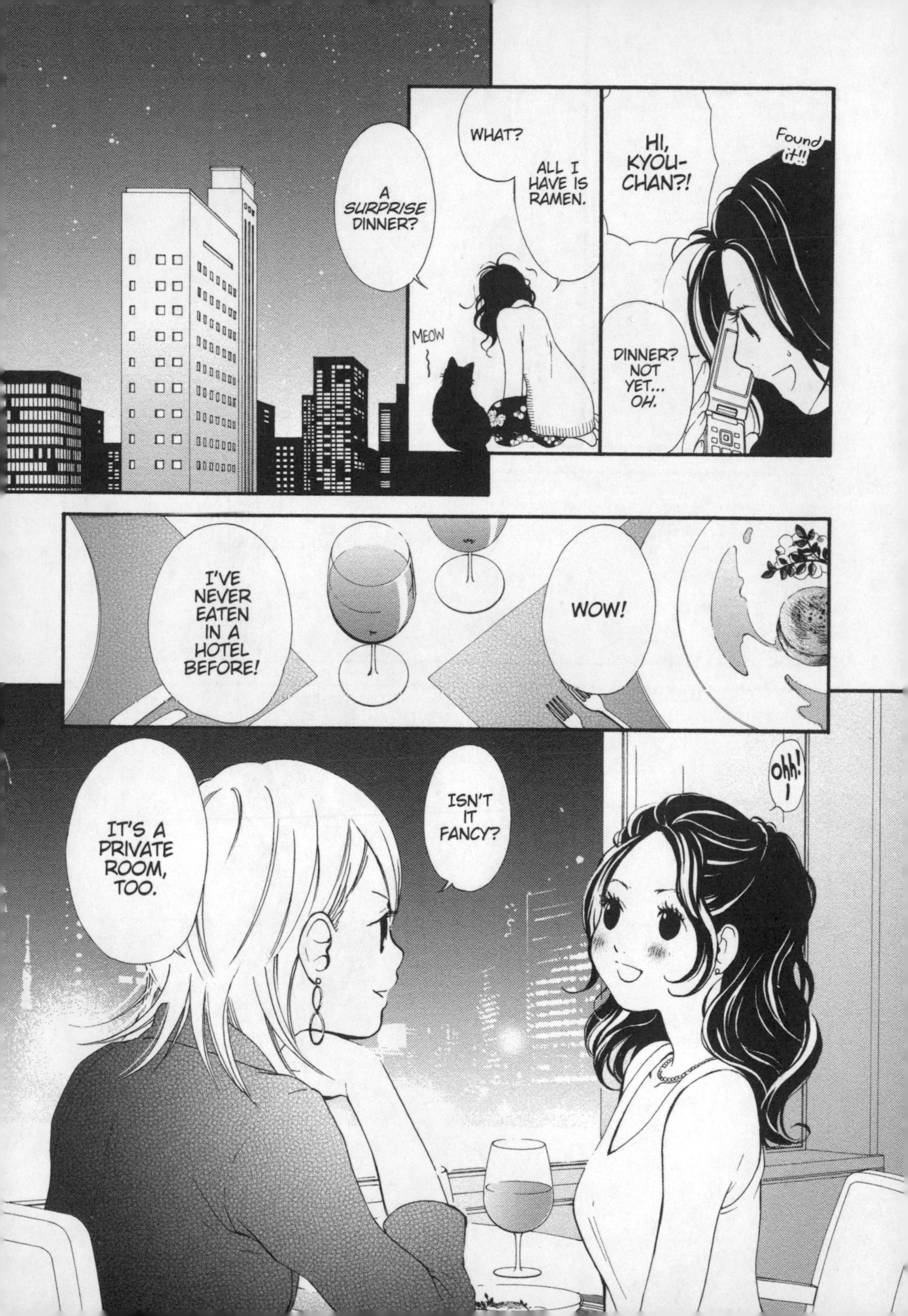
Found it!!
HI, KYOU-CHAN?!
DINNER? NOT YET... OH.
WHAT?
ALL I HAVE IS RAMEN.
MEOW
A SURPRISE DINNER?
WOW!
I'VE NEVER EATEN IN A HOTEL BEFORE!
Ohh! I
ISN'T IT FANCY?
IT'S A PRIVATE ROOM, TOO.

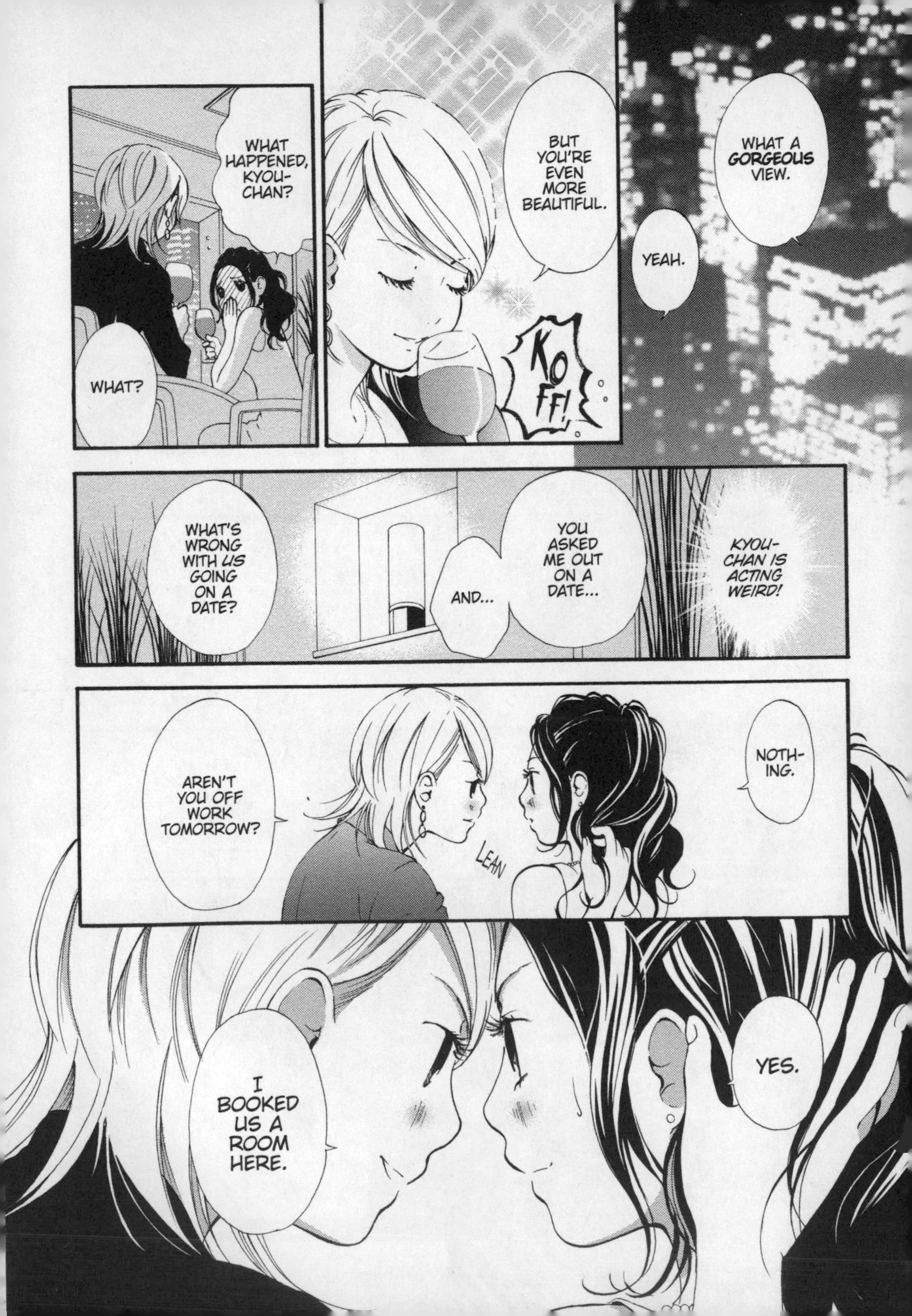
WHAT A GORGEOUS VIEW.
YEAH.
BUT YOU'RE EVEN MORE BEAUTIFUL.
KOFF!
WHAT HAPPENED, KYOU-CHAN?
WHAT?
KYOU-CHAN IS ACTING WEIRD!
YOU ASKED ME OUT ON A DATE...
AND...
WHAT'S WRONG WITH US GOING ON A DATE?
NOTH-ING.
LEAN
AREN'T YOU OFF WORK TOMORROW?
YES.
I BOOKED US A ROOM HERE.

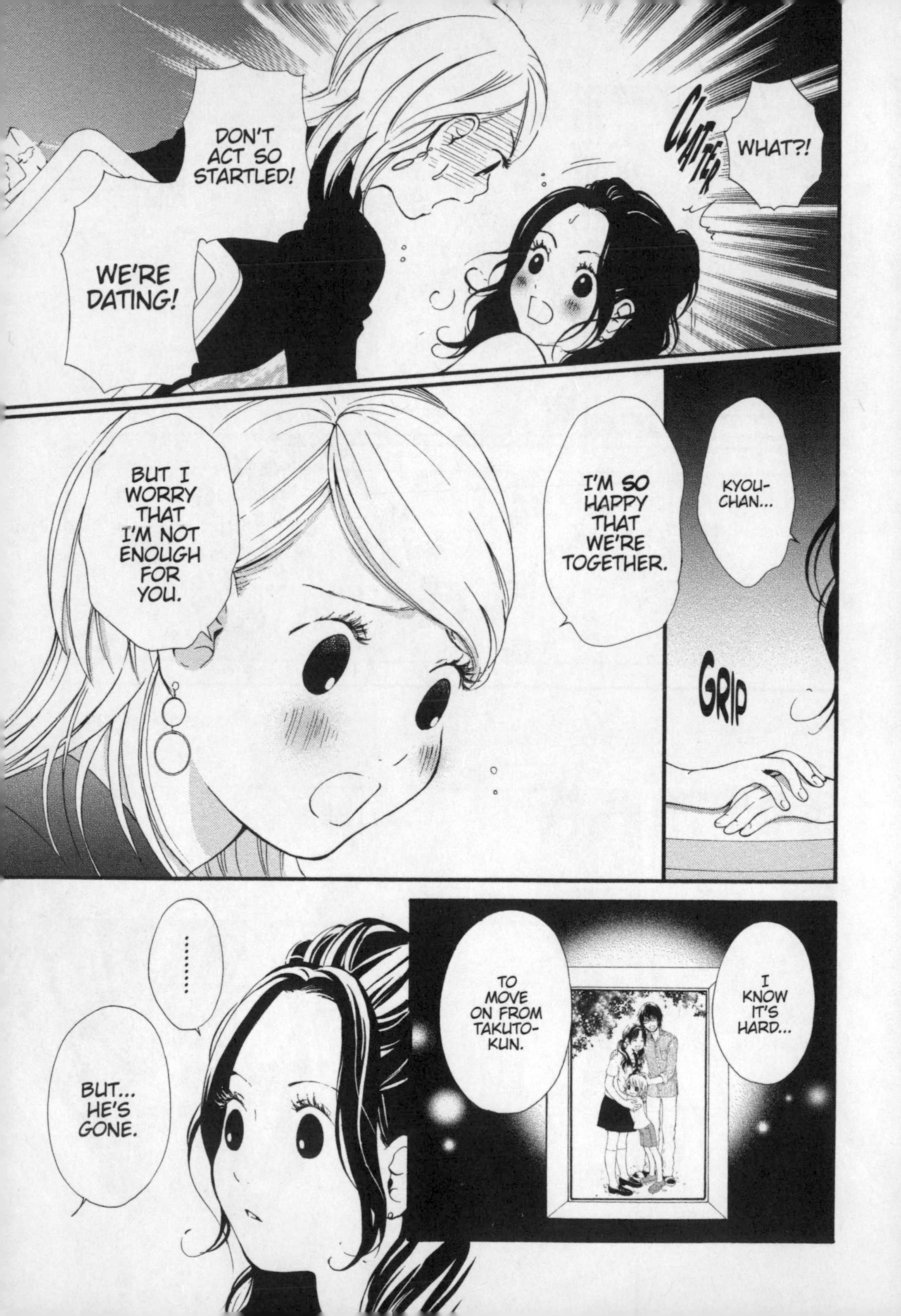
CLATTER
WHAT?!
DON'T ACT SO STARTLED!
WE'RE DATING!
KYOU-CHAN...
GRIP
I'M SO HAPPY THAT WE'RE TOGETHER.
BUT I WORRY THAT I'M NOT ENOUGH FOR YOU.
I KNOW IT'S HARD...
TO MOVE ON FROM TAKUTO-KUN.
......
BUT... HE'S GONE.

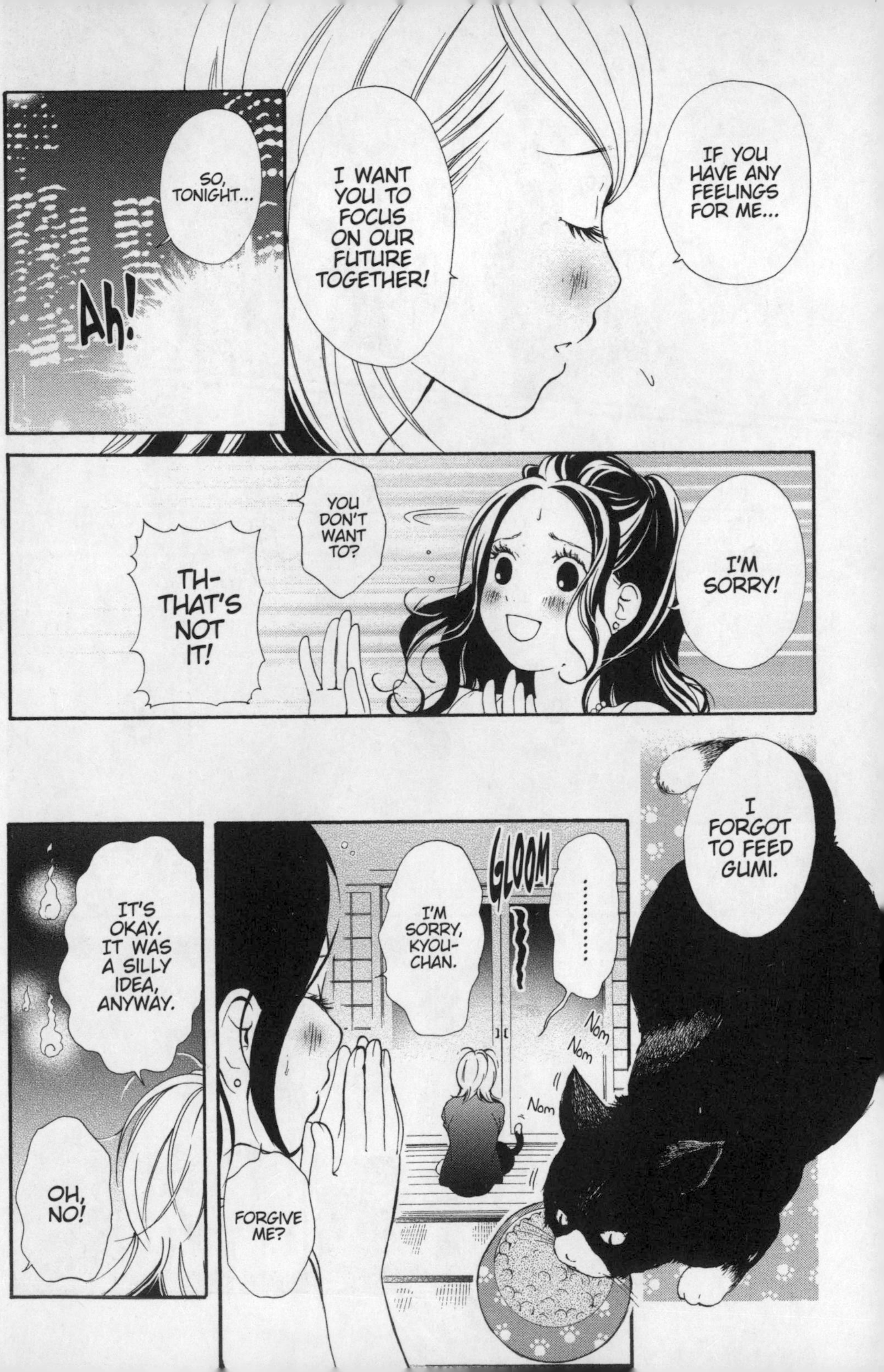
IF YOU HAVE ANY FEELINGS FOR ME...
I WANT YOU TO FOCUS ON OUR FUTURE TOGETHER!
SO, TONIGHT...
Ah!
I'M SORRY!
YOU DON'T WANT TO?
TH-THAT'S NOT IT!
I FORGOT TO FEED GUMI.
......
GLOOM
I'M SORRY, KYOU-CHAN.
Nom Nom
Nom
FORGIVE ME?
IT'S OKAY. IT WAS A SILLY IDEA, ANYWAY.
OH, NO!

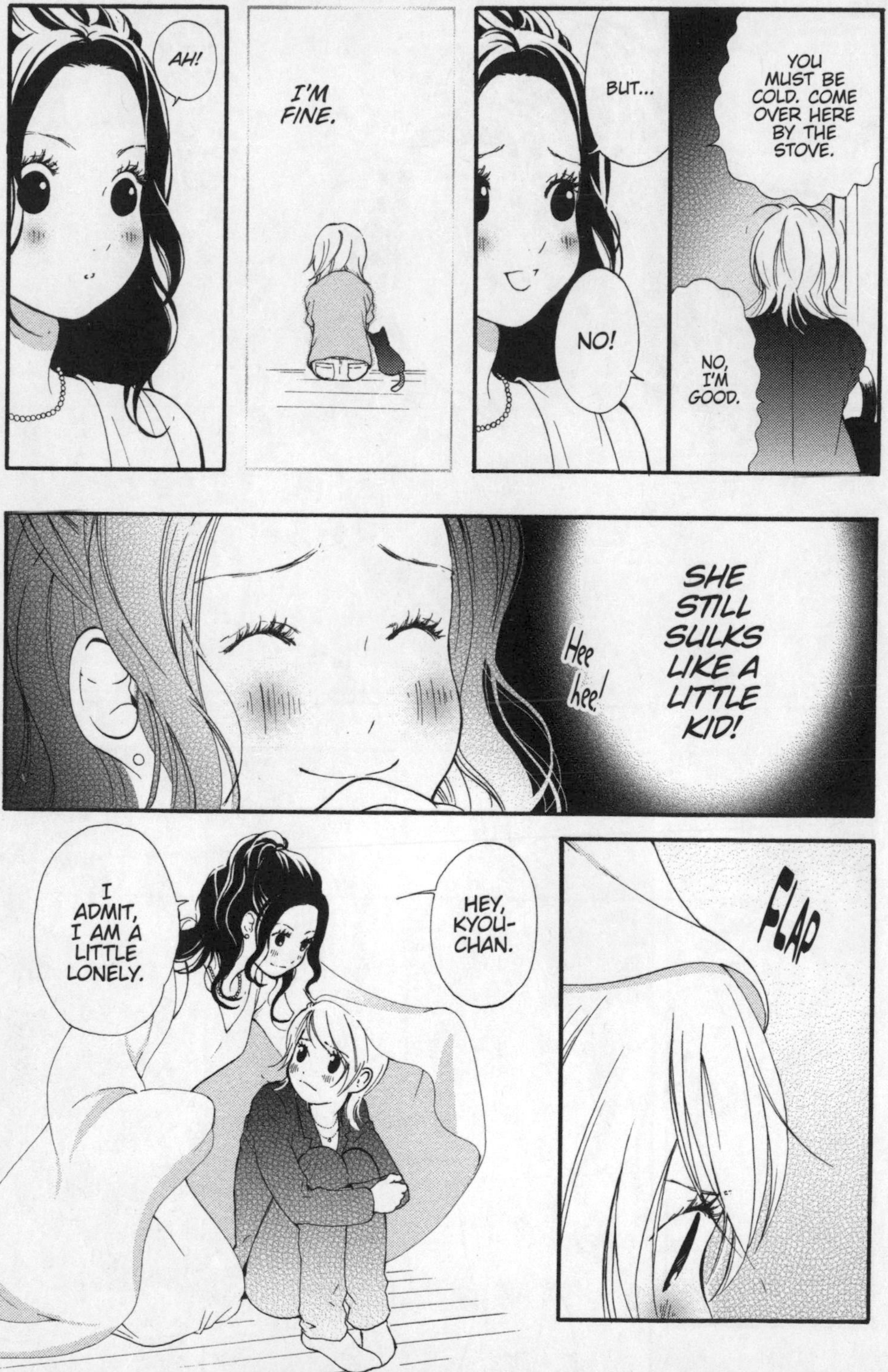
YOU MUST BE COLD. COME OVER HERE BY THE STOVE.
NO, I'M GOOD.
BUT...
NO!
I'M FINE.
AH!
SHE STILL SULKS LIKE A LITTLE KID!
Hee hee!
FLAP
HEY, KYOU-CHAN.
I ADMIT, I AM A LITTLE LONELY.

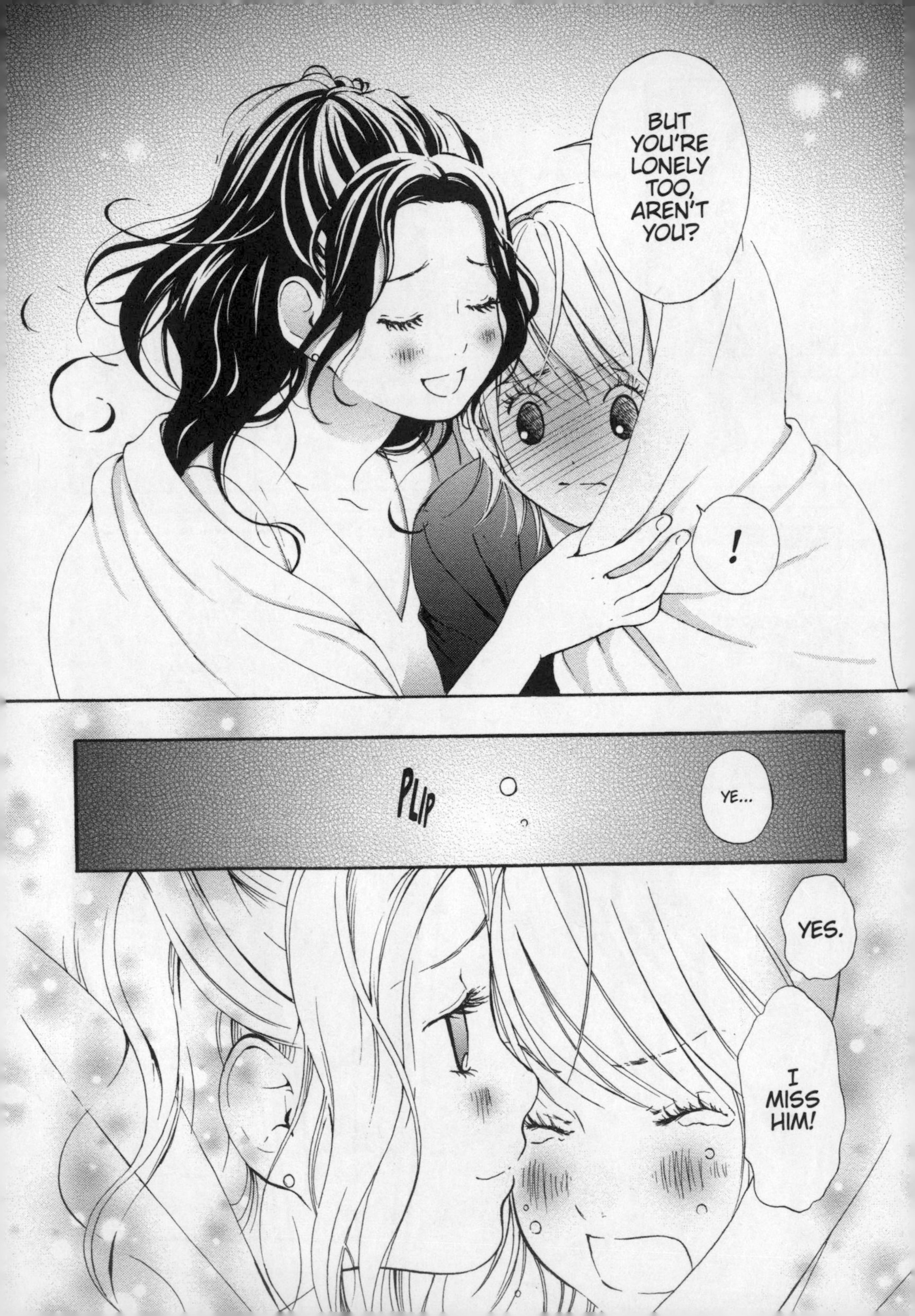
BUT YOU'RE LONELY TOO, AREN'T YOU?
!
YE...
PLIP
YES.
I MISS HIM!

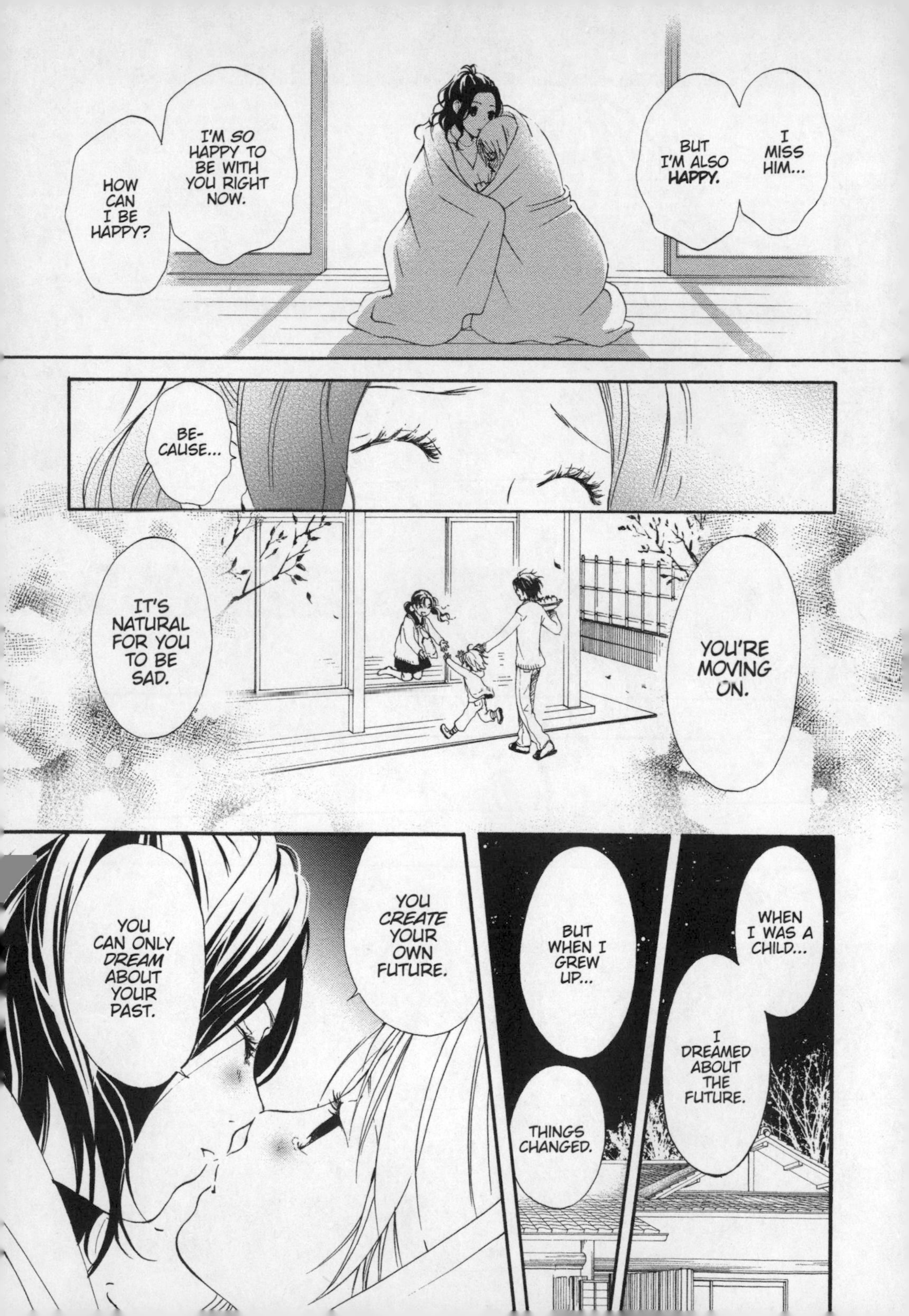
I MISS HIM...
BUT I'M ALSO **HAPPY.**
I'M SO HAPPY TO BE WITH YOU RIGHT NOW.
HOW CAN I BE HAPPY?
BE-CAUSE...
YOU'RE MOVING ON.
IT'S NATURAL FOR YOU TO BE SAD.
WHEN I WAS A CHILD...
I DREAMED ABOUT THE FUTURE.
BUT WHEN I GREW UP...
THINGS CHANGED.
YOU *CREATE* YOUR OWN FUTURE.
YOU CAN ONLY *DREAM* ABOUT YOUR PAST.

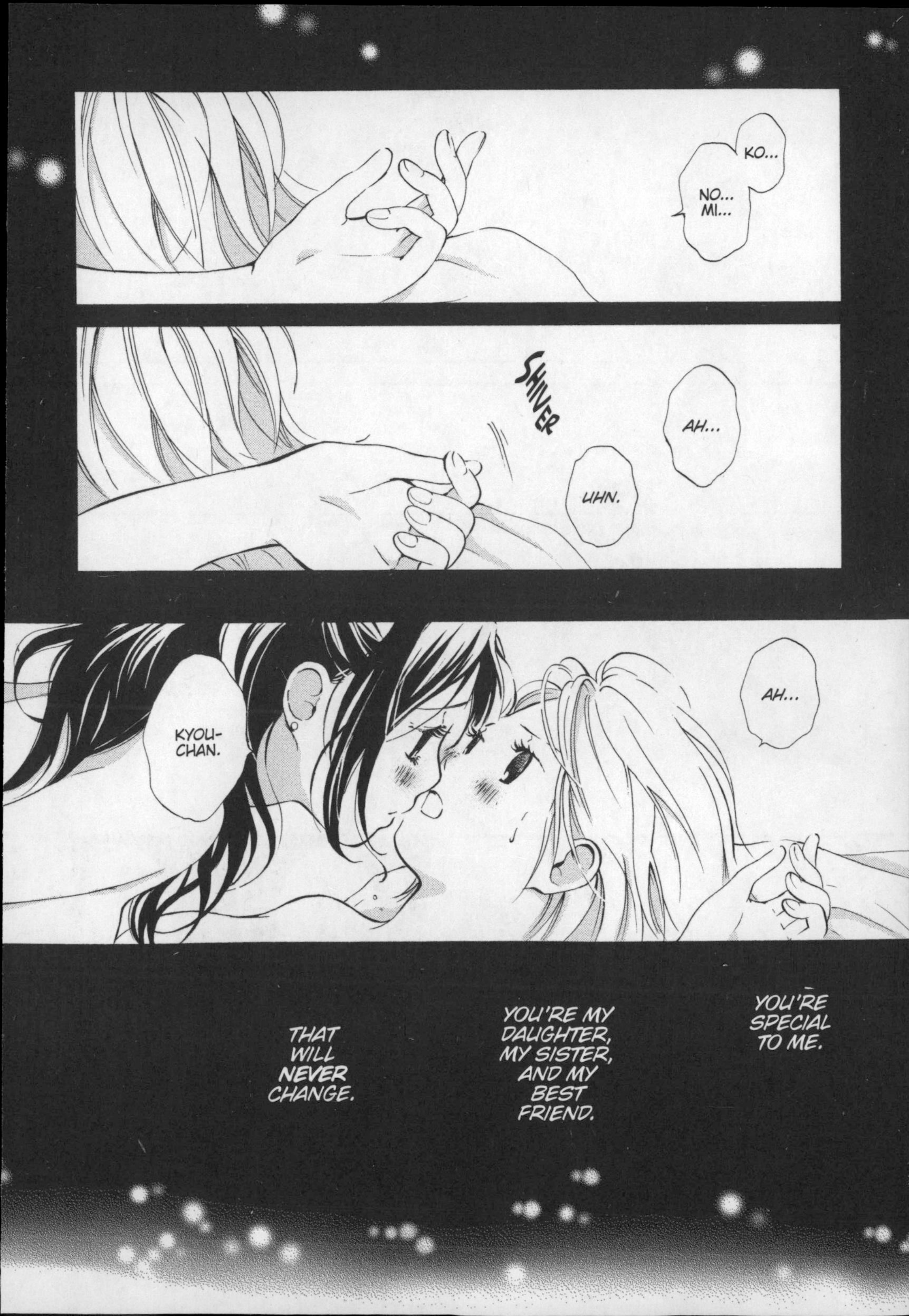
KO... NO... MI...
AH...
SHIVER
UHN.
AH...
KYOU-CHAN.
YOU'RE SPECIAL TO ME.
YOU'RE MY DAUGHTER, MY SISTER, AND MY BEST FRIEND.
THAT WILL NEVER CHANGE.

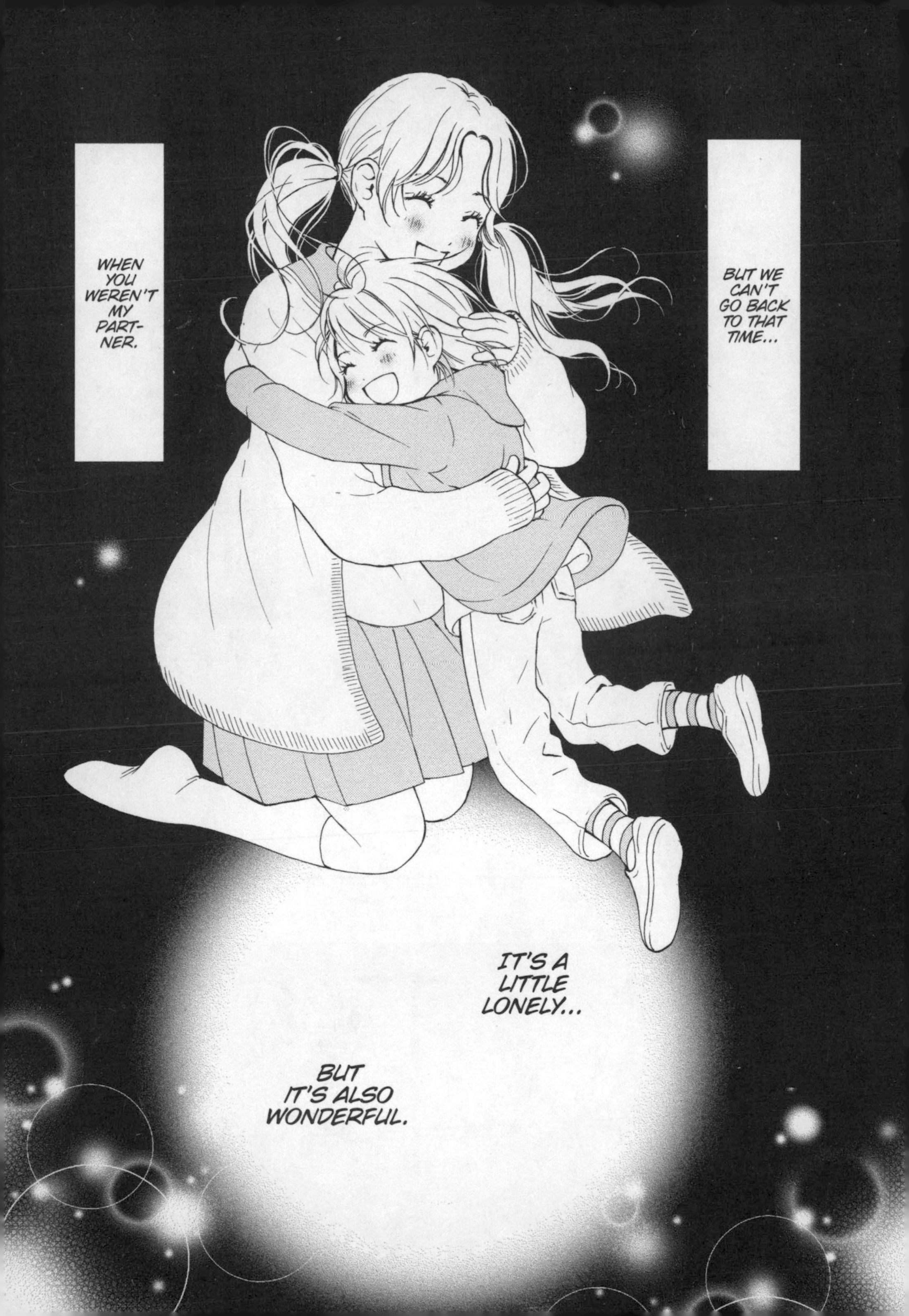
BUT WE CAN'T GO BACK TO THAT TIME...
WHEN YOU WEREN'T MY PART-NER.
IT'S A LITTLE LONELY...
BUT IT'S ALSO WONDERFUL.

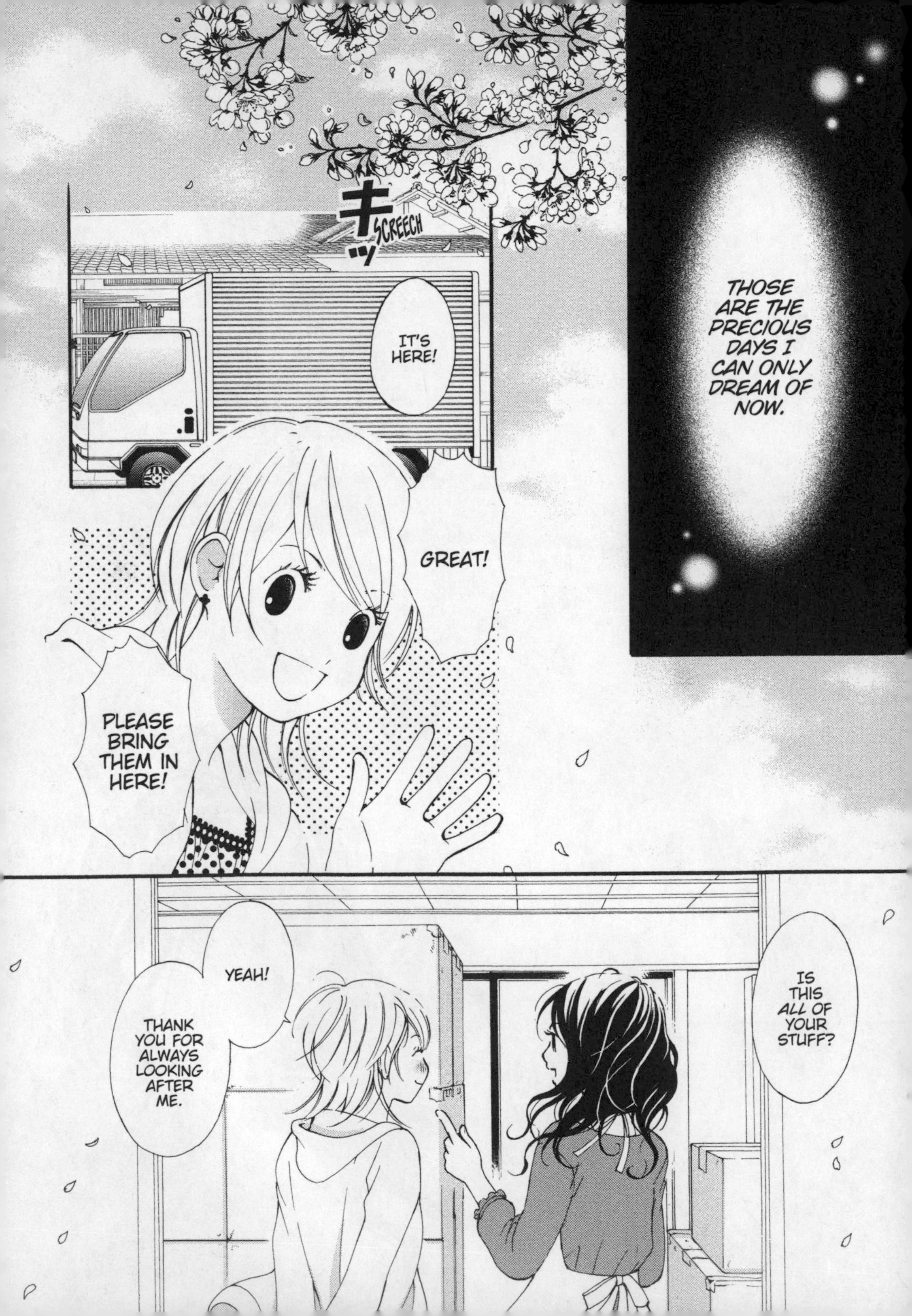
THOSE ARE THE PRECIOUS DAYS I CAN ONLY DREAM OF NOW.
キッ
SCREECH
IT'S HERE!
GREAT!
PLEASE BRING THEM IN HERE!
IS THIS ALL OF YOUR STUFF?
YEAH!
THANK YOU FOR ALWAYS LOOKING AFTER ME.

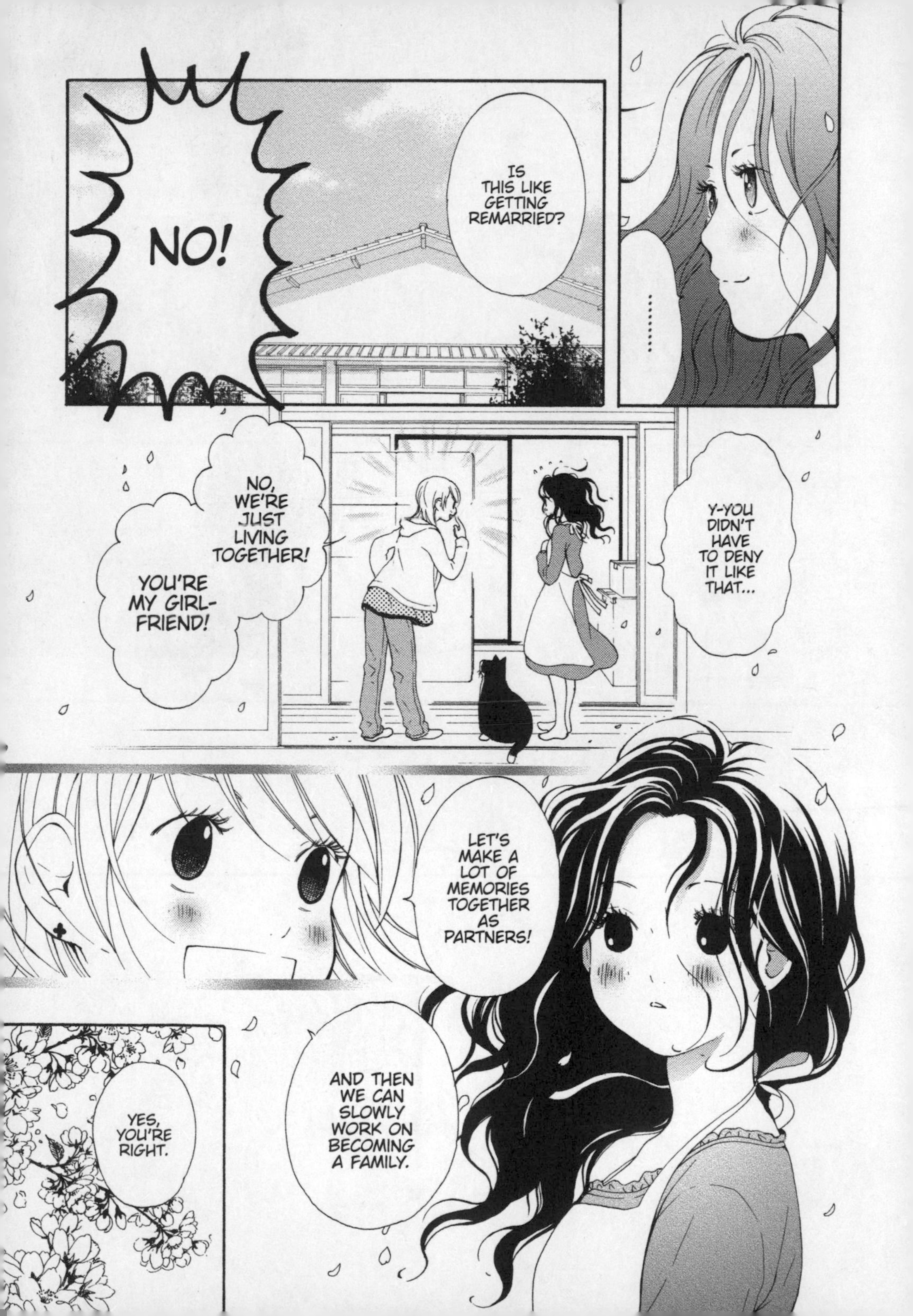
......
IS THIS LIKE GETTING REMARRIED?
NO!
Y-YOU DIDN'T HAVE TO DENY IT LIKE THAT...
NO, WE'RE JUST LIVING TOGETHER!
YOU'RE MY GIRL-FRIEND!
LET'S MAKE A LOT OF MEMORIES TOGETHER AS PARTNERS!
AND THEN WE CAN SLOWLY WORK ON BECOMING A FAMILY.
YES, YOU'RE RIGHT.

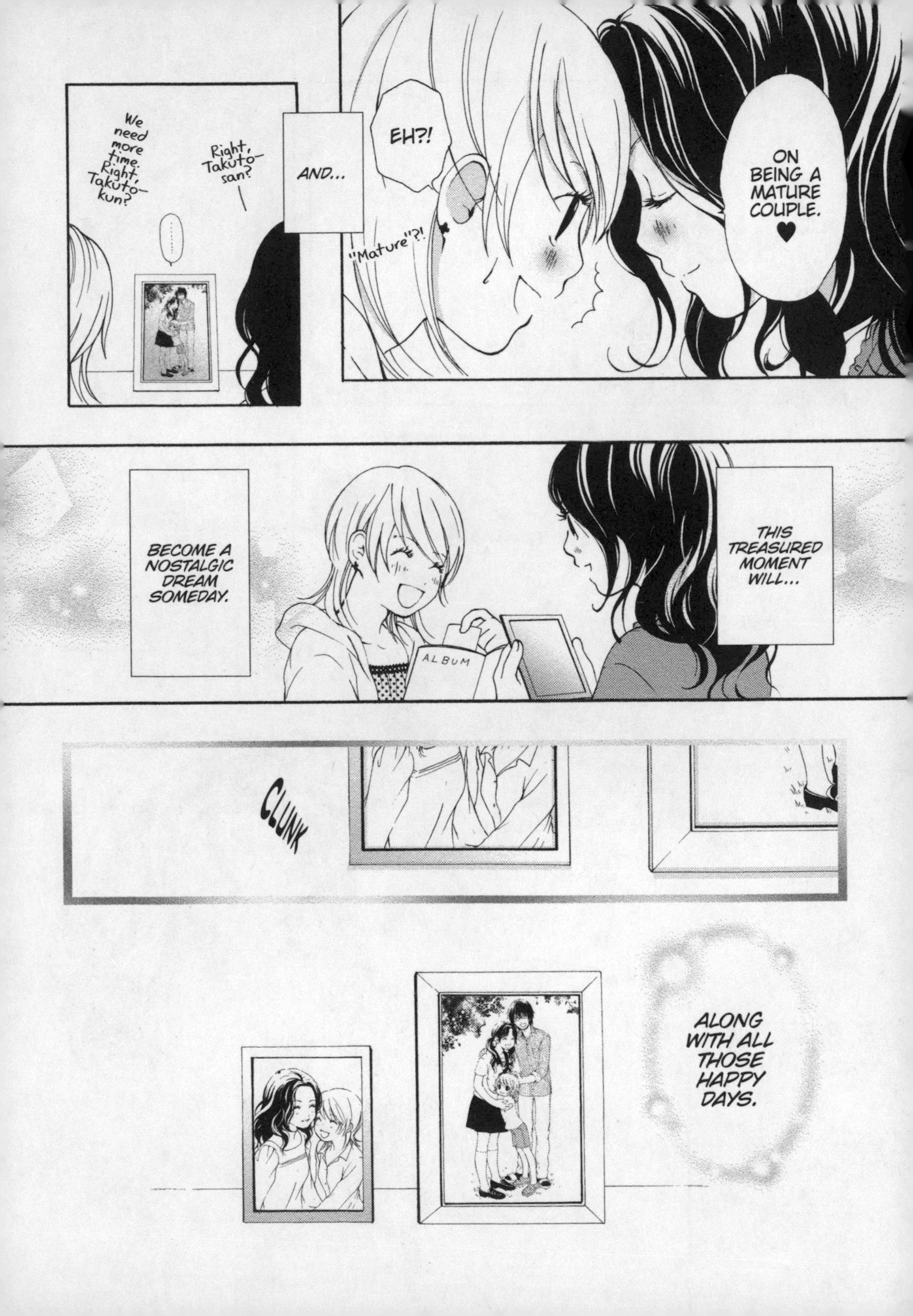
ON BEING A MATURE COUPLE. ♥
EH?!
"Mature"?!
AND...
Right, Takuto-san?
We need more time. Right, Takuto-kun?
......
THIS TREASURED MOMENT WILL...
ALBUM
BECOME A NOSTALGIC DREAM SOMEDAY.
CLUNK
ALONG WITH ALL THOSE HAPPY DAYS.

The Conditions
of Paradise*

AZURE DREAMS

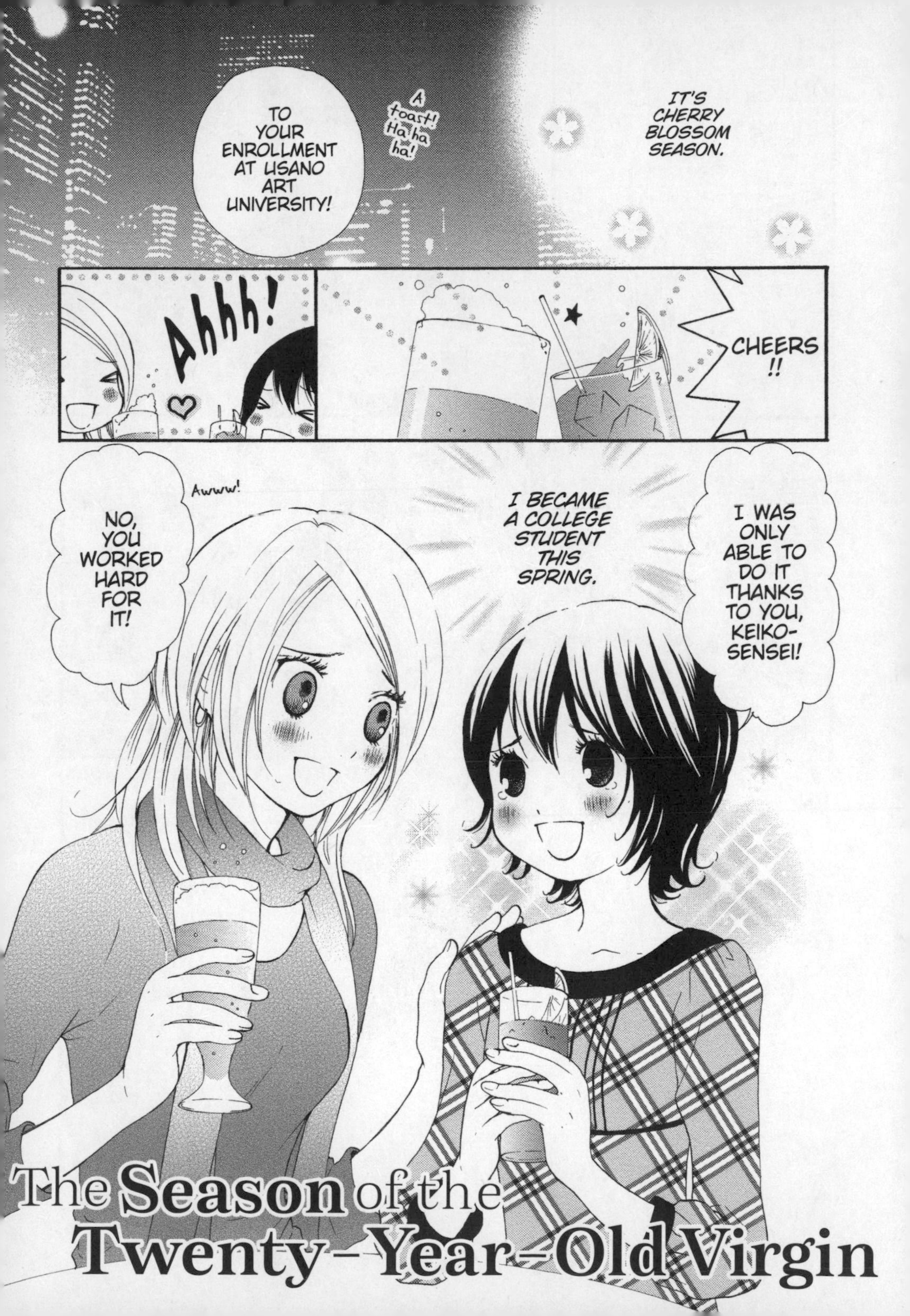
IT'S CHERRY BLOSSOM SEASON.
A toast! Ha ha ha!
TO YOUR ENROLLMENT AT USANO ART UNIVERSITY!
CHEERS!!
Ahhh!
I WAS ONLY ABLE TO DO IT THANKS TO YOU, KEIKO-SENSEI!
I BECAME A COLLEGE STUDENT THIS SPRING.
Awww!
NO, YOU WORKED HARD FOR IT!
The Season of the Twenty-Year-Old Virgin

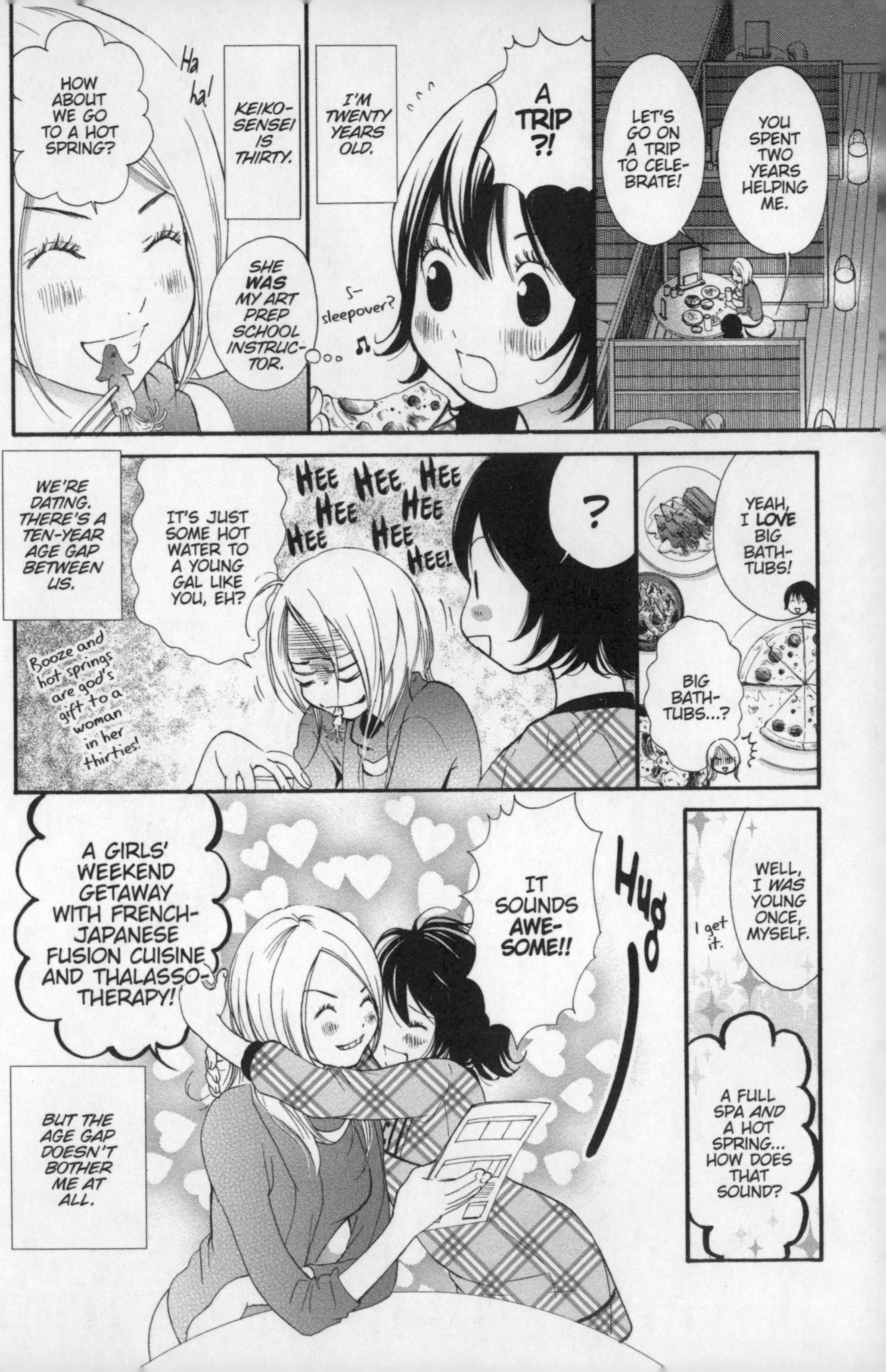
YOU SPENT TWO YEARS HELPING ME.
LET'S GO ON A TRIP TO CELEBRATE!
A TRIP ?!
I'M TWENTY YEARS OLD.
S-sleepover? ♫
SHE WAS MY ART PREP SCHOOL INSTRUCTOR.
KEIKO-SENSEI IS THIRTY.
Ha ha!
HOW ABOUT WE GO TO A HOT SPRING?
YEAH, I LOVE BIG BATHTUBS!
BIG BATHTUBS...?
?
HEE HEE HEE HEE HEE HEE HEE HEE!
IT'S JUST SOME HOT WATER TO A YOUNG GAL LIKE YOU, EH?
Booze and hot springs are god's gift to a woman in her thirties!
WE'RE DATING. THERE'S A TEN-YEAR AGE GAP BETWEEN US.
WELL, I WAS YOUNG ONCE, MYSELF.
I get it.
A FULL SPA AND A HOT SPRING... HOW DOES THAT SOUND?
Hug
IT SOUNDS AWESOME!!
A GIRLS' WEEKEND GETAWAY WITH FRENCH-JAPANESE FUSION CUISINE AND THALASSOTHERAPY!
BUT THE AGE GAP DOESN'T BOTHER ME AT ALL.

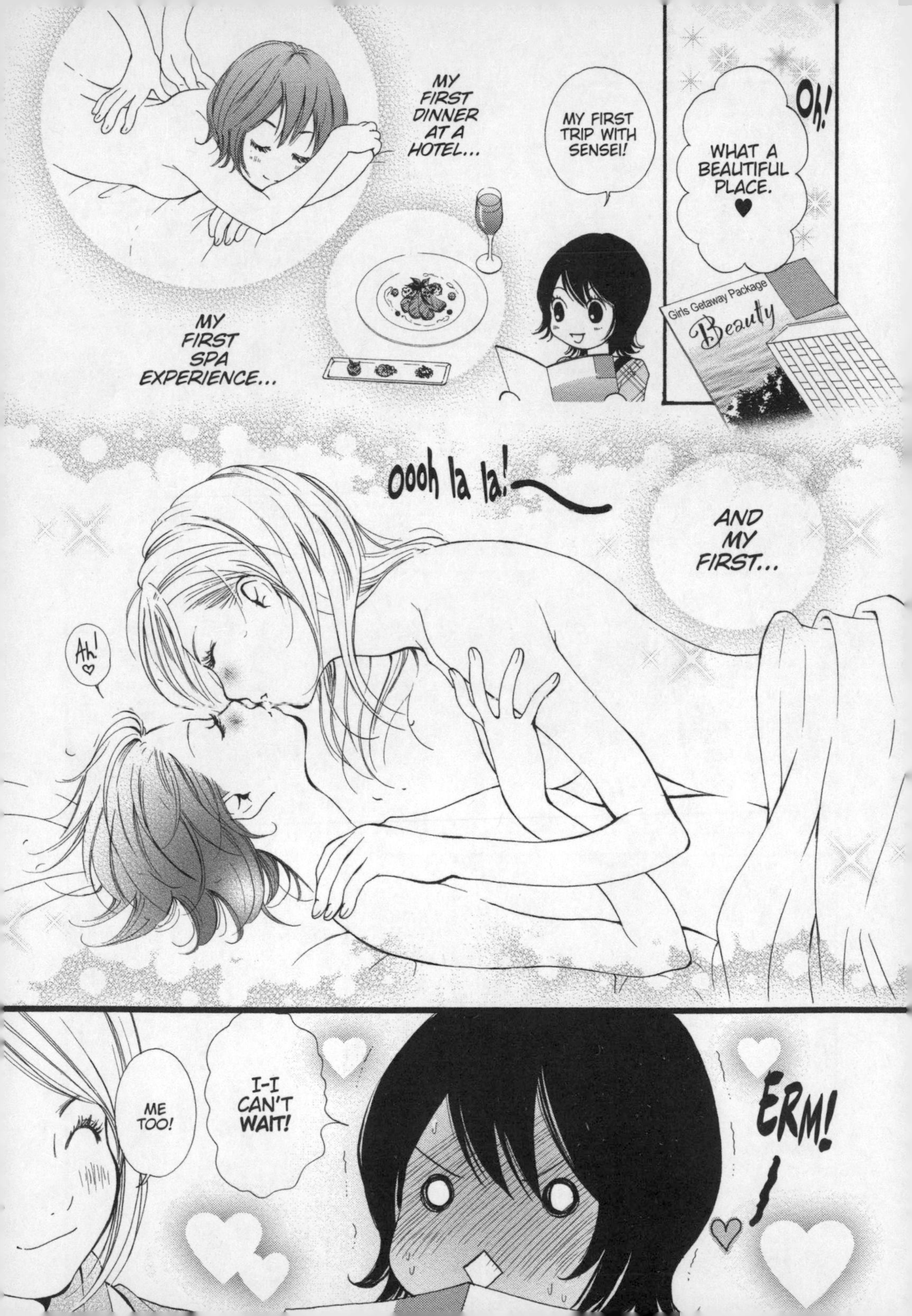
Oh!
WHAT A BEAUTIFUL PLACE. ♥
Girls Getaway Package
Beauty
MY FIRST TRIP WITH SENSEI!
MY FIRST DINNER AT A HOTEL...
MY FIRST SPA EXPERIENCE...
AND MY FIRST...
Oooh la la!~
Ah! ♡
ERM!
I-I CAN'T WAIT!
ME TOO!

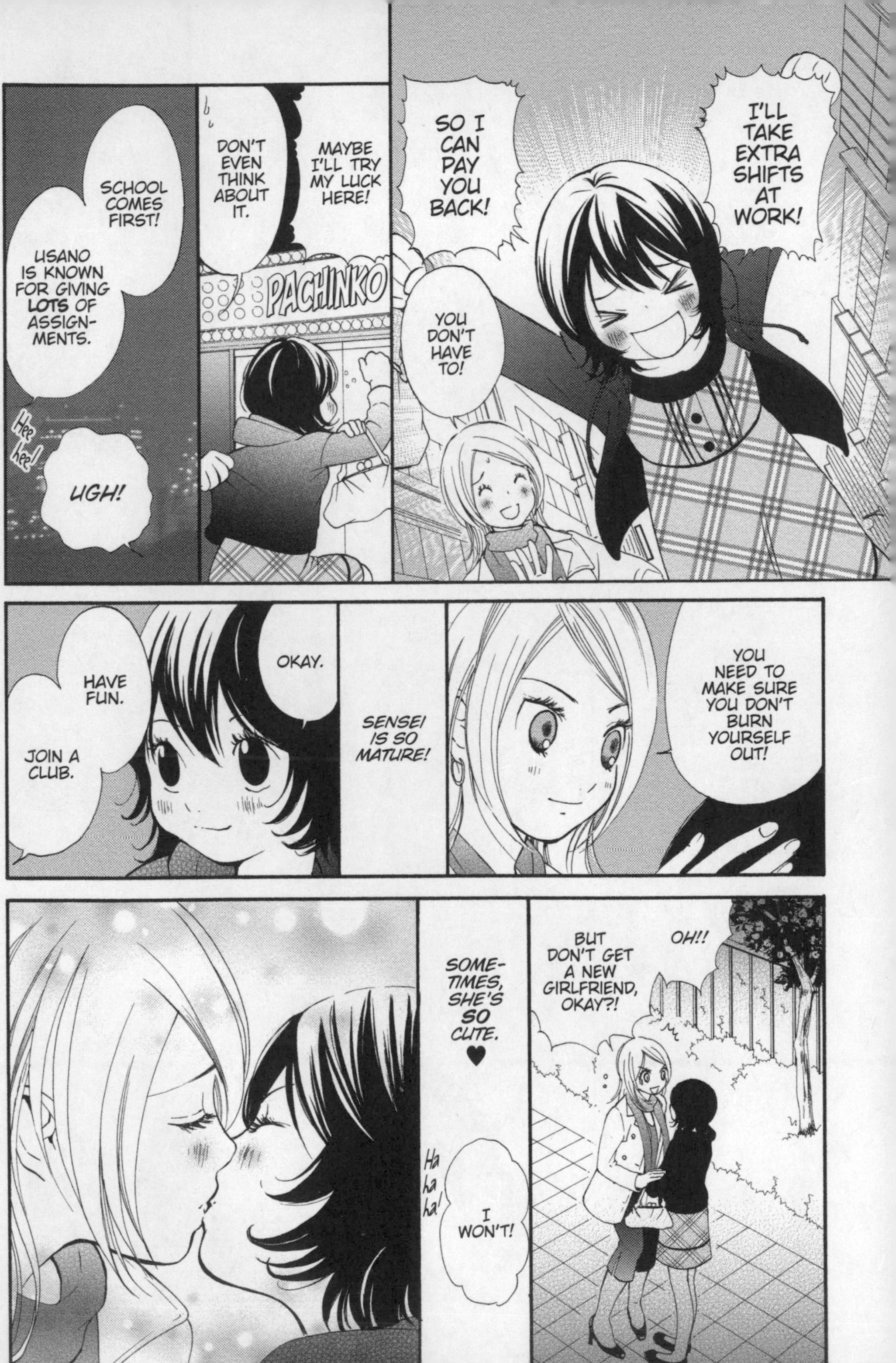
I'LL TAKE EXTRA SHIFTS AT WORK!
SO I CAN PAY YOU BACK!
YOU DON'T HAVE TO!
MAYBE I'LL TRY MY LUCK HERE!
DON'T EVEN THINK ABOUT IT.
PACHINKO
SCHOOL COMES FIRST!
USANO IS KNOWN FOR GIVING **LOTS** OF ASSIGNMENTS.
Hee hee!
UGH!
YOU NEED TO MAKE SURE YOU DON'T BURN YOURSELF OUT!
SENSEI IS SO MATURE!
OKAY.
HAVE FUN.
JOIN A CLUB.
OH!!
BUT DON'T GET A NEW GIRLFRIEND, OKAY?!
SOME-TIMES, SHE'S **SO** CUTE. ♥
Ha ha ha!
I WON'T!

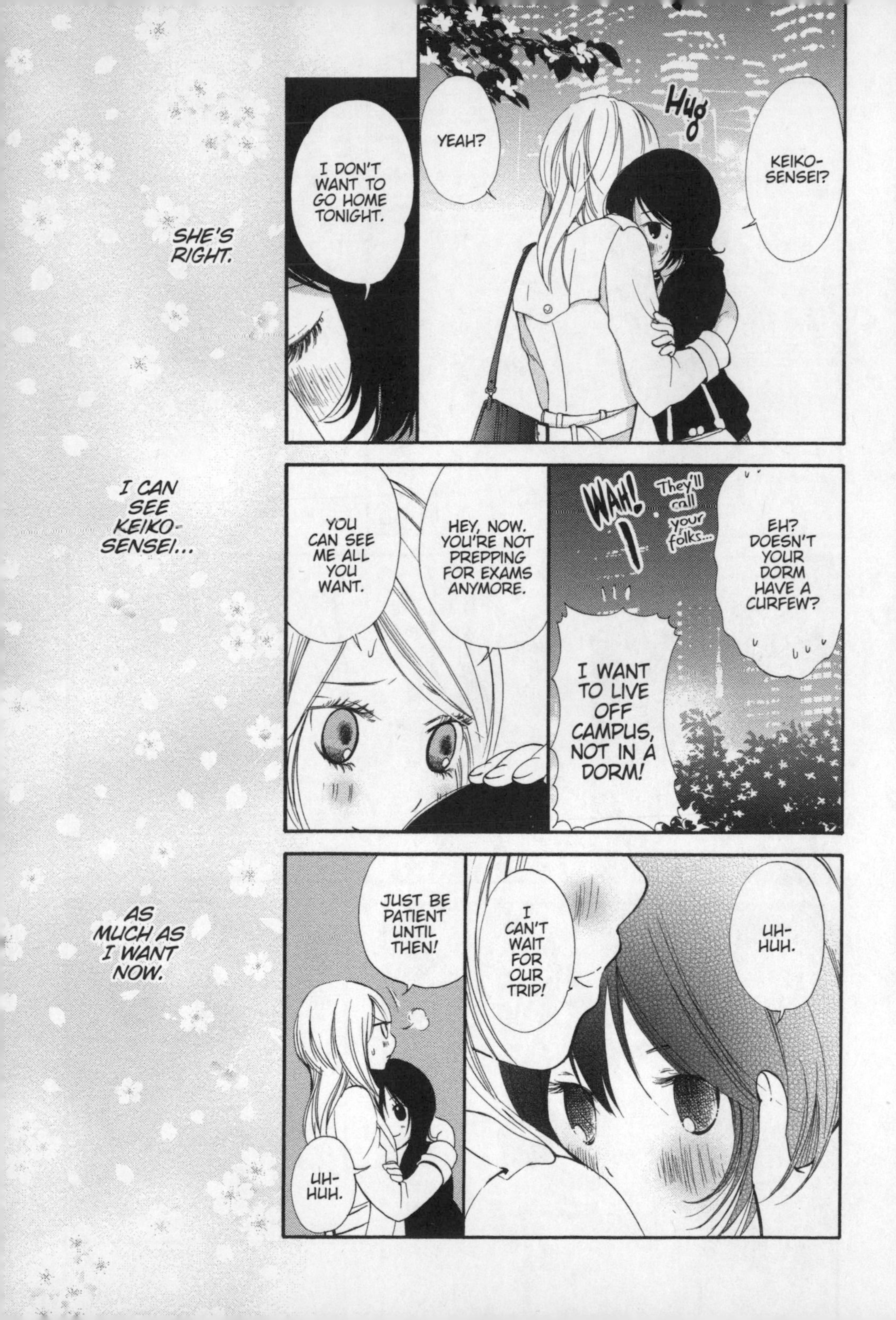
Hug
KEIKO-SENSEI?
YEAH?
I DON'T WANT TO GO HOME TONIGHT.
EH? DOESN'T YOUR DORM HAVE A CURFEW?
WAH!
They'll call your folks...
I WANT TO LIVE OFF CAMPUS, NOT IN A DORM!
HEY, NOW. YOU'RE NOT PREPPING FOR EXAMS ANYMORE.
YOU CAN SEE ME ALL YOU WANT.
UH-HUH.
I CAN'T WAIT FOR OUR TRIP!
JUST BE PATIENT UNTIL THEN!
UH-HUH.
SHE'S RIGHT.
I CAN SEE KEIKO-SENSEI...
AS MUCH AS I WANT NOW.

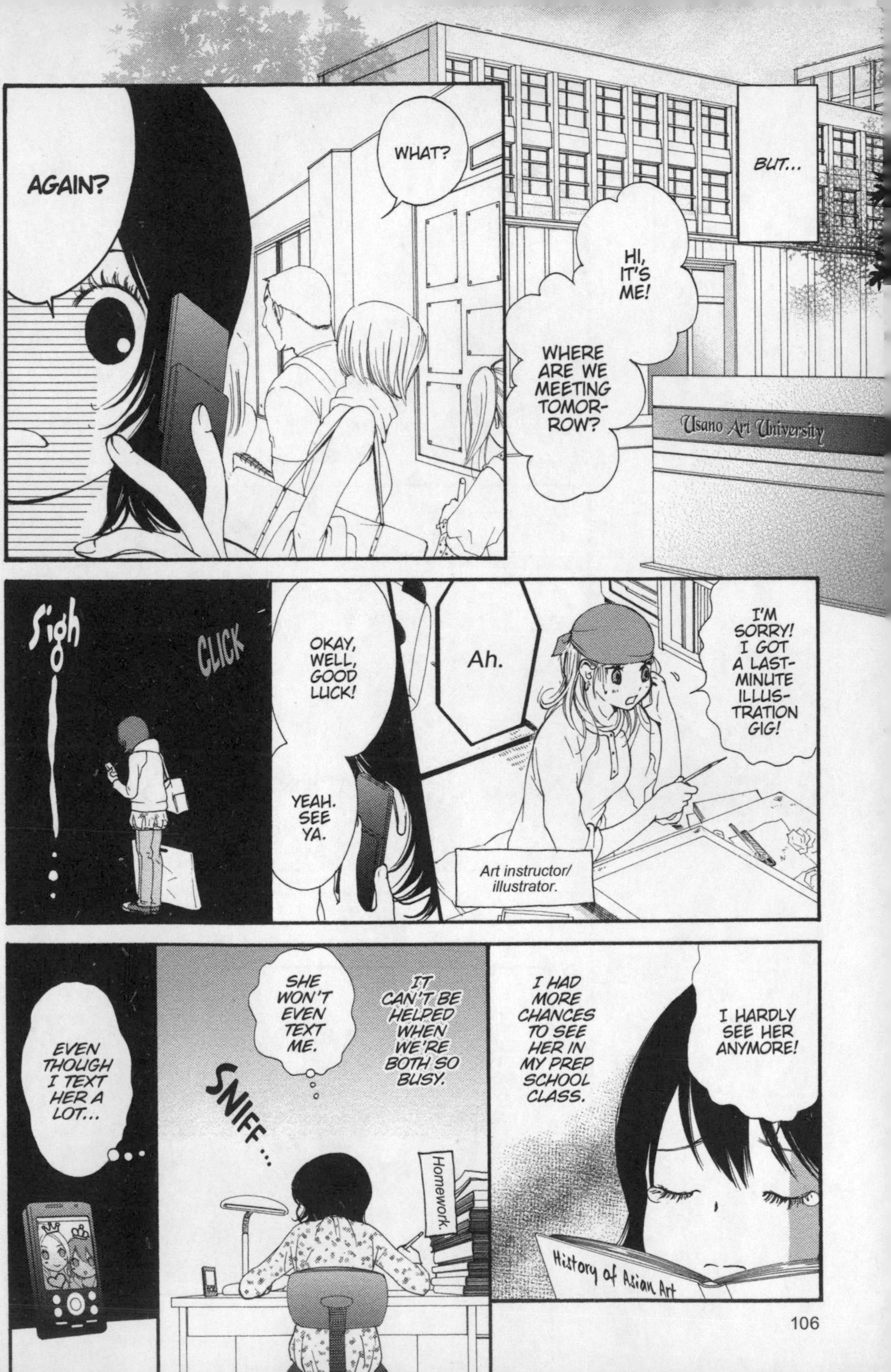
BUT...
HI, IT'S ME!
WHERE ARE WE MEETING TOMORROW?
Usano Art University
WHAT?
AGAIN?
I'M SORRY! I GOT A LAST-MINUTE ILLUSTRATION GIG!
Art instructor/ illustrator.
Ah.
OKAY, WELL, GOOD LUCK!
YEAH. SEE YA.
CLICK
Sigh
I HARDLY SEE HER ANYMORE!
I HAD MORE CHANCES TO SEE HER IN MY PREP SCHOOL CLASS.
History of Asian Art
IT CAN'T BE HELPED WHEN WE'RE BOTH SO BUSY.
SHE WON'T EVEN TEXT ME.
SNIFF...
Homework.
EVEN THOUGH I TEXT HER A LOT...

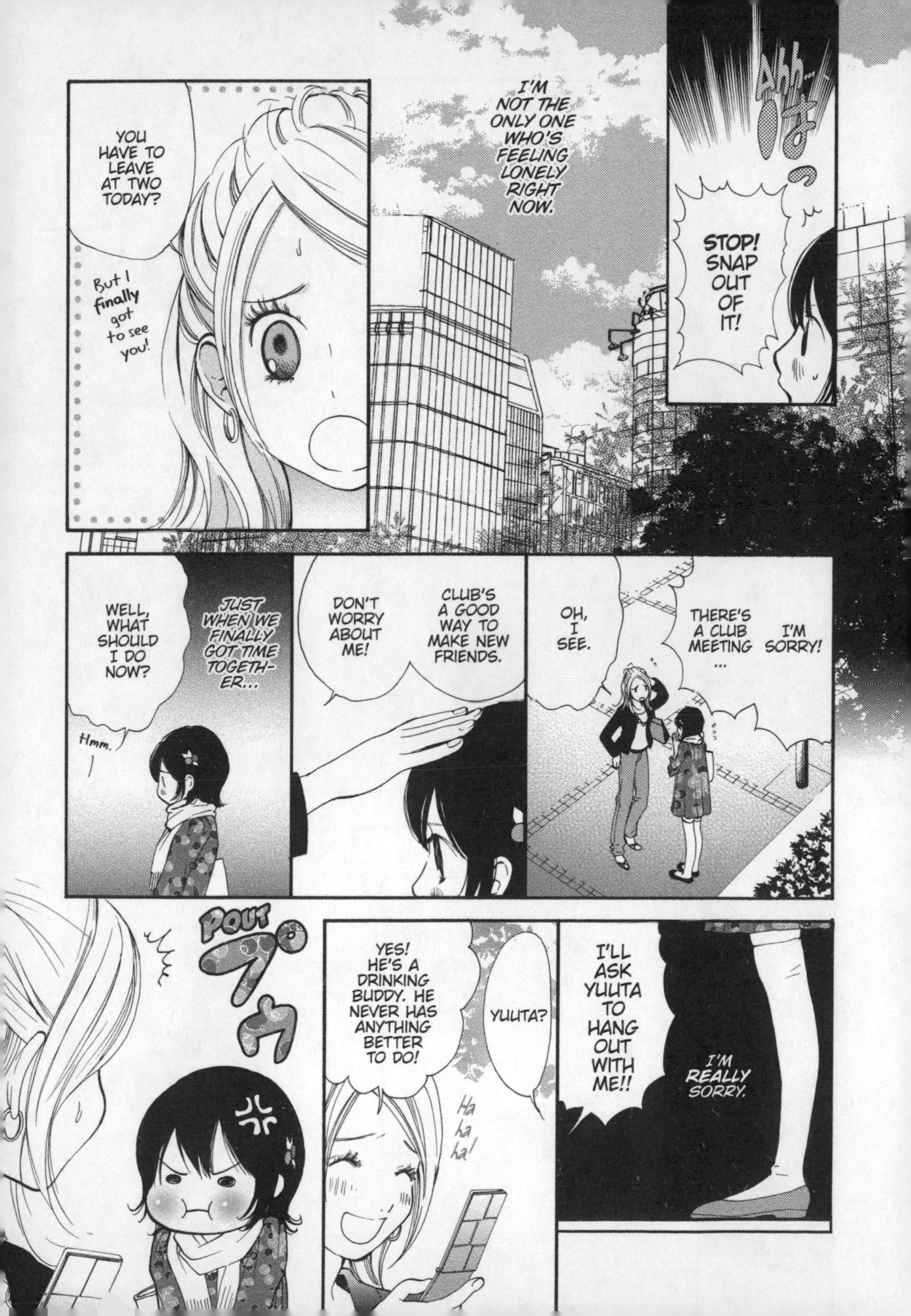
Ahh...
STOP! SNAP OUT OF IT!
I'M NOT THE ONLY ONE WHO'S FEELING LONELY RIGHT NOW.
YOU HAVE TO LEAVE AT TWO TODAY?
But I finally got to see you!
I'M SORRY!
THERE'S A CLUB MEETING...
OH, I SEE.
CLUB'S A GOOD WAY TO MAKE NEW FRIENDS.
DON'T WORRY ABOUT ME!
JUST WHEN WE FINALLY GOT TIME TOGETHER...
WELL, WHAT SHOULD I DO NOW?
Hmm.
I'LL ASK YUUTA TO HANG OUT WITH ME!!
I'M REALLY SORRY.
YUUTA?
YES! HE'S A DRINKING BUDDY. HE NEVER HAS ANYTHING BETTER TO DO!
Ha ha ha!
POUT

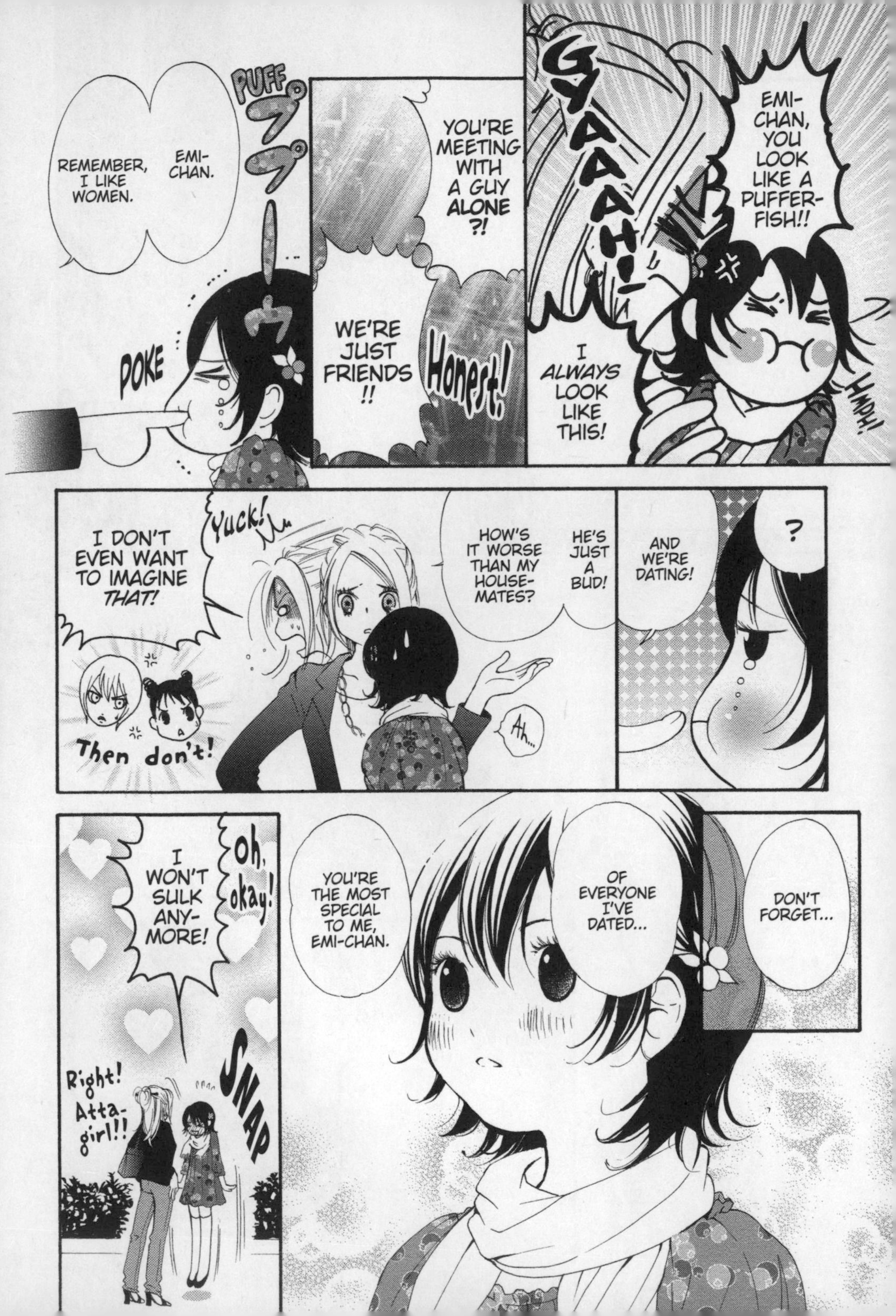
EMI-CHAN, YOU LOOK LIKE A PUFFER-FISH!!
GYAAAH!!
I ALWAYS LOOK LIKE THIS!
HMPH!
YOU'RE MEETING WITH A GUY ALONE?!
WE'RE JUST FRIENDS!!
Honest!
PUFF
EMI-CHAN.
REMEMBER, I LIKE WOMEN.
POKE
?
AND WE'RE DATING!
HE'S JUST A BUD!
HOW'S IT WORSE THAN MY HOUSE-MATES?
Yuck!
I DON'T EVEN WANT TO IMAGINE THAT!
Ah...
Then don't!
DON'T FORGET...
OF EVERYONE I'VE DATED...
YOU'RE THE MOST SPECIAL TO ME, EMI-CHAN.
Oh, okay!
I WON'T SULK ANYMORE!
SNAP
Right! Atta-girl!!

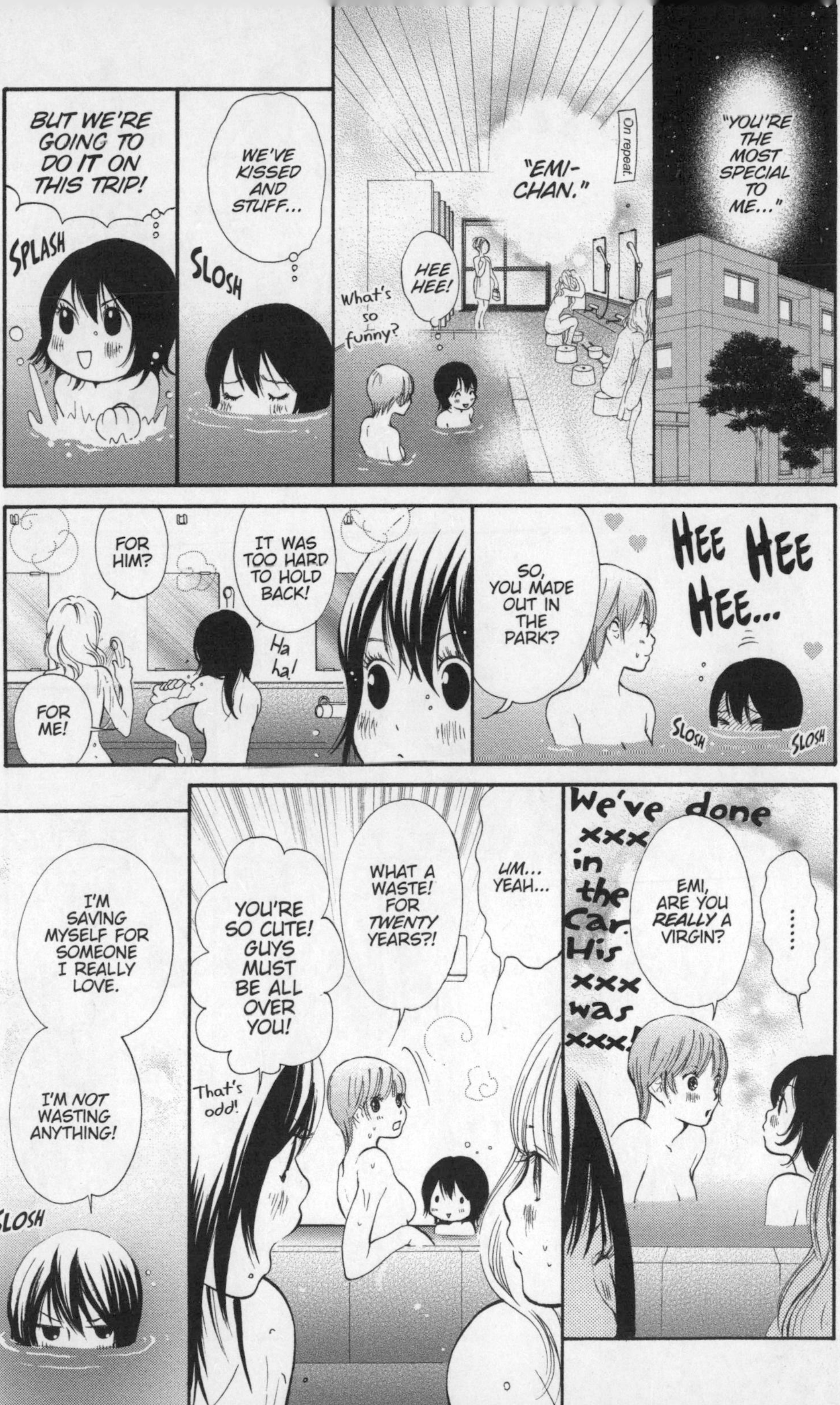
"YOU'RE THE MOST SPECIAL TO ME..."
"EMI-CHAN."
On repeat.
HEE HEE!
What's so funny?
WE'VE KISSED AND STUFF...
SLOSH
BUT WE'RE GOING TO DO IT ON THIS TRIP!
SPLASH
HEE HEE HEE...
SO, YOU MADE OUT IN THE PARK?
SLOSH
SLOSH
IT WAS TOO HARD TO HOLD BACK!
FOR HIM?
Ha ha!
FOR ME!
......
EMI, ARE YOU REALLY A VIRGIN?
We've done xxx in the car. His xxx was xxx!
UM... YEAH...
WHAT A WASTE! FOR TWENTY YEARS?!
YOU'RE SO CUTE! GUYS MUST BE ALL OVER YOU!
That's odd!
I'M SAVING MYSELF FOR SOMEONE I REALLY LOVE.
I'M NOT WASTING ANYTHING!
SLOSH

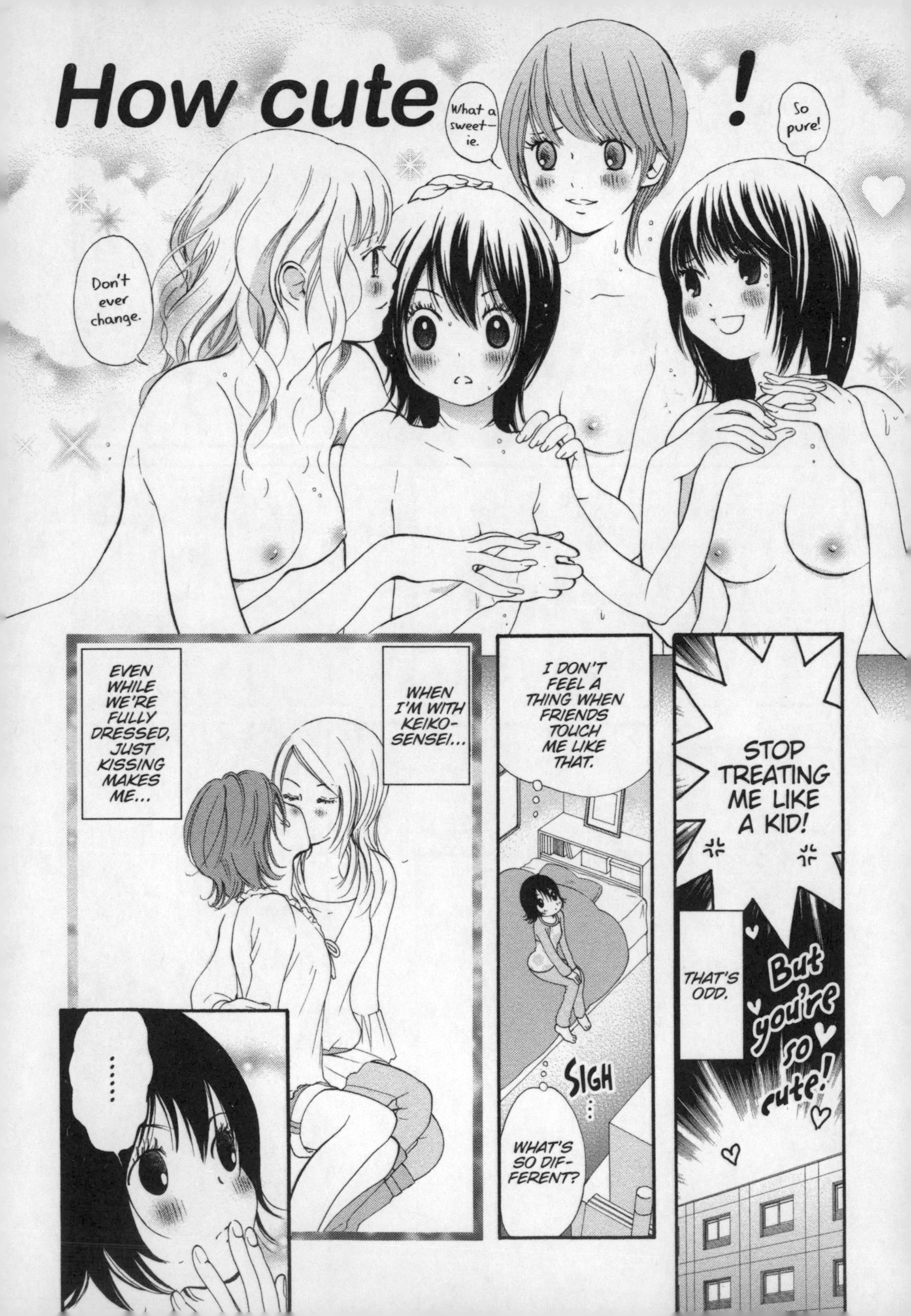
So pure!
What a sweetie.
How cute!
Don't ever change.
STOP TREATING ME LIKE A KID!
But you're so cute!
THAT'S ODD.
I DON'T FEEL A THING WHEN FRIENDS TOUCH ME LIKE THAT.
SIGH...
WHAT'S SO DIFFERENT?
WHEN I'M WITH KEIKO-SENSEI...
EVEN WHILE WE'RE FULLY DRESSED, JUST KISSING MAKES ME...
......

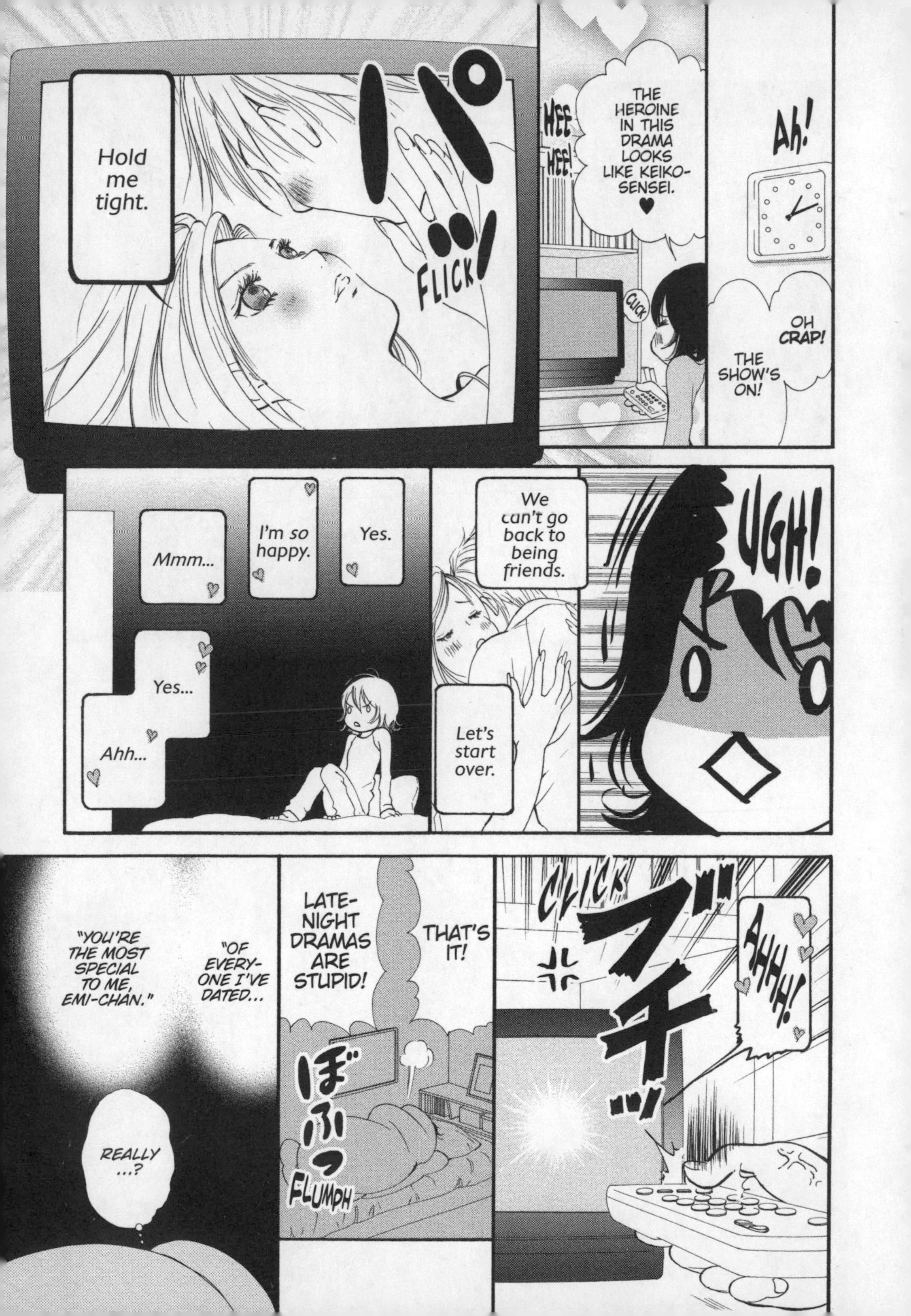

Ah!
OH CRAP!
THE SHOW'S ON!
THE HEROINE IN THIS DRAMA LOOKS LIKE KEIKO-SENSEI. ♥
HEE HEE!
CLICK
パッ
FLICK
Hold me tight.
UGH!
We can't go back to being friends.
Let's start over.
Yes.
I'm so happy.
Mmm...
Yes...
Ahh...
CLICK
ブチッ
AHHH!
THAT'S IT!
LATE-NIGHT DRAMAS ARE STUPID!
ぼふっ
FLUMPH
"OF EVERYONE I'VE DATED...
"YOU'RE THE MOST SPECIAL TO ME, EMI-CHAN."
REALLY ...?

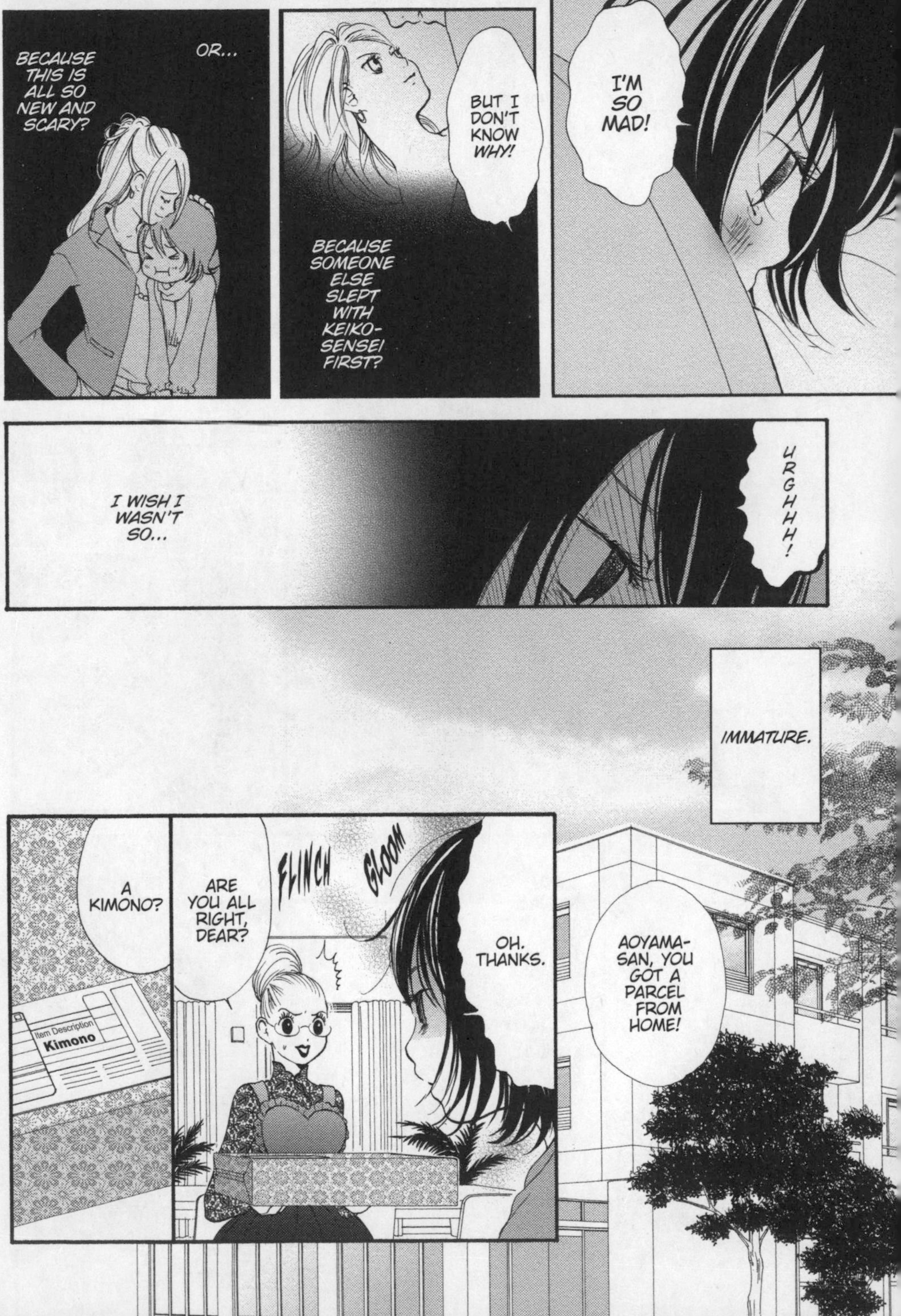
I'M SO MAD!
BUT I DON'T KNOW WHY!
BECAUSE SOMEONE ELSE SLEPT WITH KEIKO-SENSEI FIRST?
OR...
BECAUSE THIS IS ALL SO NEW AND SCARY?
URGHHH!
I WISH I WASN'T SO...
IMMATURE.
AOYAMA-SAN, YOU GOT A PARCEL FROM HOME!
OH. THANKS.
GLOOM
FLINCH
ARE YOU ALL RIGHT, DEAR?
A KIMONO?
Item Description
Kimono

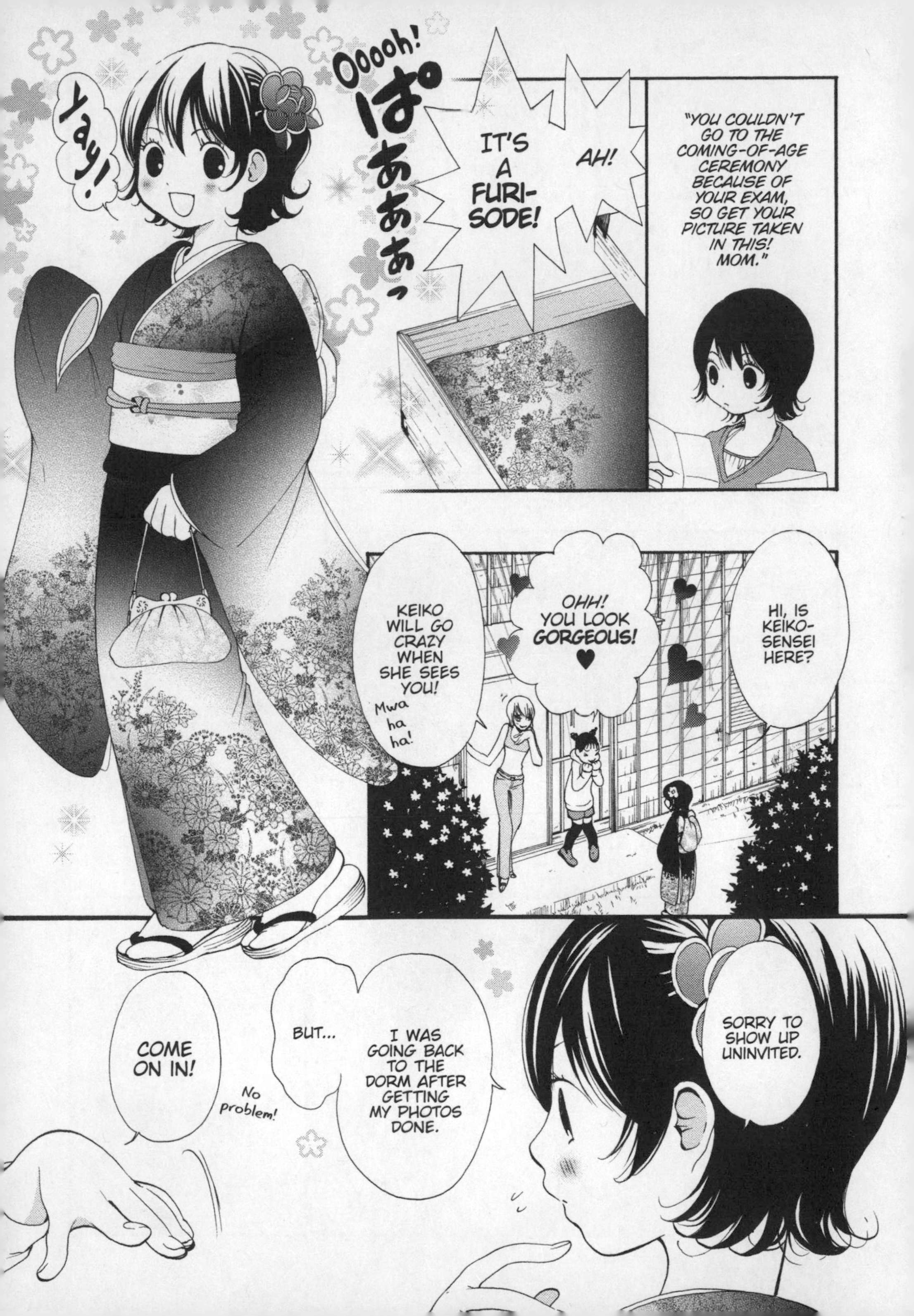
"YOU COULDN'T GO TO THE COMING-OF-AGE CEREMONY BECAUSE OF YOUR EXAM, SO GET YOUR PICTURE TAKEN IN THIS! MOM."
AH!
IT'S A FURI-SODE!
HI, IS KEIKO-SENSEI HERE?
OHH! YOU LOOK GORGEOUS! ♥
KEIKO WILL GO CRAZY WHEN SHE SEES YOU!
Mwa ha ha!
Ooooh!
ぱあああっ
Yay!
SORRY TO SHOW UP UNINVITED.
I WAS GOING BACK TO THE DORM AFTER GETTING MY PHOTOS DONE.
BUT...
COME ON IN!
No problem!

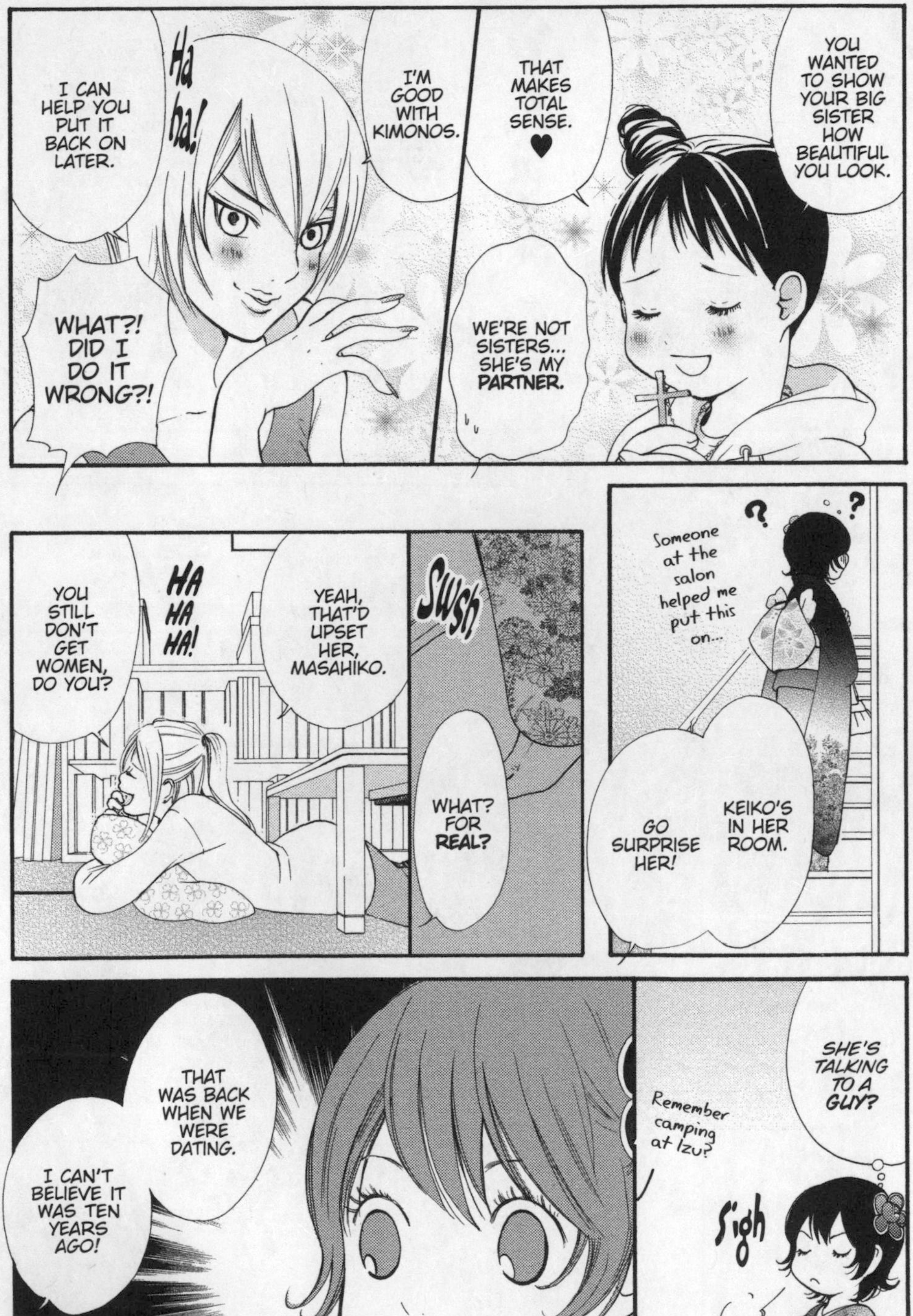
YOU WANTED TO SHOW YOUR BIG SISTER HOW BEAUTIFUL YOU LOOK.
THAT MAKES TOTAL SENSE. ♥
WE'RE NOT SISTERS... SHE'S MY **PARTNER.**
I'M GOOD WITH KIMONOS.
Ha ha!
I CAN HELP YOU PUT IT BACK ON LATER.
WHAT?! DID I DO IT WRONG?!
Someone at the salon helped me put this on...
KEIKO'S IN HER ROOM.
GO SURPRISE HER!
Swsh
WHAT? FOR **REAL?**
YEAH, THAT'D UPSET HER, MASAHIKO.
HA HA HA!
YOU STILL DON'T GET WOMEN, DO YOU?
SHE'S TALKING TO A **GUY?**
Remember camping at Izu?
Sigh
THAT WAS BACK WHEN WE WERE DATING.
I CAN'T BELIEVE IT WAS TEN YEARS AGO!

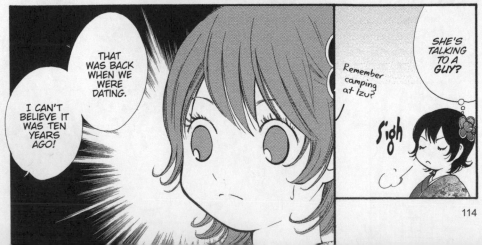

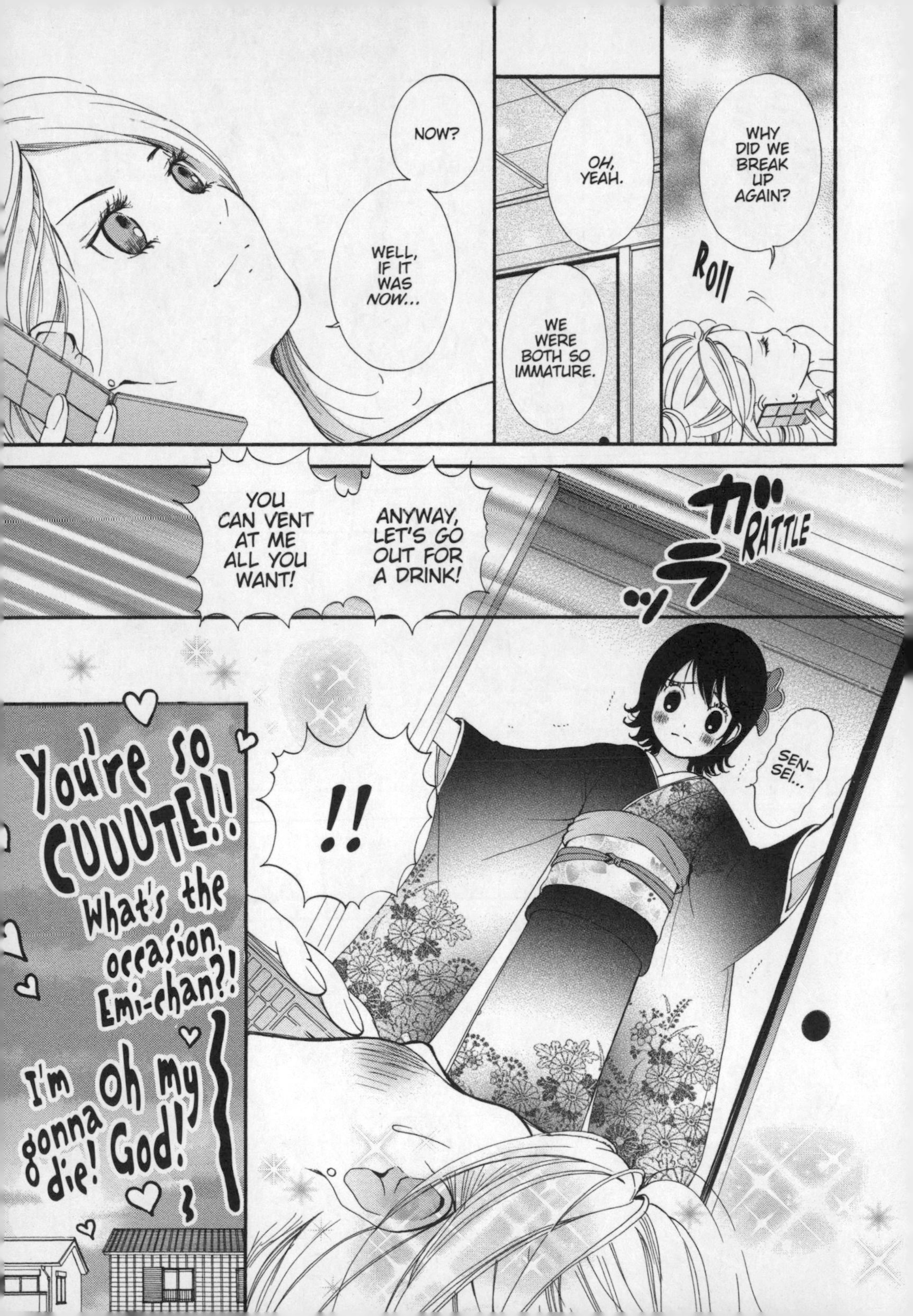
WHY DID WE BREAK UP AGAIN?
ROll
OH, YEAH.
WE WERE BOTH SO IMMATURE.
NOW?
WELL, IF IT WAS NOW...
ガラッ
RATTLE
ANYWAY, LET'S GO OUT FOR A DRINK!
YOU CAN VENT AT ME ALL YOU WANT!
SEN-SEI...
!!
You're so CUUUTE!! What's the occasion, Emi-chan?! I'm gonna die! Oh my God!

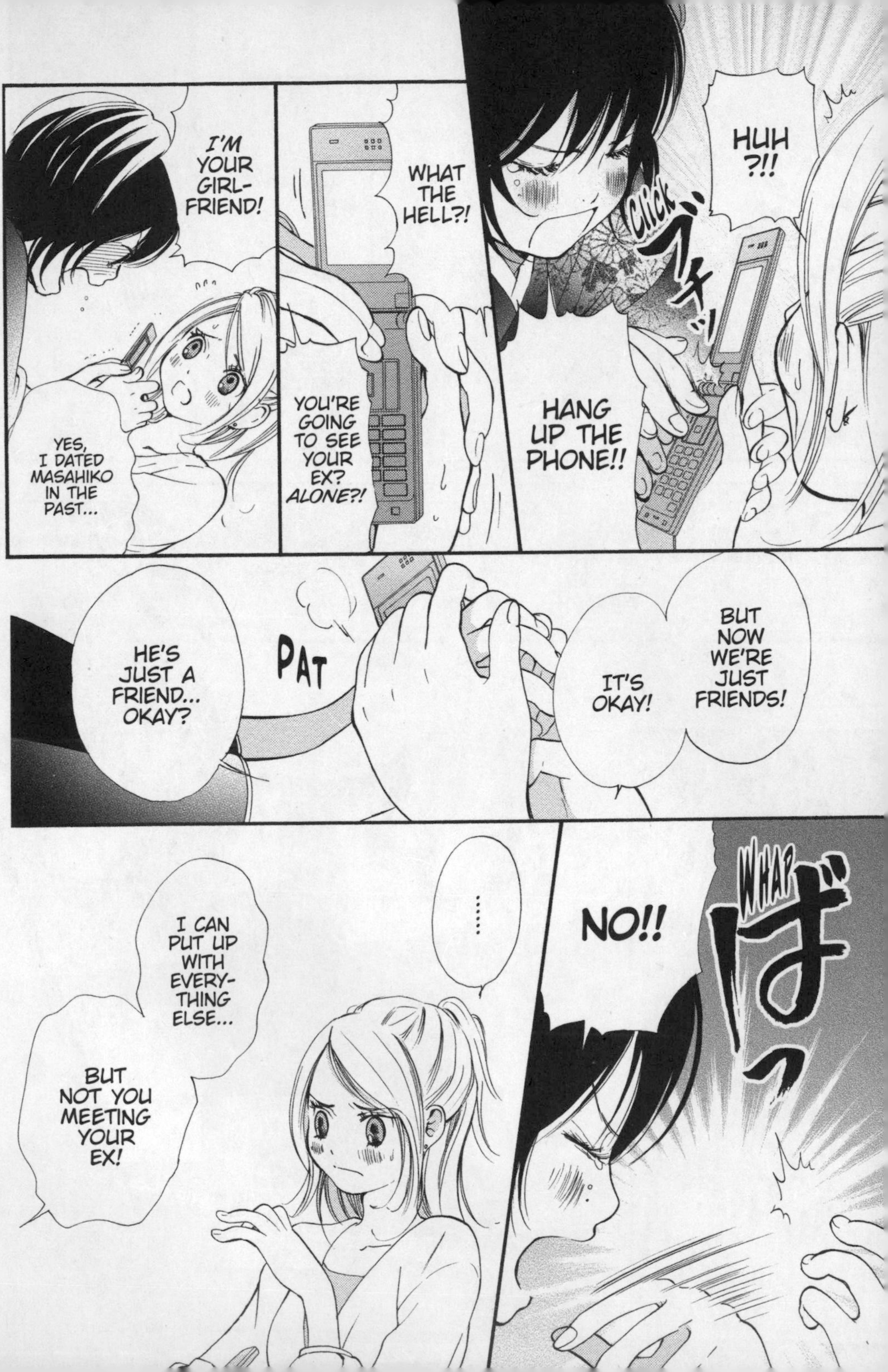
HUH ?!!
CLICK
HANG UP THE PHONE!!
WHAT THE HELL?!
YOU'RE GOING TO SEE YOUR EX? ALONE?!
I'M YOUR GIRL-FRIEND!
YES, I DATED MASAHIKO IN THE PAST...
BUT NOW WE'RE JUST FRIENDS!
IT'S OKAY!
PAT
HE'S JUST A FRIEND... OKAY?
WHAP
ばっ
NO!!
......
I CAN PUT UP WITH EVERY-THING ELSE...
BUT NOT YOU MEETING YOUR EX!

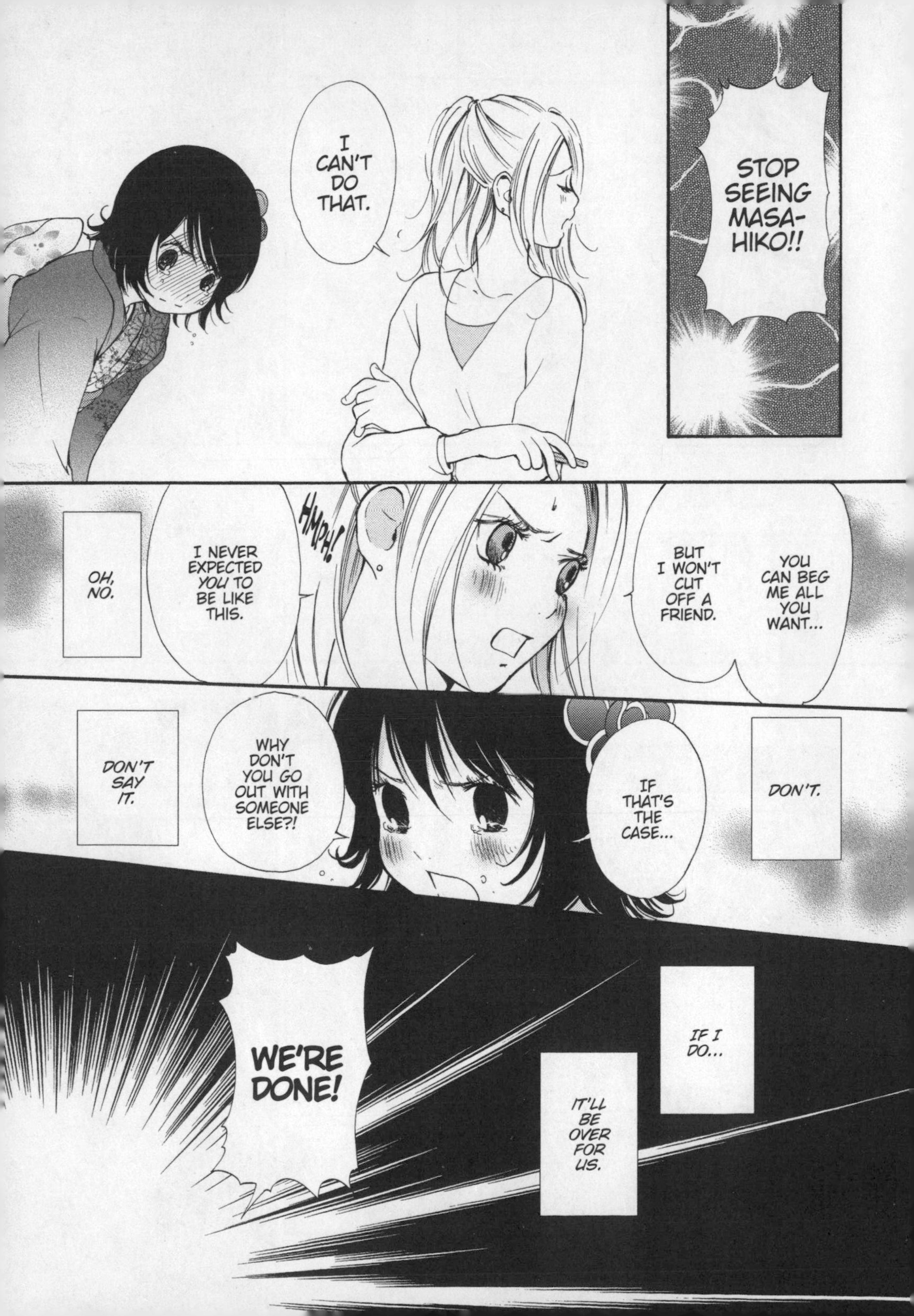
STOP SEEING MASA-HIKO!!
I CAN'T DO THAT.
YOU CAN BEG ME ALL YOU WANT...
BUT I WON'T CUT OFF A FRIEND.
HMPH!
I NEVER EXPECTED YOU TO BE LIKE THIS.
OH, NO.
DON'T.
IF THAT'S THE CASE...
WHY DON'T YOU GO OUT WITH SOMEONE ELSE?!
DON'T SAY IT.
IF I DO...
IT'LL BE OVER FOR US.
WE'RE DONE!

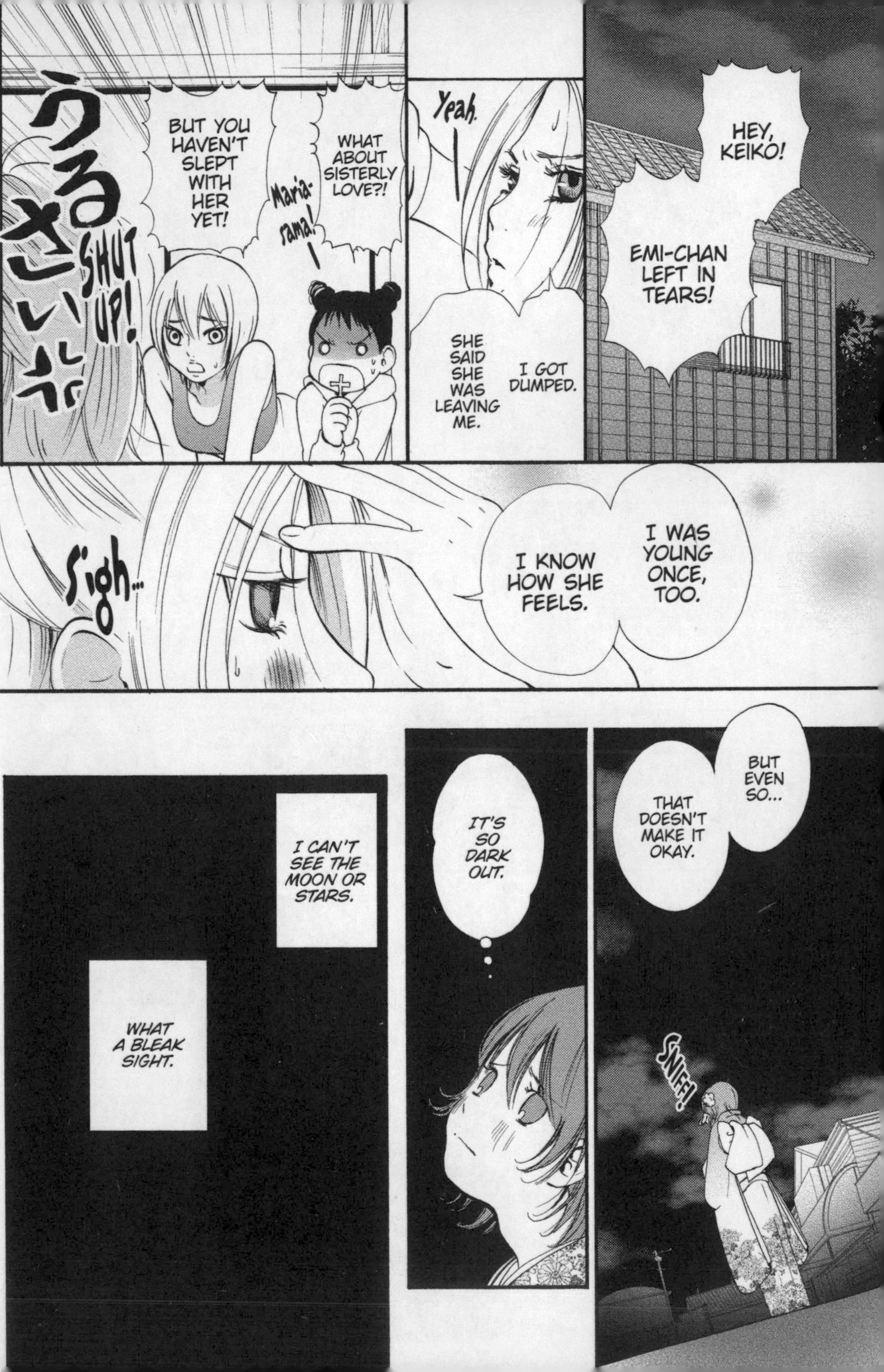
HEY, KEIKO!
EMI-CHAN LEFT IN TEARS!
Yeah.
I GOT DUMPED.
SHE SAID SHE WAS LEAVING ME.
WHAT ABOUT SISTERLY LOVE?!
Maria-sama!
BUT YOU HAVEN'T SLEPT WITH HER YET!
うるさい
SHUT UP!
I WAS YOUNG ONCE, TOO.
I KNOW HOW SHE FEELS.
Sigh...
BUT EVEN SO...
THAT DOESN'T MAKE IT OKAY.
SNIFF!
IT'S SO DARK OUT.
I CAN'T SEE THE MOON OR STARS.
WHAT A BLEAK SIGHT.

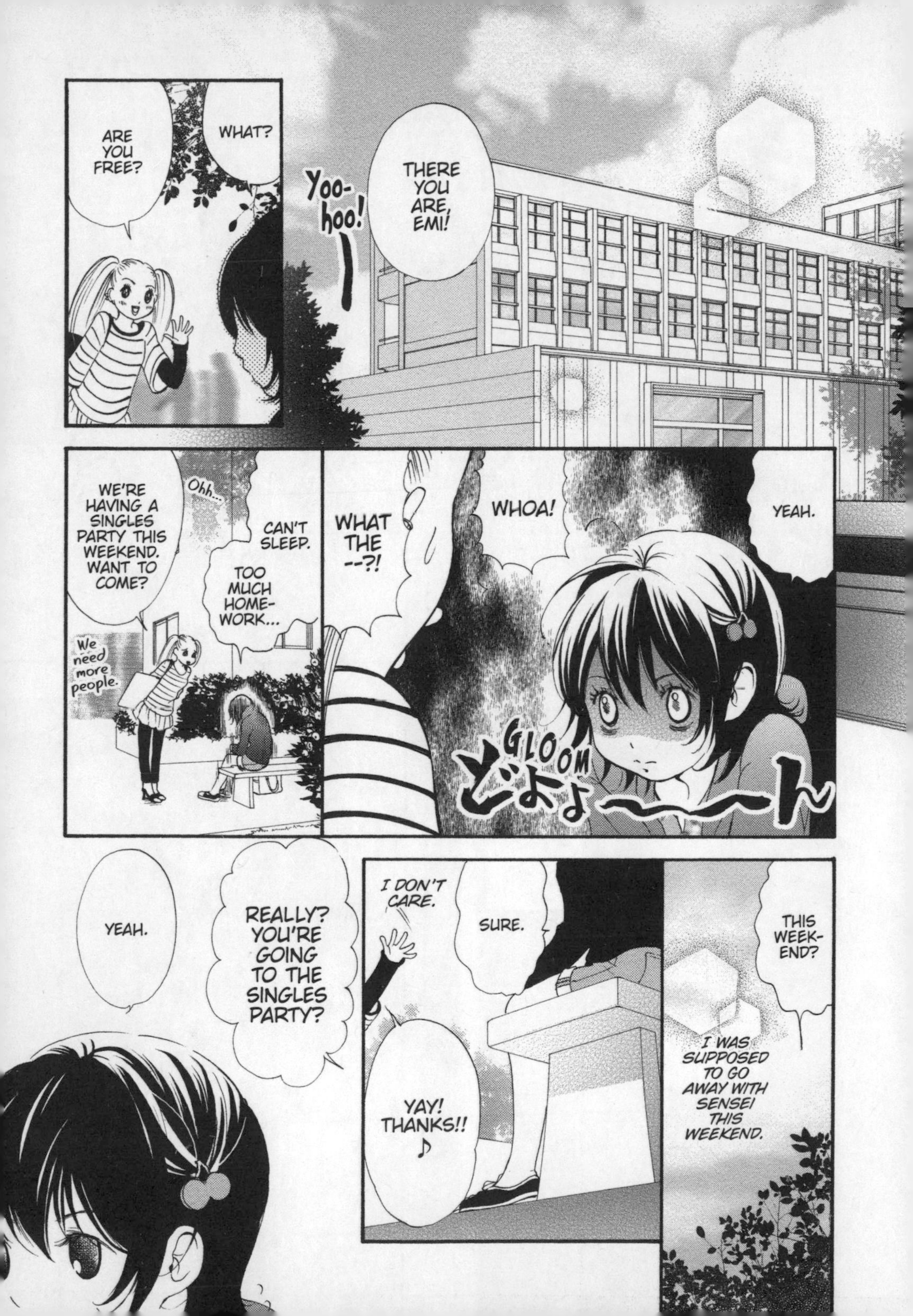
Yoo-hoo!
THERE YOU ARE, EMI!
WHAT?
ARE YOU FREE?
YEAH.
WHOA!
WHAT THE --?!
GLOOM
Ohh...
CAN'T SLEEP.
TOO MUCH HOMEWORK...
WE'RE HAVING A SINGLES PARTY THIS WEEKEND. WANT TO COME?
We need more people.
THIS WEEKEND?
I WAS SUPPOSED TO GO AWAY WITH SENSEI THIS WEEKEND.
SURE.
I DON'T CARE.
YAY! THANKS!! ♪
REALLY? YOU'RE GOING TO THE SINGLES PARTY?
YEAH.

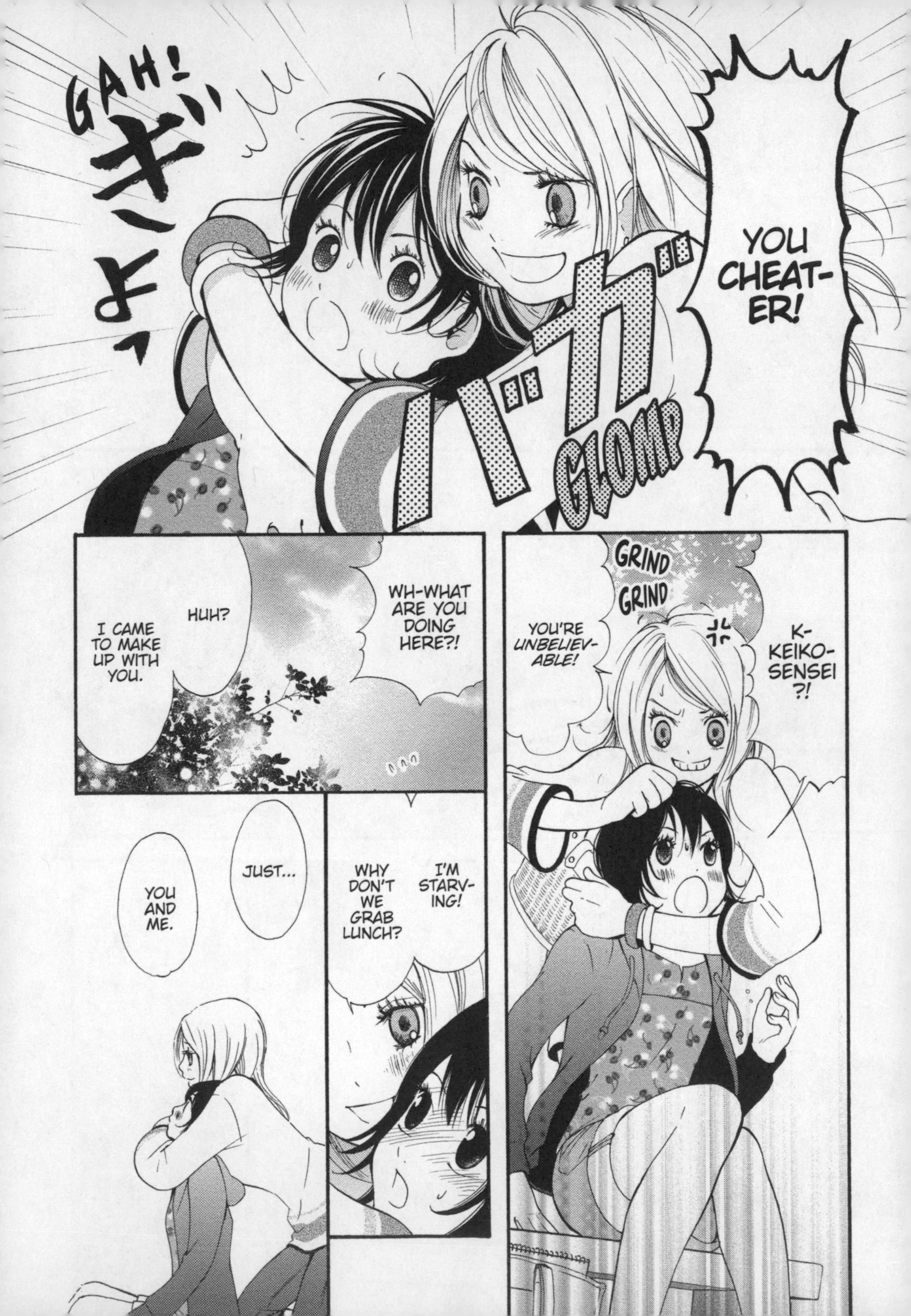
YOU CHEATER!
GAH!
GLOMP
GRIND GRIND
K-KEIKO-SENSEI?!
YOU'RE UNBELIEVABLE!
WH-WHAT ARE YOU DOING HERE?!
HUH?
I CAME TO MAKE UP WITH YOU.
I'M STARVING!
WHY DON'T WE GRAB LUNCH?
JUST...
YOU AND ME.

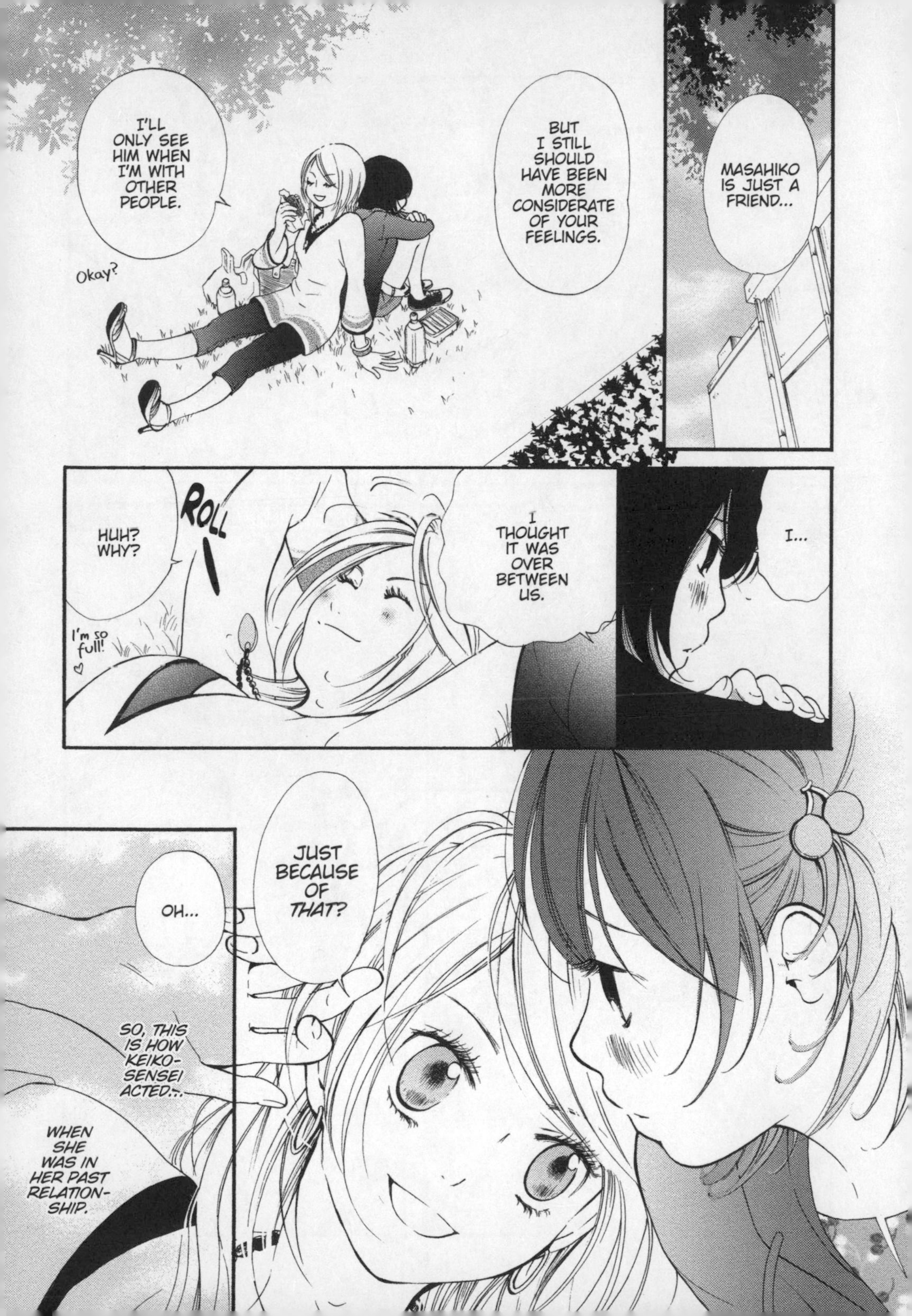
MASAHIKO IS JUST A FRIEND...
BUT I STILL SHOULD HAVE BEEN MORE CONSIDERATE OF YOUR FEELINGS.
I'LL ONLY SEE HIM WHEN I'M WITH OTHER PEOPLE.
Okay?
I...
I THOUGHT IT WAS OVER BETWEEN US.
ROLL
HUH? WHY?
I'm so full! ♡
JUST BECAUSE OF *THAT*?
OH...
SO, THIS IS HOW KEIKO-SENSEI ACTED...
WHEN SHE WAS IN HER PAST RELATIONSHIP.

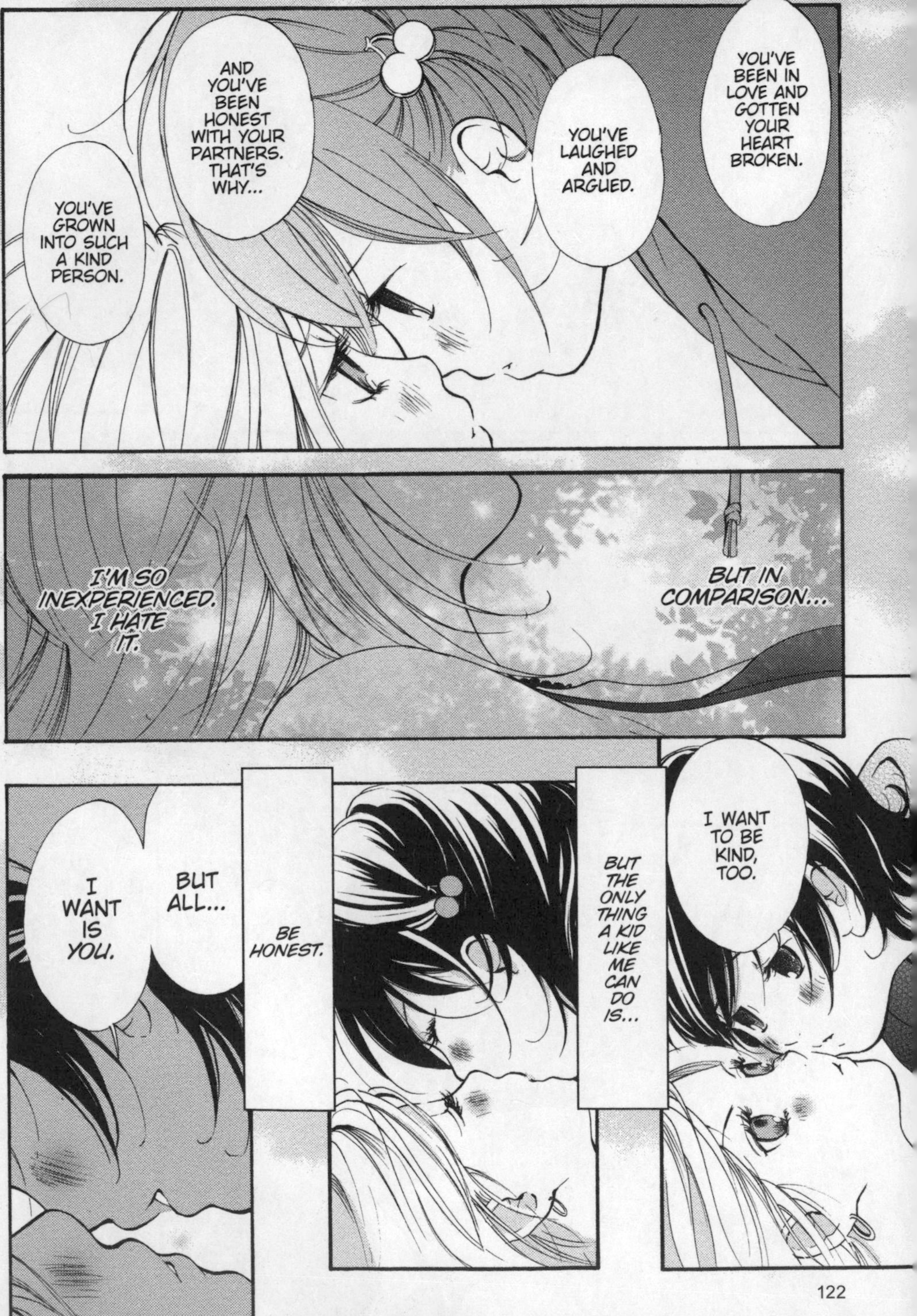
YOU'VE BEEN IN LOVE AND GOTTEN YOUR HEART BROKEN.
YOU'VE LAUGHED AND ARGUED.
AND YOU'VE BEEN HONEST WITH YOUR PARTNERS. THAT'S WHY...
YOU'VE GROWN INTO SUCH A KIND PERSON.
BUT IN COMPARISON...
I'M SO INEXPERIENCED. I HATE IT.
I WANT TO BE KIND, TOO.
BUT THE ONLY THING A KID LIKE ME CAN DO IS...
BE HONEST.
BUT ALL...
I WANT IS *YOU*.

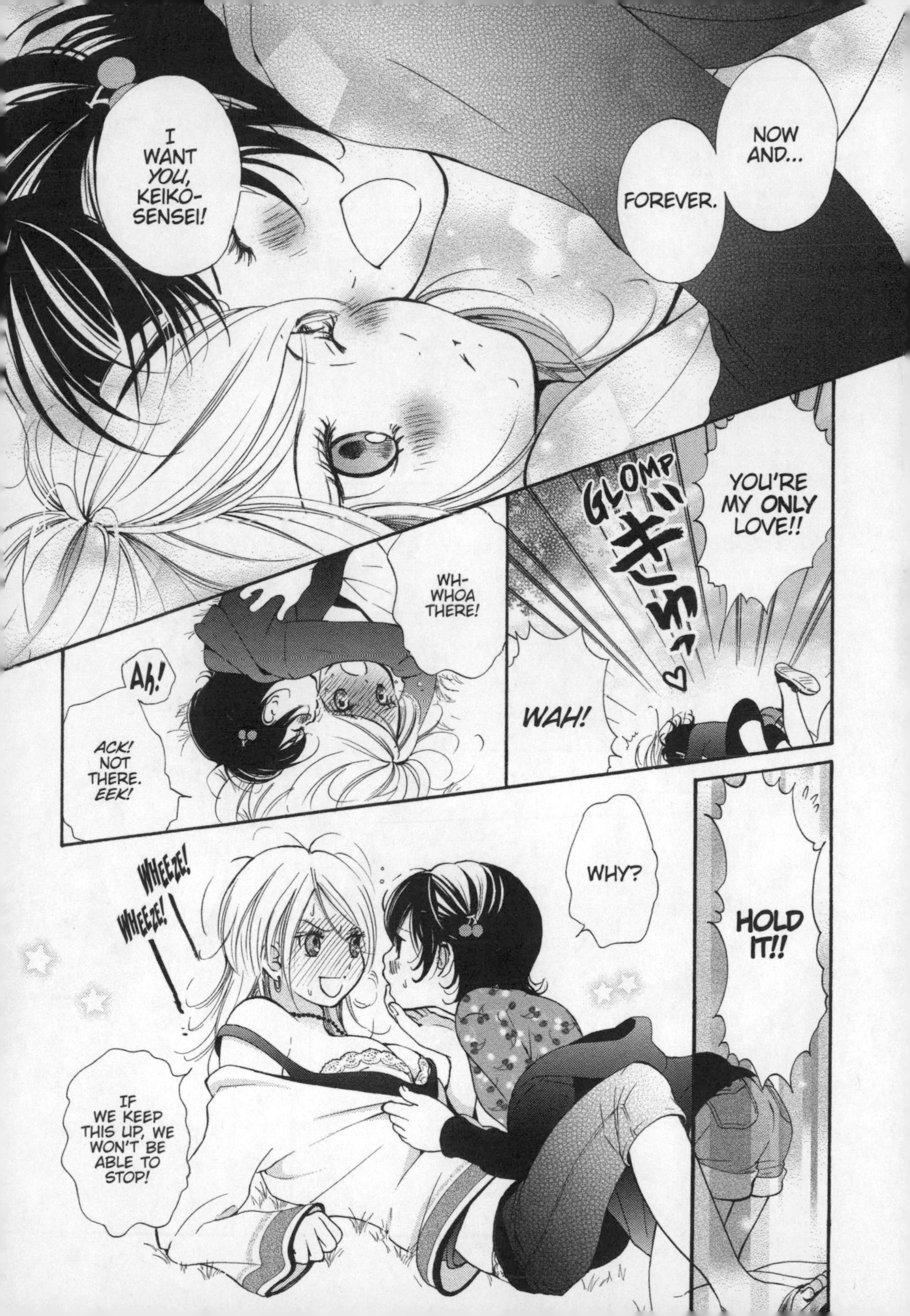
NOW AND...
FOREVER.
I WANT YOU, KEIKO-SENSEI!
YOU'RE MY ONLY LOVE!!
GLOMP
ぎゅっ
WAH!
WH-WHOA THERE!
Ah!
ACK! NOT THERE. EEK!
HOLD IT!!
WHY?
WHEEZE!
WHEEZE!
IF WE KEEP THIS UP, WE WON'T BE ABLE TO STOP!

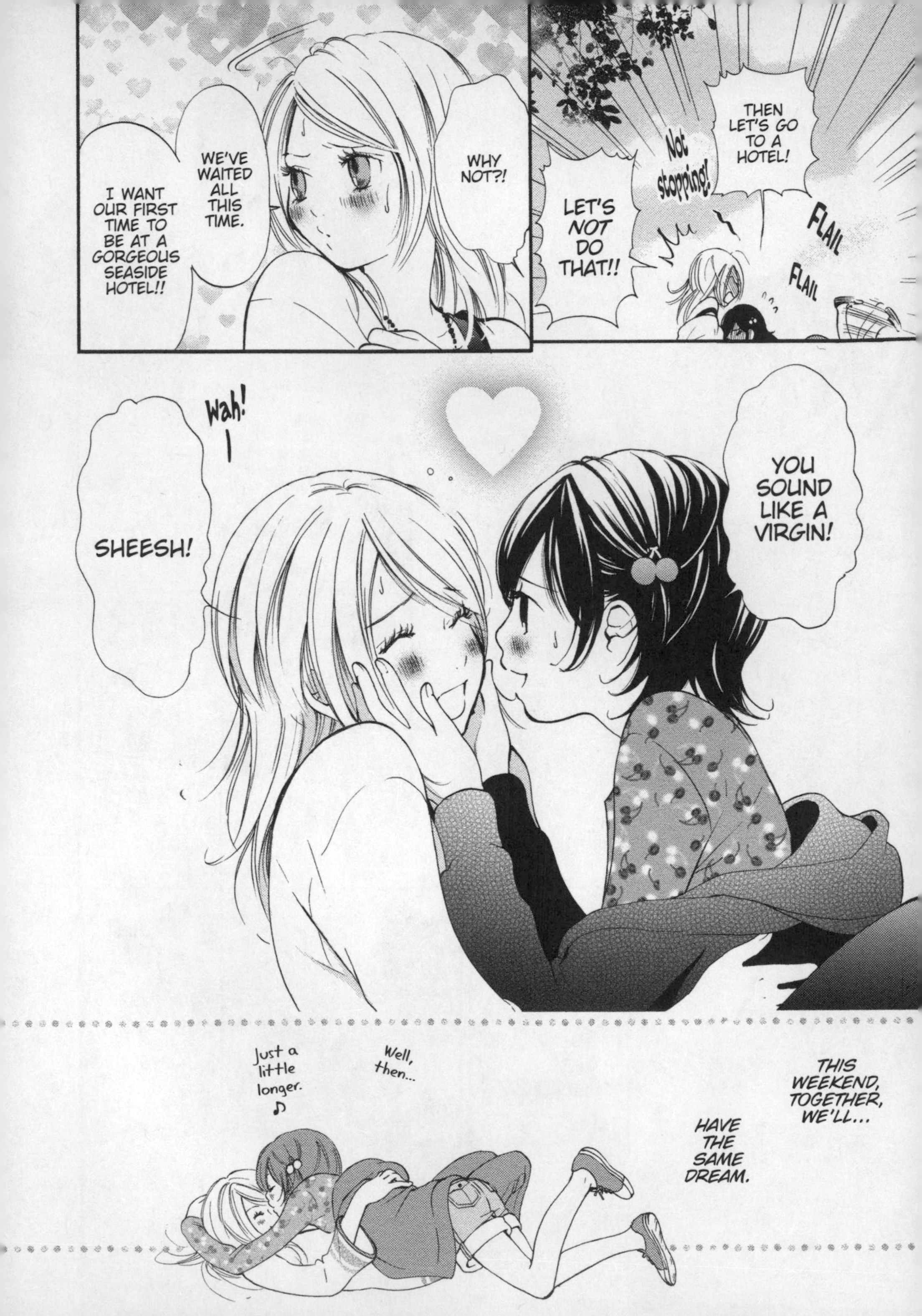
THEN LET'S GO TO A HOTEL!
Not stopping!
FLAIL
FLAIL
LET'S NOT DO THAT!!
WHY NOT?!
WE'VE WAITED ALL THIS TIME.
I WANT OUR FIRST TIME TO BE AT A GORGEOUS SEASIDE HOTEL!!
YOU SOUND LIKE A VIRGIN!
Wah!
SHEESH!
THIS WEEKEND, TOGETHER, WE'LL...
HAVE THE SAME DREAM.
Well, then...
Just a little longer. ♪

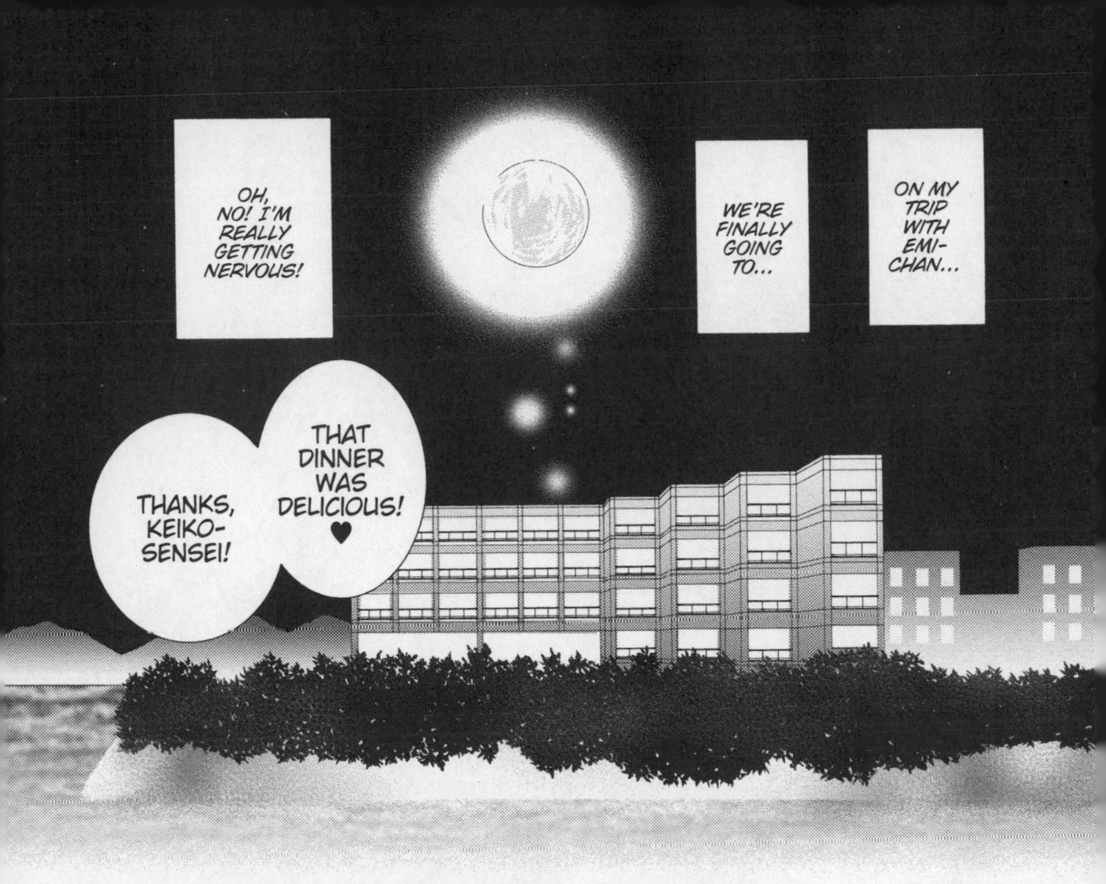
ON MY TRIP WITH EMI-CHAN...
WE'RE FINALLY GOING TO...
OH, NO! I'M REALLY GETTING NERVOUS!
THAT DINNER WAS DELICIOUS! ♥
THANKS, KEIKO-SENSEI!

Under a Full Moon

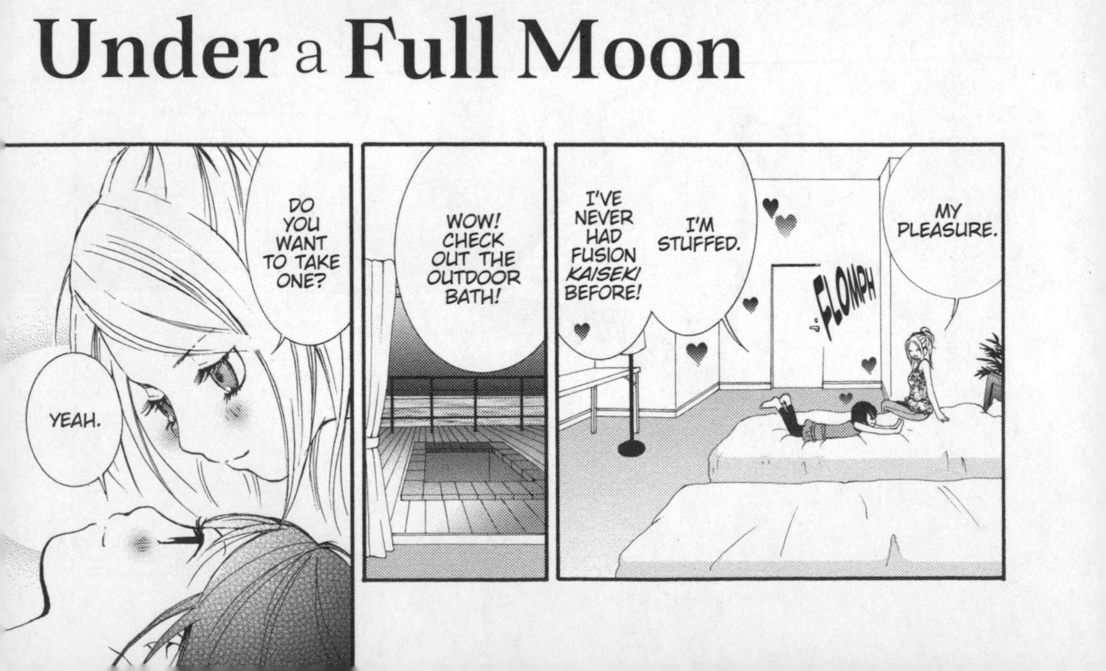
MY PLEASURE.
FLOMPH
I'M STUFFED.
I'VE NEVER HAD FUSION *KAISEKI* BEFORE!
WOW! CHECK OUT THE OUTDOOR BATH!
DO YOU WANT TO TAKE ONE?
YEAH.

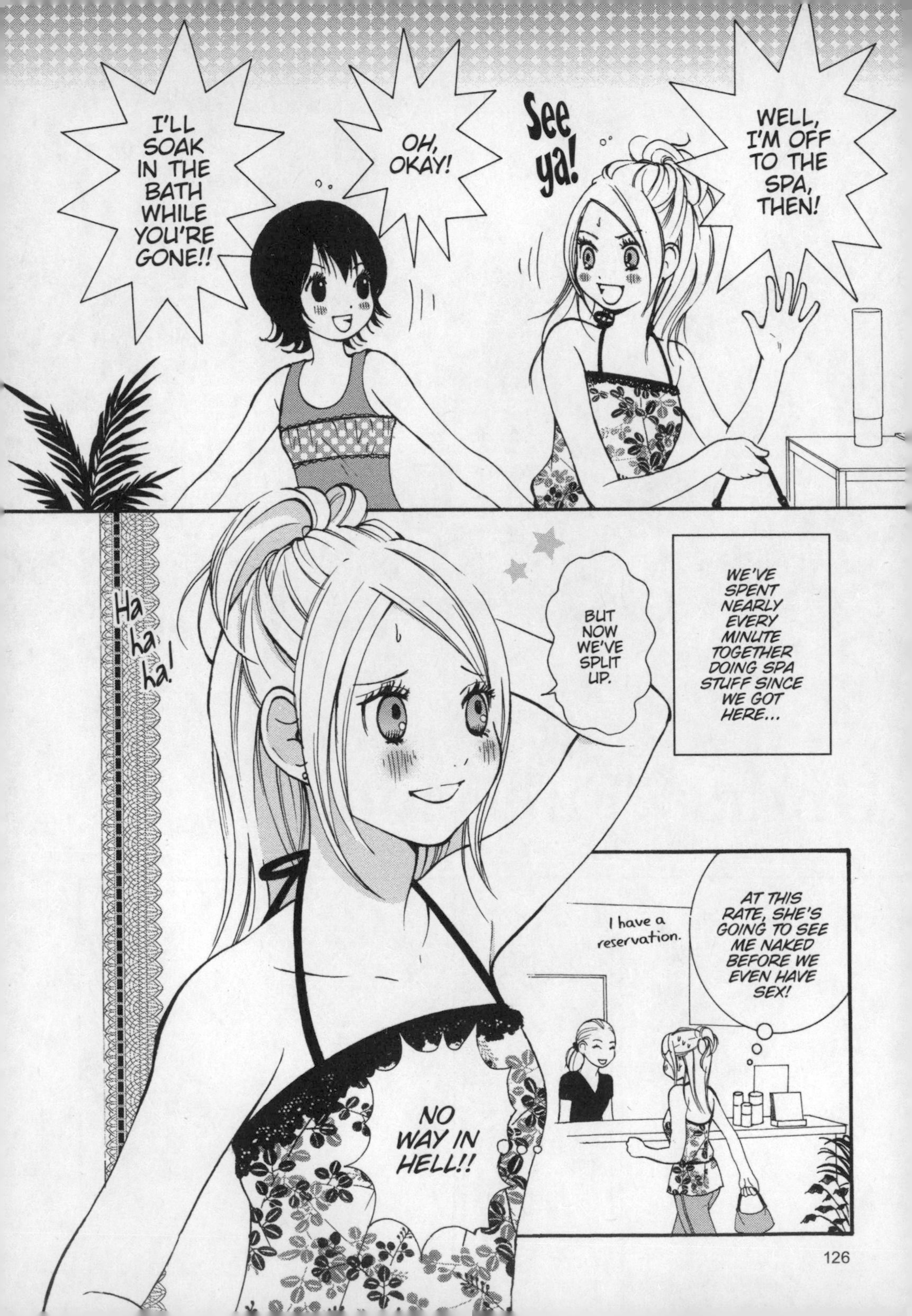
WELL, I'M OFF TO THE SPA, THEN!
See ya!
OH, OKAY!
I'LL SOAK IN THE BATH WHILE YOU'RE GONE!!
WE'VE SPENT NEARLY EVERY MINUTE TOGETHER DOING SPA STUFF SINCE WE GOT HERE...
BUT NOW WE'VE SPLIT UP.
Ha ha ha!
AT THIS RATE, SHE'S GOING TO SEE ME NAKED BEFORE WE EVEN HAVE SEX!
I have a reservation.
NO WAY IN HELL!!

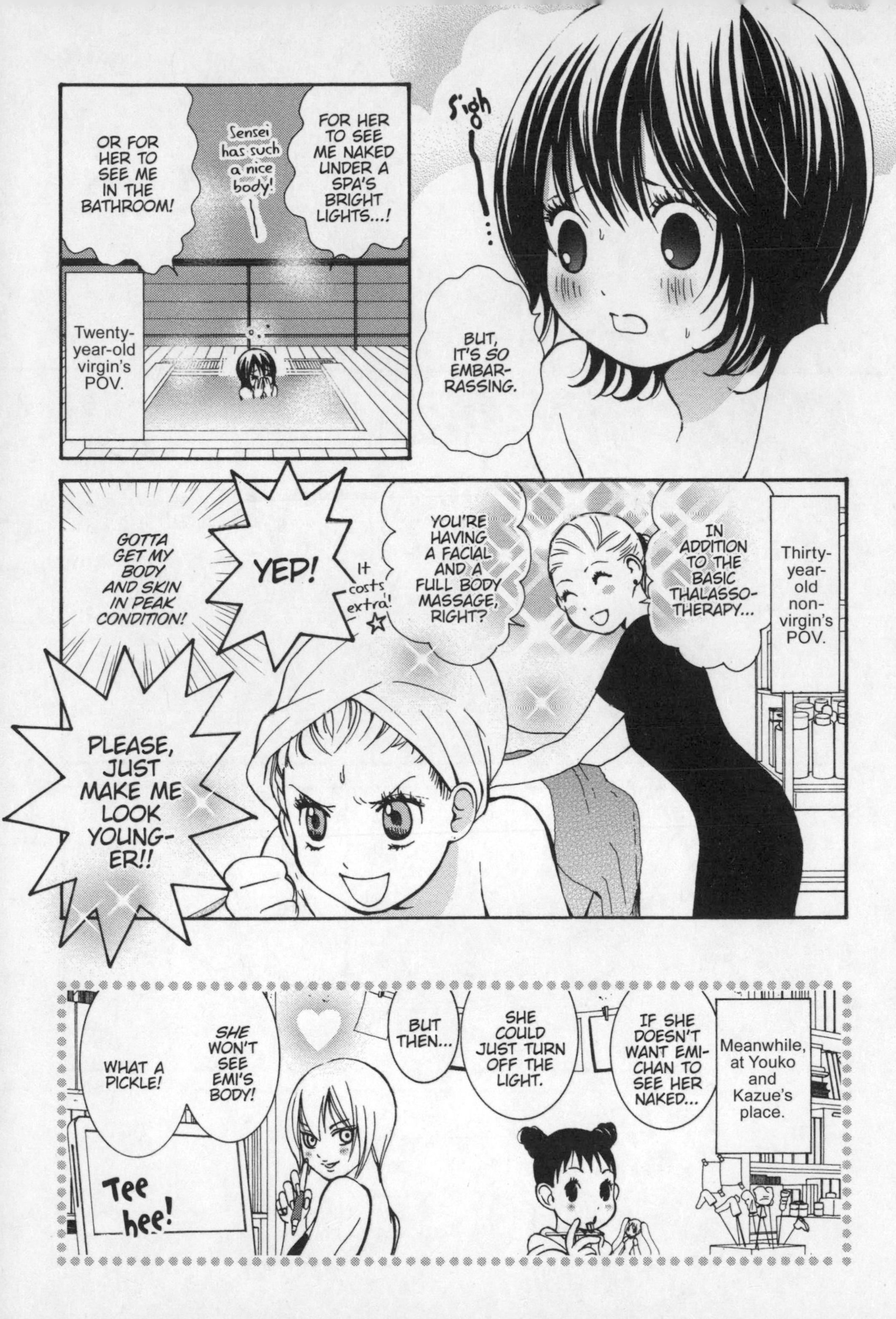
Sigh
BUT, IT'S SO EMBARRASSING.
FOR HER TO SEE ME NAKED UNDER A SPA'S BRIGHT LIGHTS...!
Sensei has such a nice body!
OR FOR HER TO SEE ME IN THE BATHROOM!
Twenty-year-old virgin's POV.
Thirty-year-old non-virgin's POV.
IN ADDITION TO THE BASIC THALASSO-THERAPY...
YOU'RE HAVING A FACIAL AND A FULL BODY MASSAGE, RIGHT?
It costs extra! ☆
YEP!
GOTTA GET MY BODY AND SKIN IN PEAK CONDITION!
PLEASE, JUST MAKE ME LOOK YOUNGER!!
Meanwhile, at Youko and Kazue's place.
IF SHE DOESN'T WANT EMI-CHAN TO SEE HER NAKED...
SHE COULD JUST TURN OFF THE LIGHT.
BUT THEN...
SHE WON'T SEE EMI'S BODY!
WHAT A PICKLE!
Tee hee!

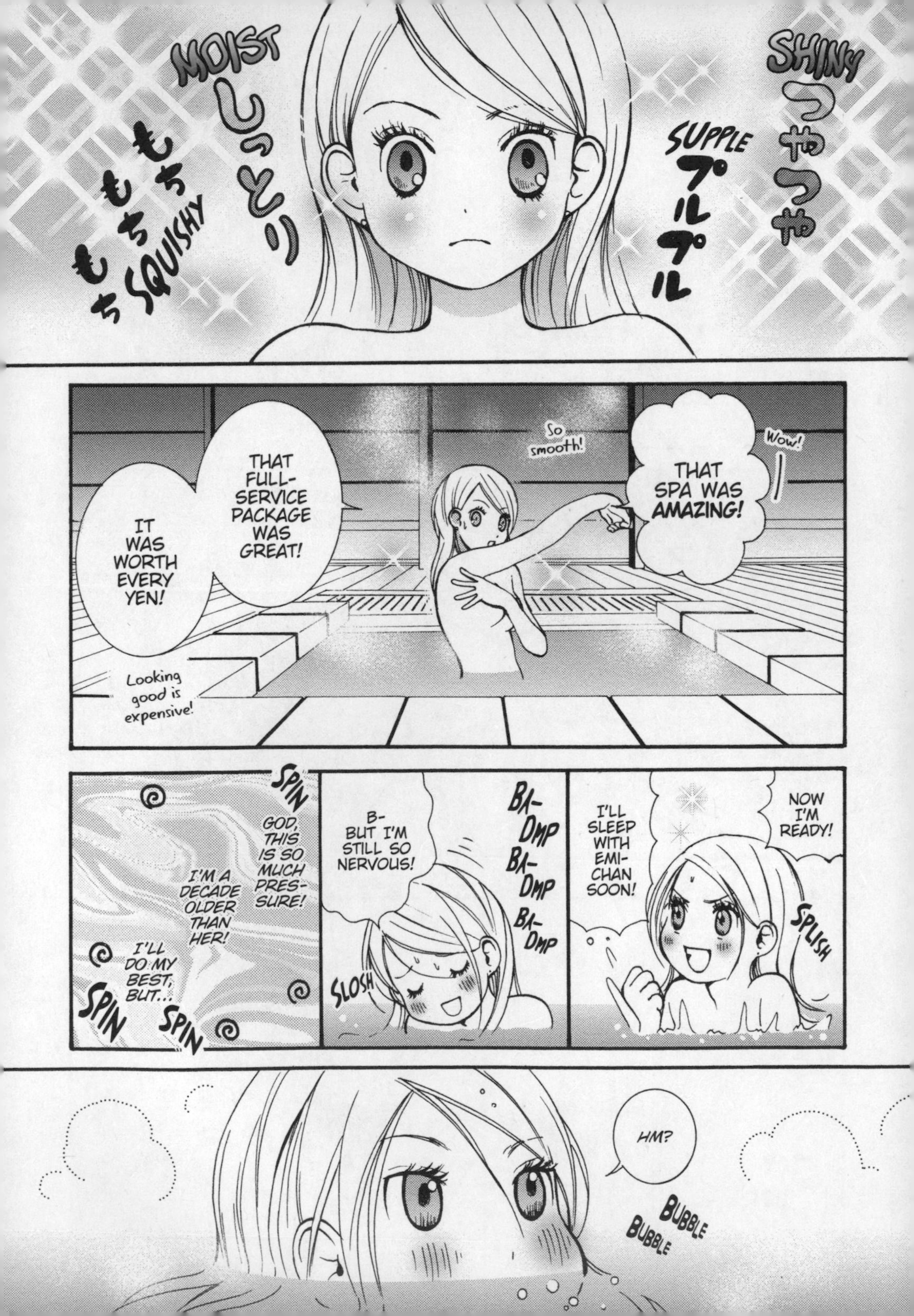
SHINY
つやつや
SUPPLE
プルプル
MOIST
しっとり
SQUISHY
もちもち
Wow!
THAT SPA WAS AMAZING!
So smooth!
THAT FULL-SERVICE PACKAGE WAS GREAT!
IT WAS WORTH EVERY YEN!
Looking good is expensive!
NOW I'M READY!
I'LL SLEEP WITH EMI-CHAN SOON!
SPLISH
BA-DMP BA-DMP BA-DMP
B- BUT I'M STILL SO NERVOUS!
SLOSH
SPIN
GOD, THIS IS SO MUCH PRES-SURE!
I'M A DECADE OLDER THAN HER!
I'LL DO MY BEST, BUT...
SPIN SPIN
HM?
BUBBLE BUBBLE

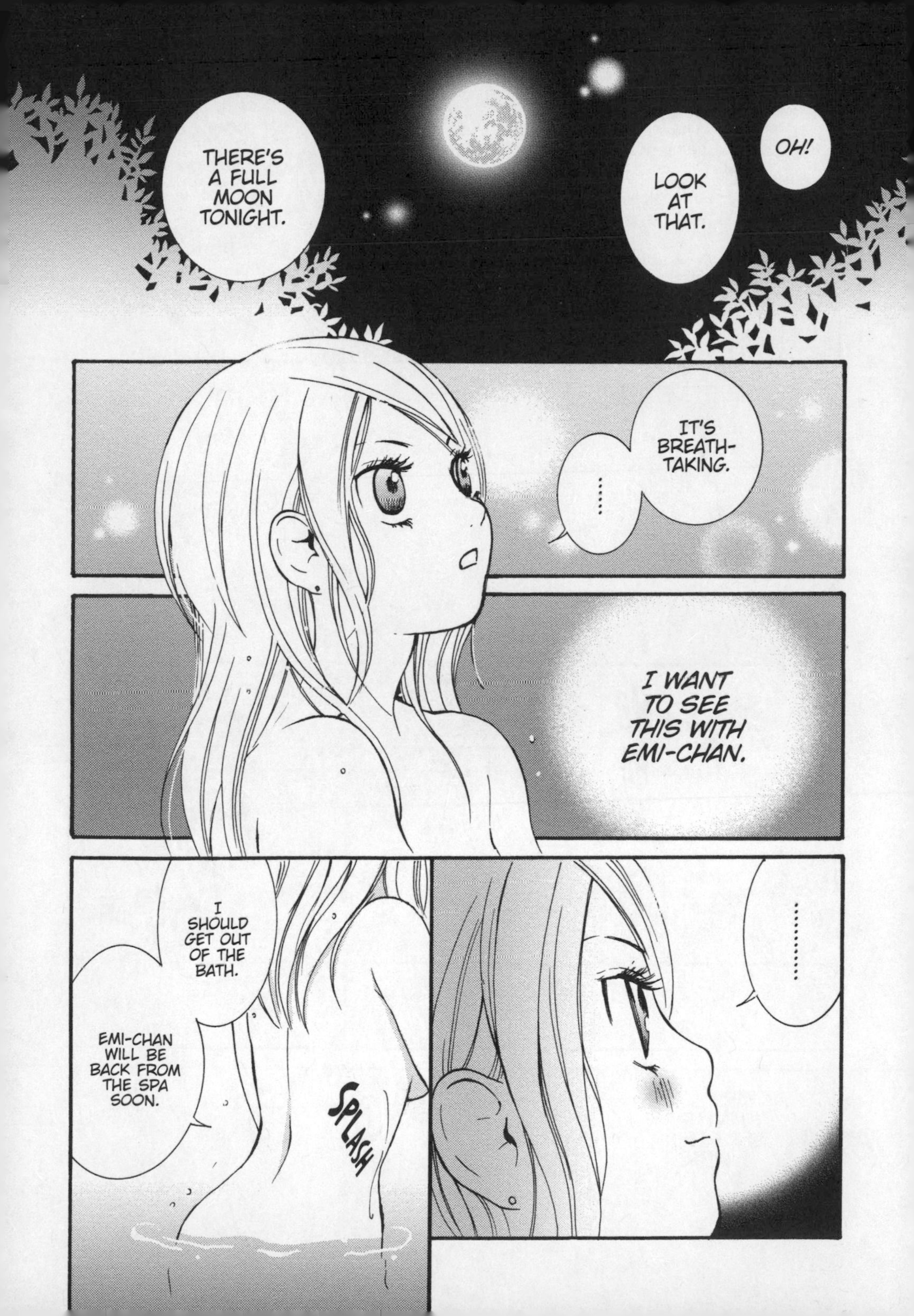
OH!
LOOK AT THAT.
THERE'S A FULL MOON TONIGHT.
IT'S BREATH-TAKING.
......
I WANT TO SEE THIS WITH EMI-CHAN.
......
I SHOULD GET OUT OF THE BATH.
EMI-CHAN WILL BE BACK FROM THE SPA SOON.
SPLASH

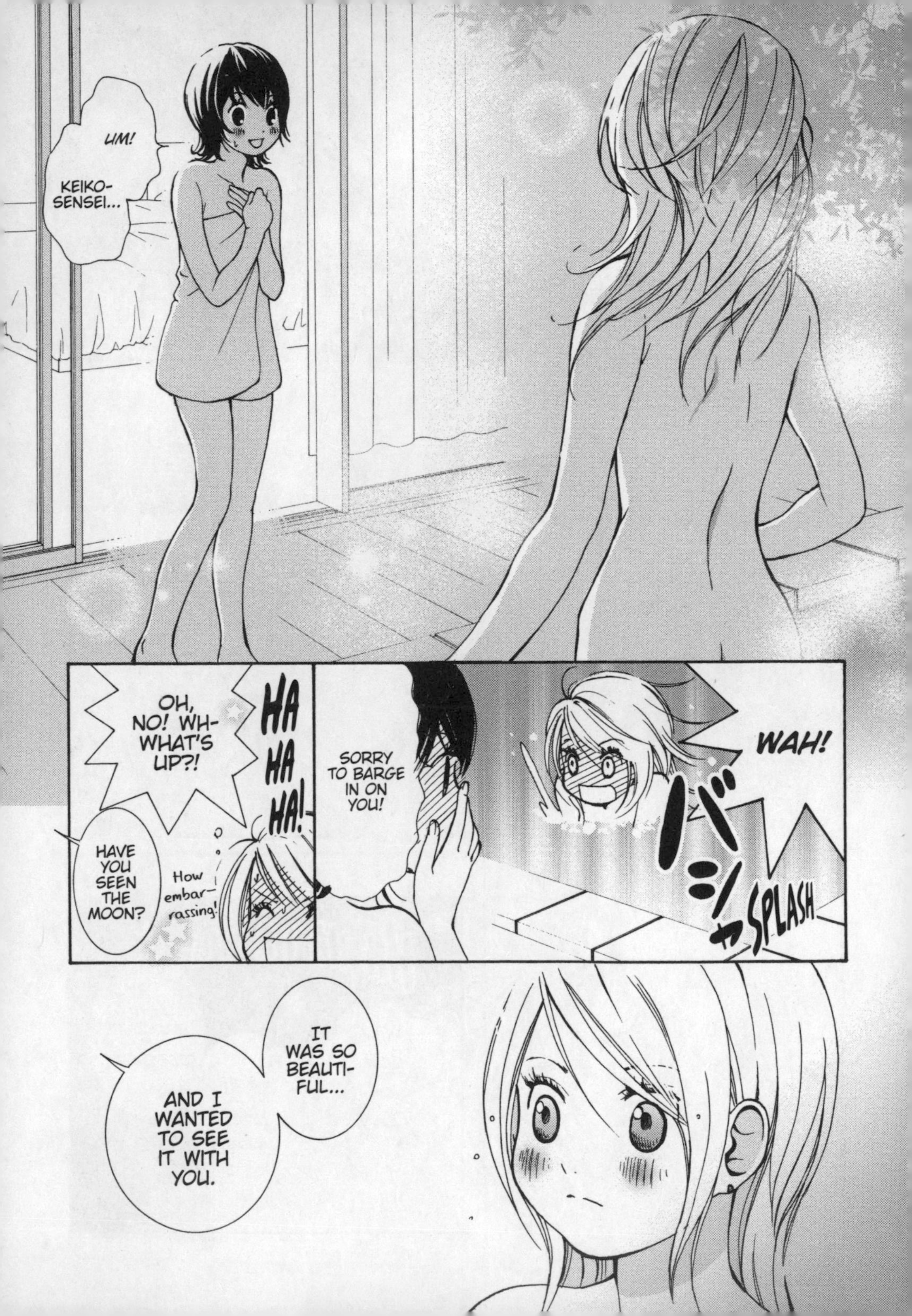
UM!
KEIKO-SENSEI...
WAH!
バシャ
SPLASH
SORRY TO BARGE IN ON YOU!
HA HA HA HA!
OH, NO! WH-WHAT'S UP?!
How embarrassing!
HAVE YOU SEEN THE MOON?
IT WAS SO BEAUTIFUL...
AND I WANTED TO SEE IT WITH YOU.

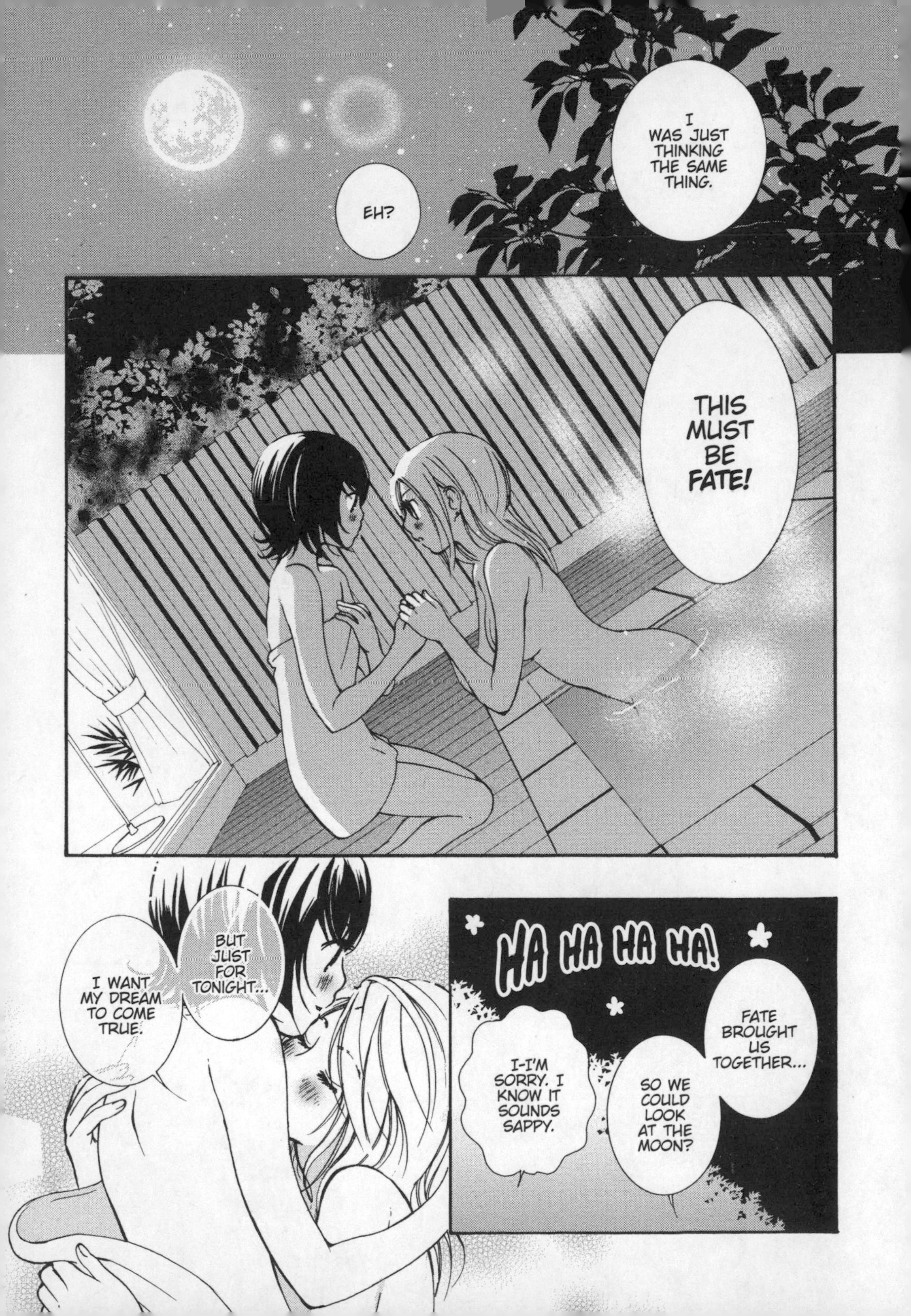
I WAS JUST THINKING THE SAME THING.
EH?
THIS MUST BE FATE!
HA HA HA HA!
FATE BROUGHT US TOGETHER...
SO WE COULD LOOK AT THE MOON?
I-I'M SORRY. I KNOW IT SOUNDS SAPPY.
BUT JUST FOR TONIGHT...
I WANT MY DREAM TO COME TRUE.

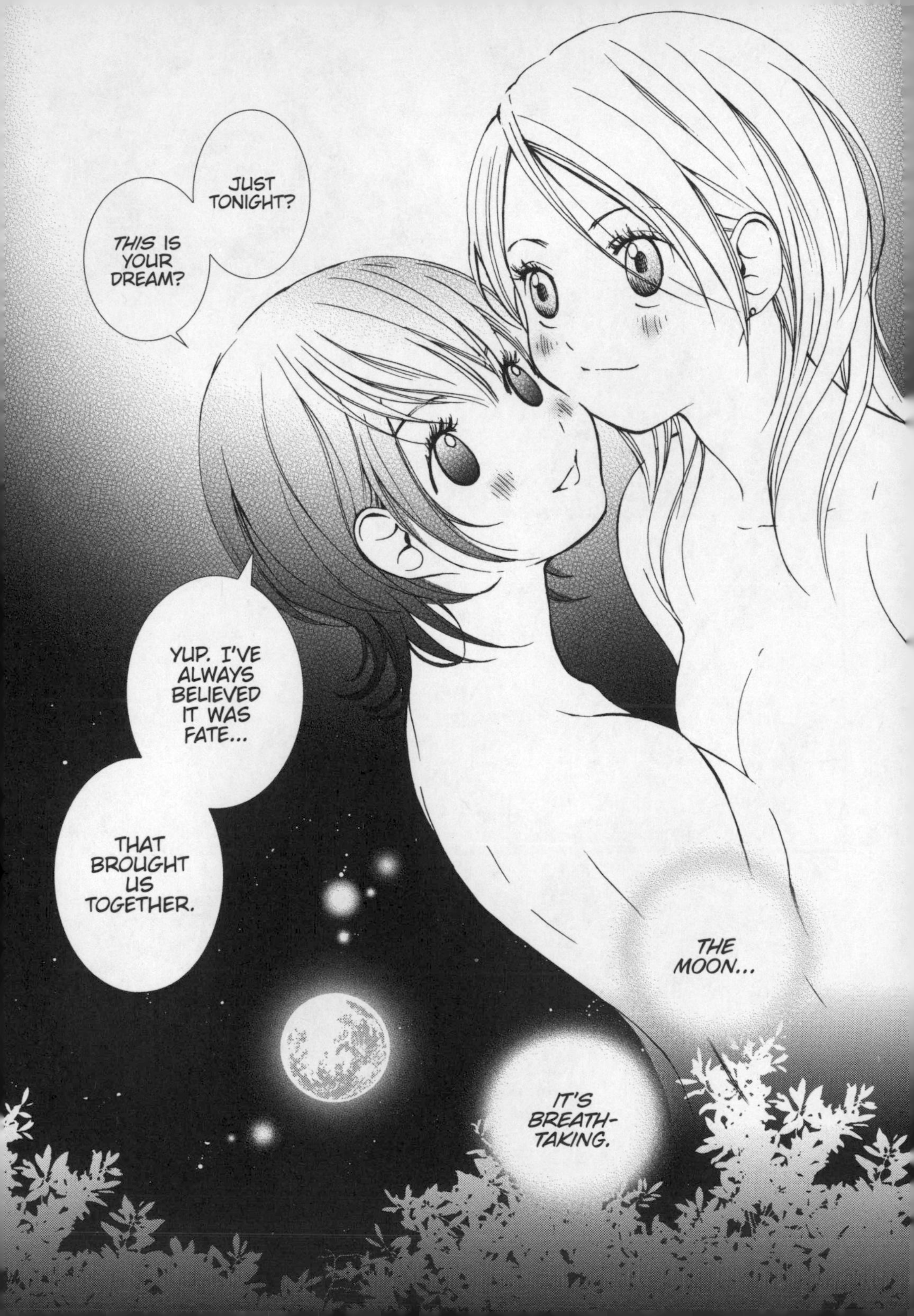
JUST TONIGHT?
THIS IS YOUR DREAM?
YUP. I'VE ALWAYS BELIEVED IT WAS FATE...
THAT BROUGHT US TOGETHER.
THE MOON...
IT'S BREATH-TAKING.

The Conditions
of Paradise

AZURE DREAMS

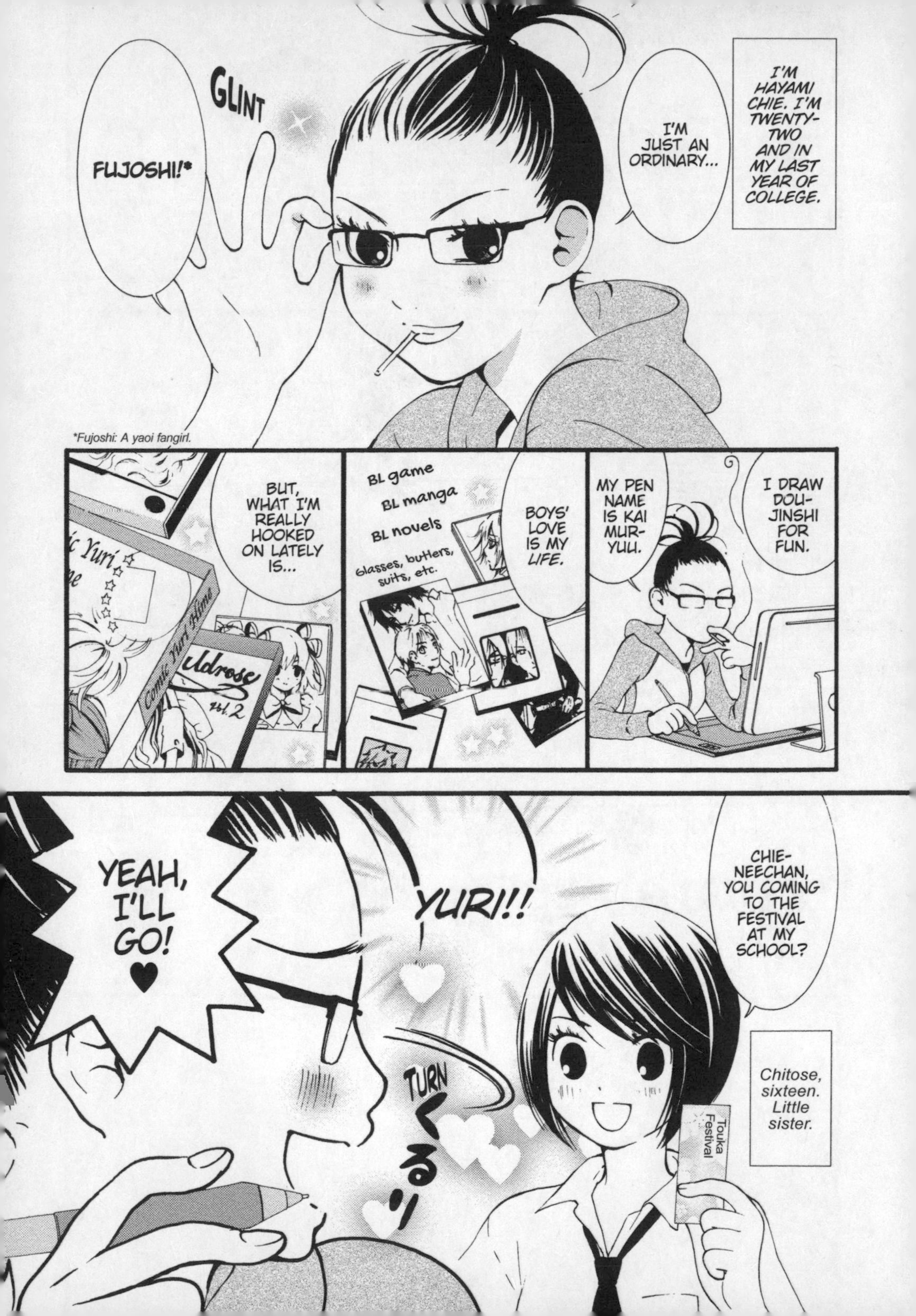
I'M HAYAMI CHIE. I'M TWENTY-TWO AND IN MY LAST YEAR OF COLLEGE.
I'M JUST AN ORDINARY...
GLINT
FUJOSHI!*
I DRAW DOUJINSHI FOR FUN.
MY PEN NAME IS KAI MURYUU.
BOYS' LOVE IS MY LIFE.
BL game
BL manga
BL novels
Glasses, butlers, suits, etc.
BUT, WHAT I'M REALLY HOOKED ON LATELY IS...
Comic Yuri Hime
vol. 2
CHIE-NEECHAN, YOU COMING TO THE FESTIVAL AT MY SCHOOL?
Chitose, sixteen. Little sister.
Touka Festival
YURI!!
TURN
くるり
YEAH, I'LL GO! ♥

*Fujoshi: A yaoi fangirl.

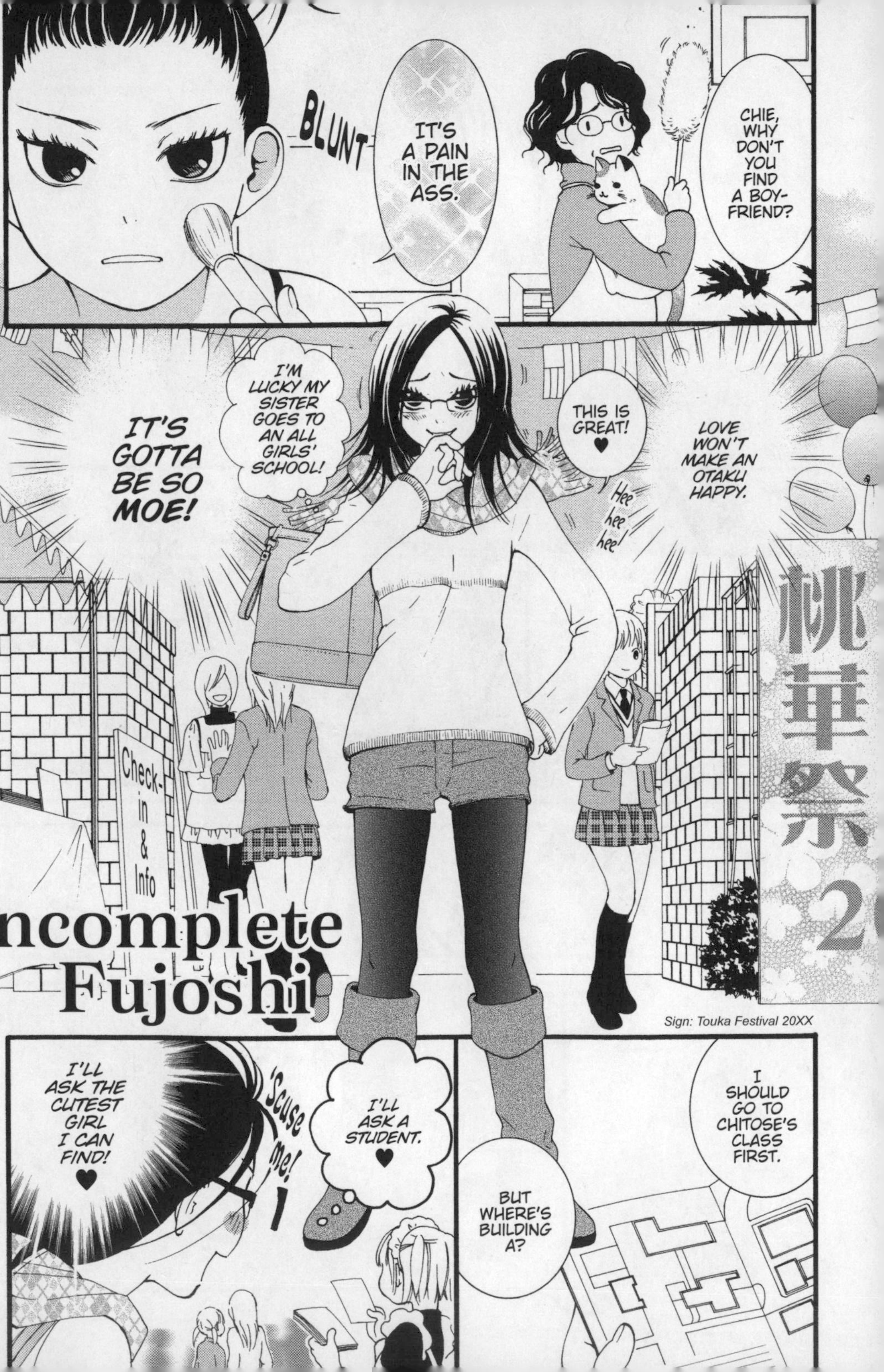
CHIE, WHY DON'T YOU FIND A BOY-FRIEND?
IT'S A PAIN IN THE ASS.
BLUNT
LOVE WON'T MAKE AN OTAKU HAPPY.
THIS IS GREAT! ♥
Hee hee hee!
I'M LUCKY MY SISTER GOES TO AN ALL GIRLS' SCHOOL!
IT'S GOTTA BE SO MOE!
桃華祭2
Check-in & Info
Incomplete Fujoshi
I SHOULD GO TO CHITOSE'S CLASS FIRST.
BUT WHERE'S BUILDING A?
I'LL ASK A STUDENT. ♥
'Scuse me!
I'LL ASK THE CUTEST GIRL I CAN FIND! ♥

Sign: Touka Festival 20XX

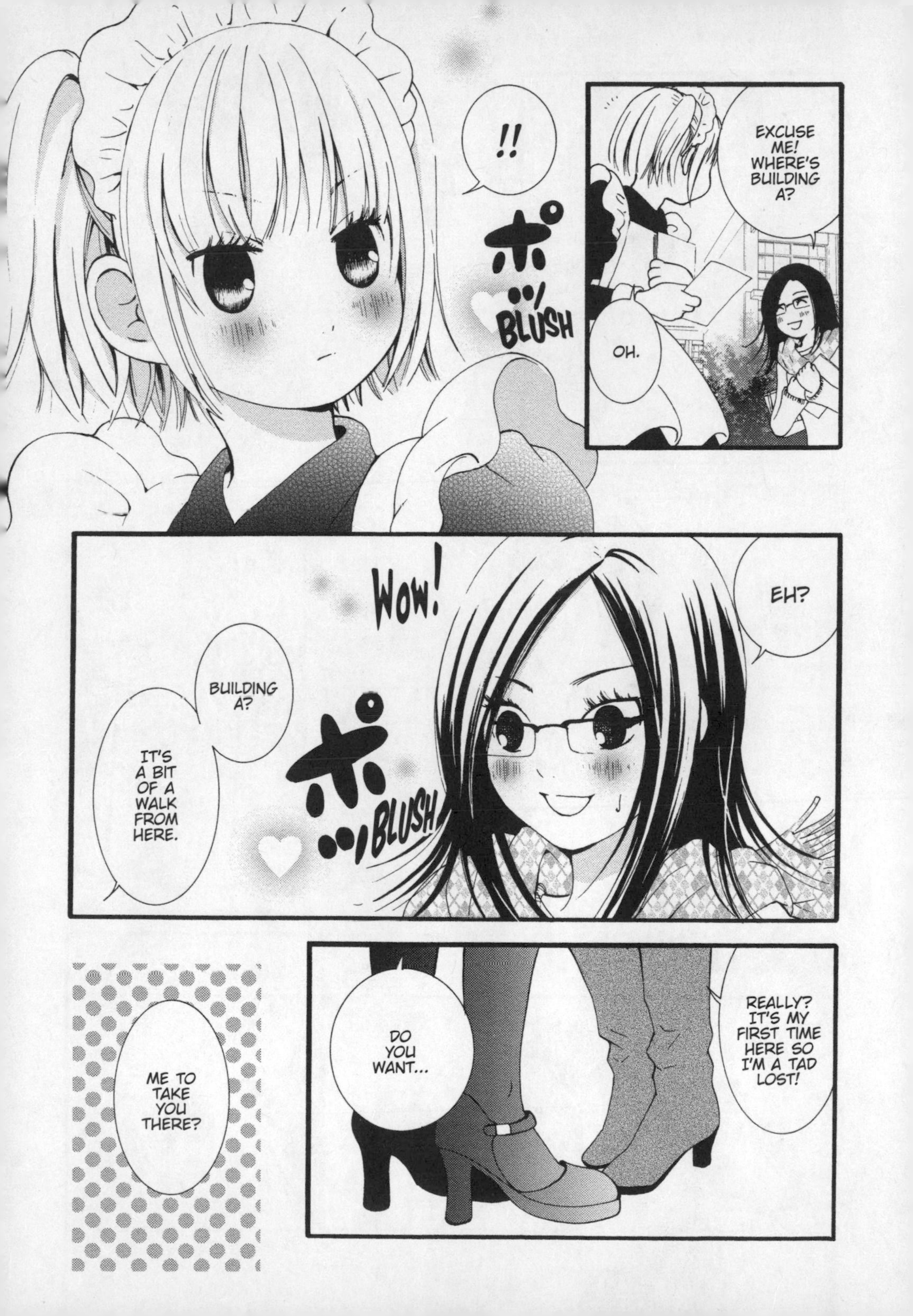
EXCUSE ME! WHERE'S BUILDING A?
OH.
!!
ポ
BLUSH
EH?
WOW!
BUILDING A?
IT'S A BIT OF A WALK FROM HERE.
ポ
BLUSH
REALLY? IT'S MY FIRST TIME HERE SO I'M A TAD LOST!
DO YOU WANT...
ME TO TAKE YOU THERE?

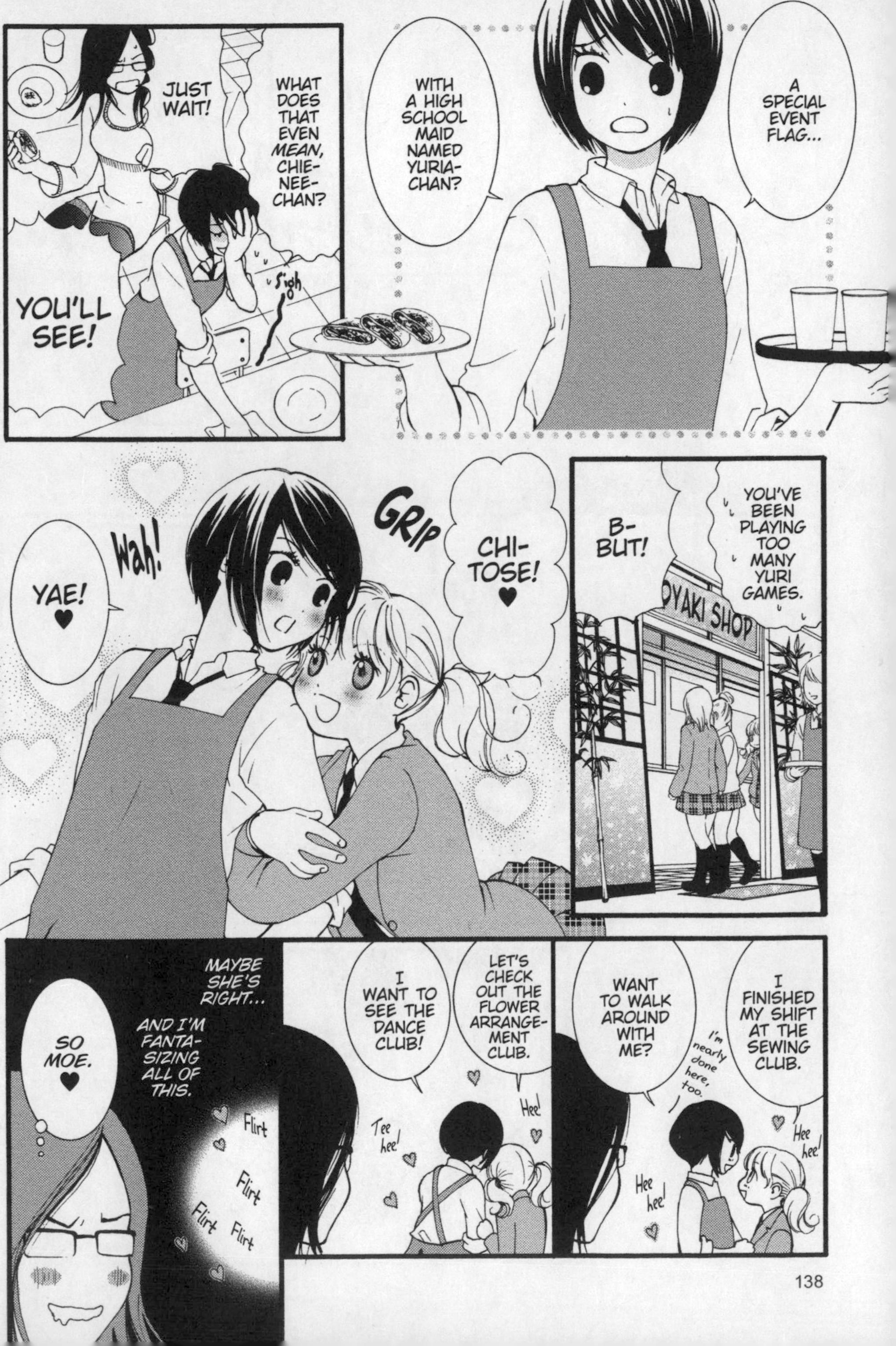
A SPECIAL EVENT FLAG...
WITH A HIGH SCHOOL MAID NAMED YURIA-CHAN?
WHAT DOES THAT EVEN MEAN, CHIE-NEE-CHAN?
JUST WAIT!
YOU'LL SEE!
Sigh
B-BUT!
YOU'VE BEEN PLAYING TOO MANY YURI GAMES.
OYAKI SHOP
CHI-TOSE! ♥
GRIP
Wah!
YAE! ♥
I FINISHED MY SHIFT AT THE SEWING CLUB.
WANT TO WALK AROUND WITH ME?
I'm nearly done here, too.
Hee hee!
Hee hee!
LET'S CHECK OUT THE FLOWER ARRANGEMENT CLUB.
I WANT TO SEE THE DANCE CLUB!
Hee!
Tee hee!
MAYBE SHE'S RIGHT...
AND I'M FANTASIZING ALL OF THIS.
SO MOE. ♥
Flirt
Flirt
Flirt Flirt

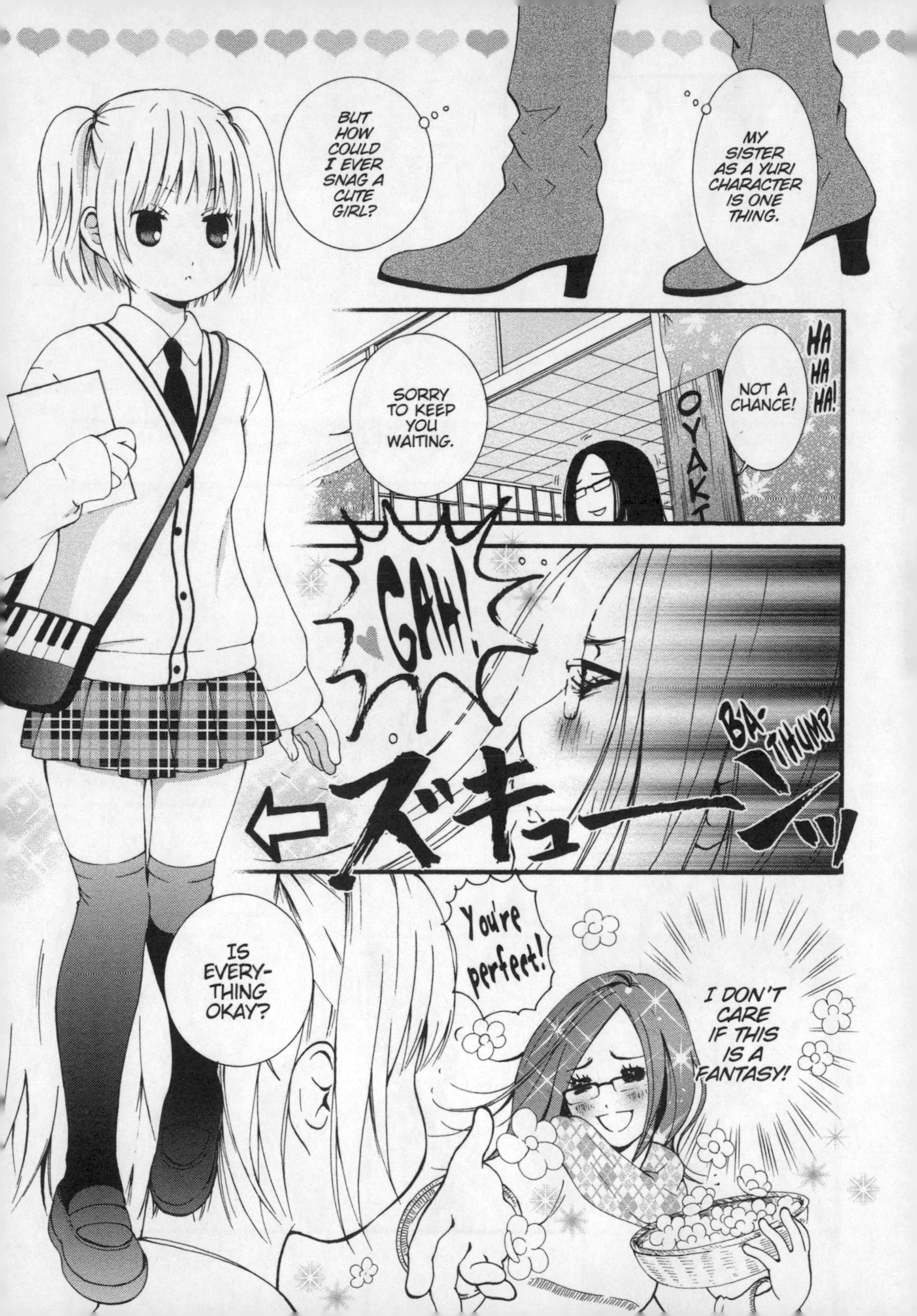
MY SISTER AS A YURI CHARACTER IS ONE THING.
BUT HOW COULD I EVER SNAG A CUTE GIRL?
HA HA HA!
NOT A CHANCE!
SORRY TO KEEP YOU WAITING.
BA-THUMP
GAH!
ズキューンッ
I DON'T CARE IF THIS IS A FANTASY!
You're perfect!
IS EVERY-THING OKAY?

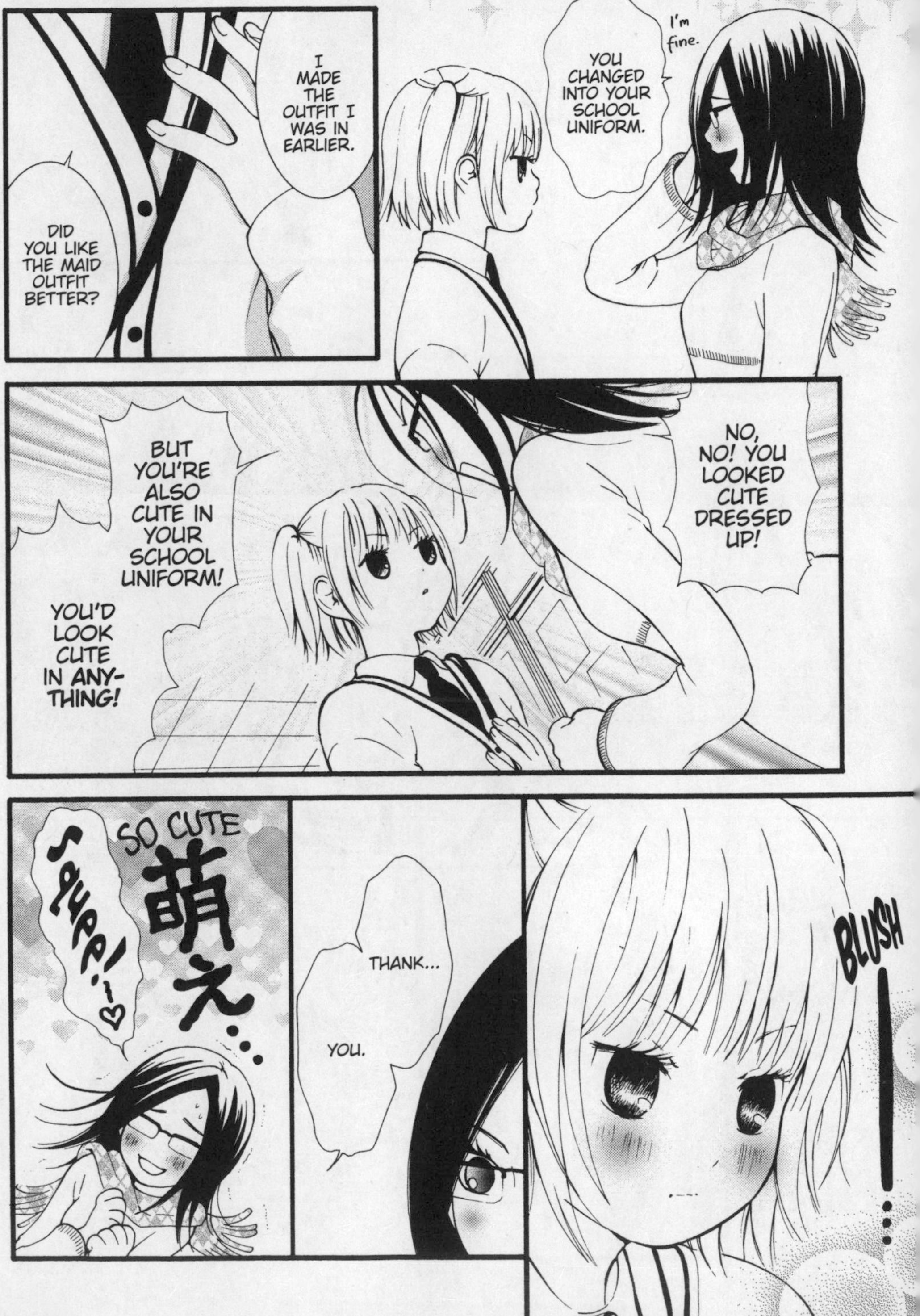
I'm fine.
YOU CHANGED INTO YOUR SCHOOL UNIFORM.
I MADE THE OUTFIT I WAS IN EARLIER.
DID YOU LIKE THE MAID OUTFIT BETTER?
NO, NO! YOU LOOKED CUTE DRESSED UP!
BUT YOU'RE ALSO CUTE IN YOUR SCHOOL UNIFORM!
YOU'D LOOK CUTE IN ANY-THING!
BLUSH
THANK...
YOU.
SO CUTE
萌え…
Squee!~♡

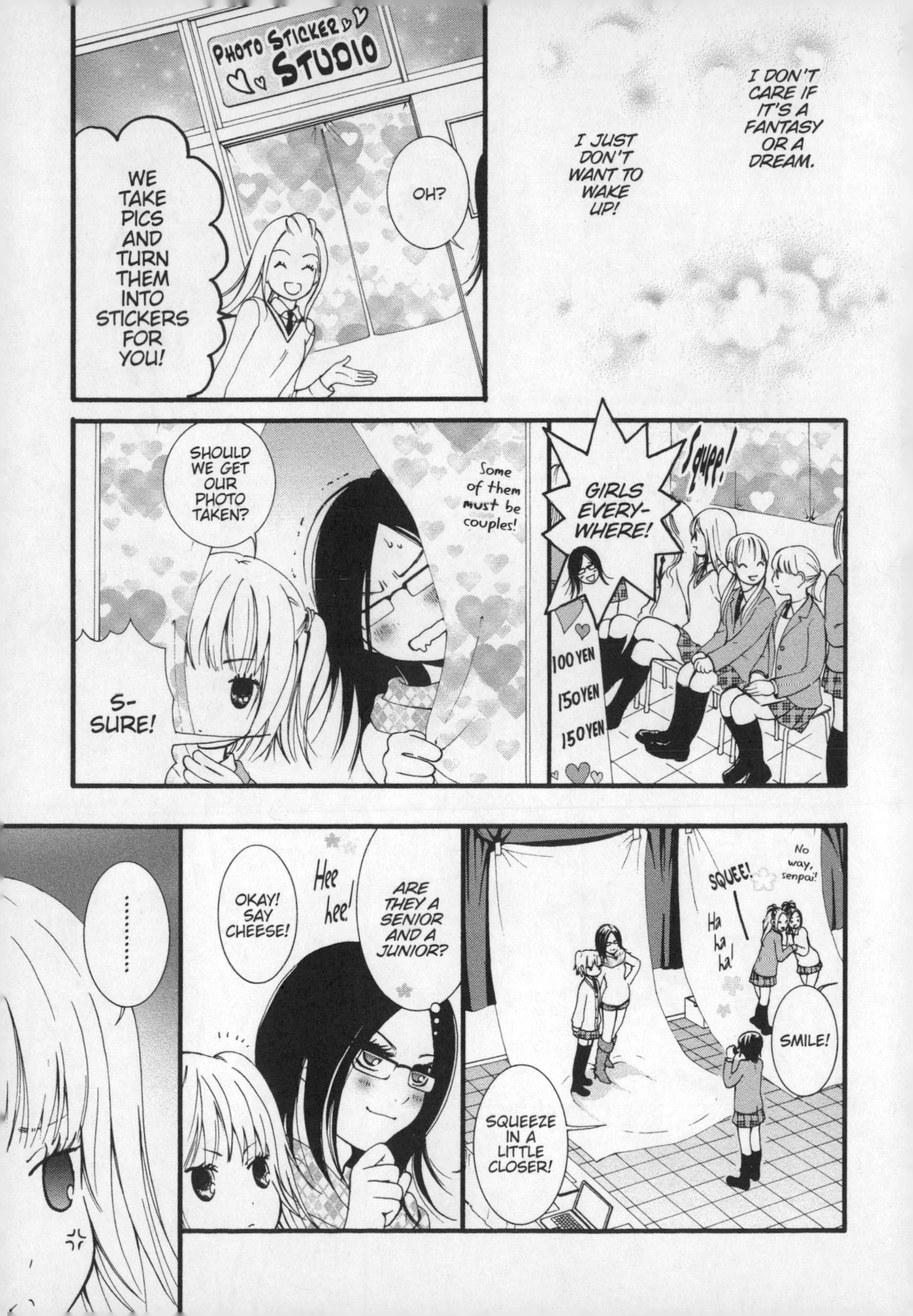
I DON'T CARE IF IT'S A FANTASY OR A DREAM.
I JUST DON'T WANT TO WAKE UP!
PHOTO STICKER STUDIO
OH?
WE TAKE PICS AND TURN THEM INTO STICKERS FOR YOU!
Squee!
GIRLS EVERYWHERE!
100 YEN
150 YEN
150 YEN
Some of them must be couples!
SHOULD WE GET OUR PHOTO TAKEN?
S-SURE!
No way, senpai!
SQUEE!
Ha ha ha!
SMILE!
SQUEEZE IN A LITTLE CLOSER!
ARE THEY A SENIOR AND A JUNIOR?
Hee hee!
OKAY! SAY CHEESE!
......

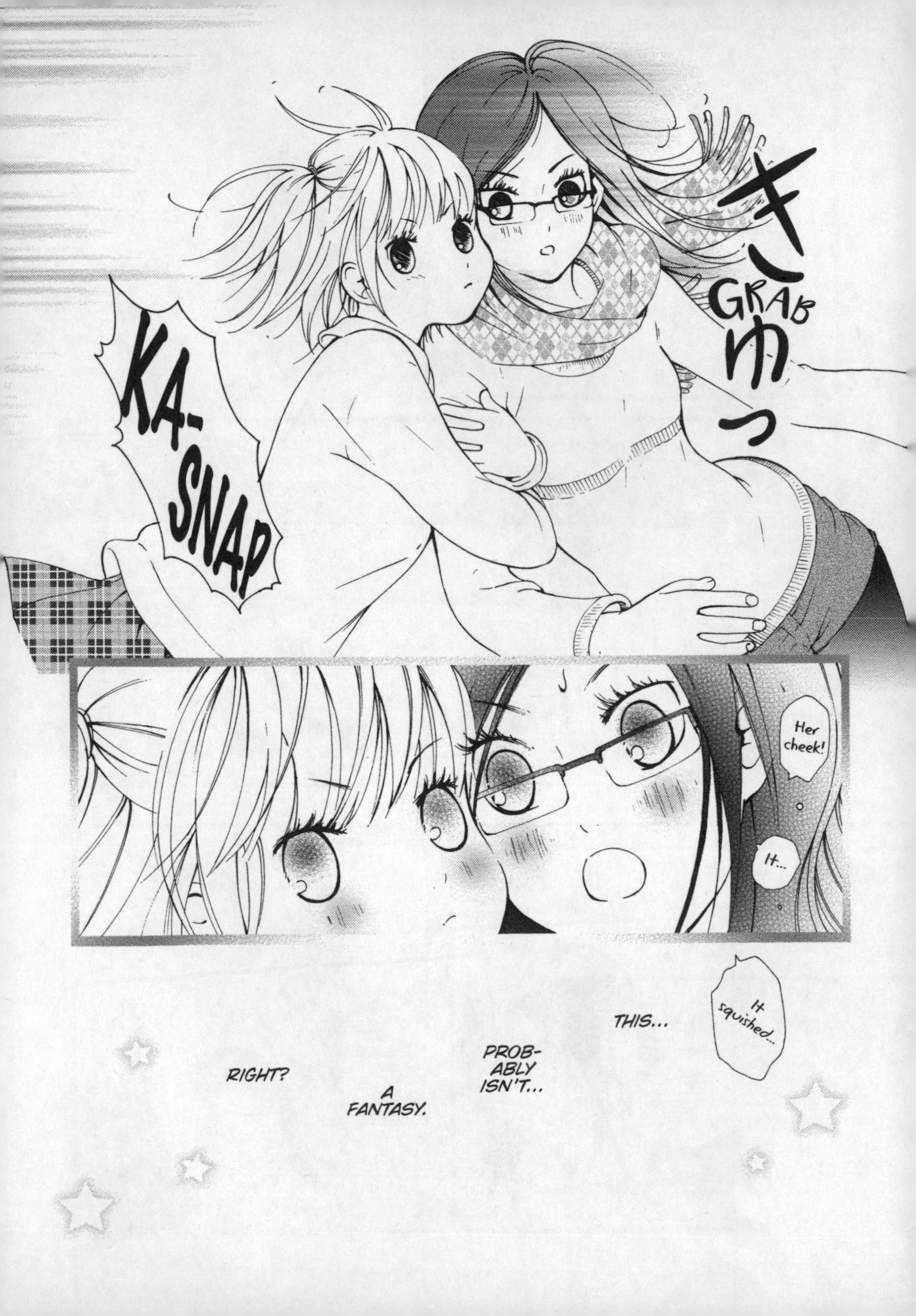
GRAB
KA-SNAP
Her cheek!
It...
It squished...
THIS...
PROB-ABLY ISN'T...
A FANTASY.
RIGHT?

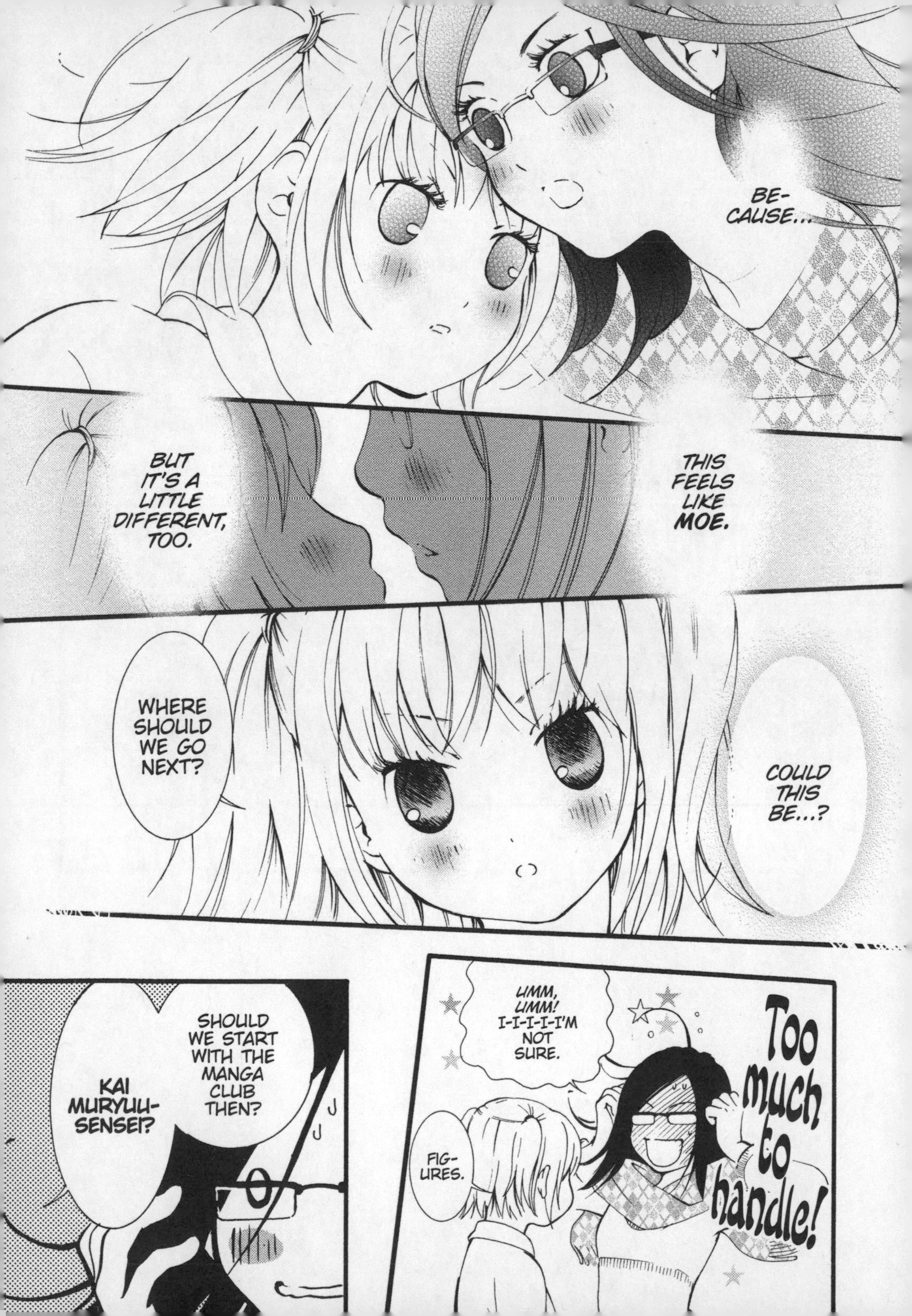
BE-CAUSE...
THIS FEELS LIKE MOE.
BUT IT'S A LITTLE DIFFERENT, TOO.
COULD THIS BE...?
WHERE SHOULD WE GO NEXT?
UMM, UMM! I-I-I-I-I'M NOT SURE.
Too much to handle!
FIG-URES.
SHOULD WE START WITH THE MANGA CLUB THEN?
KAI MURYUU-SENSEI?

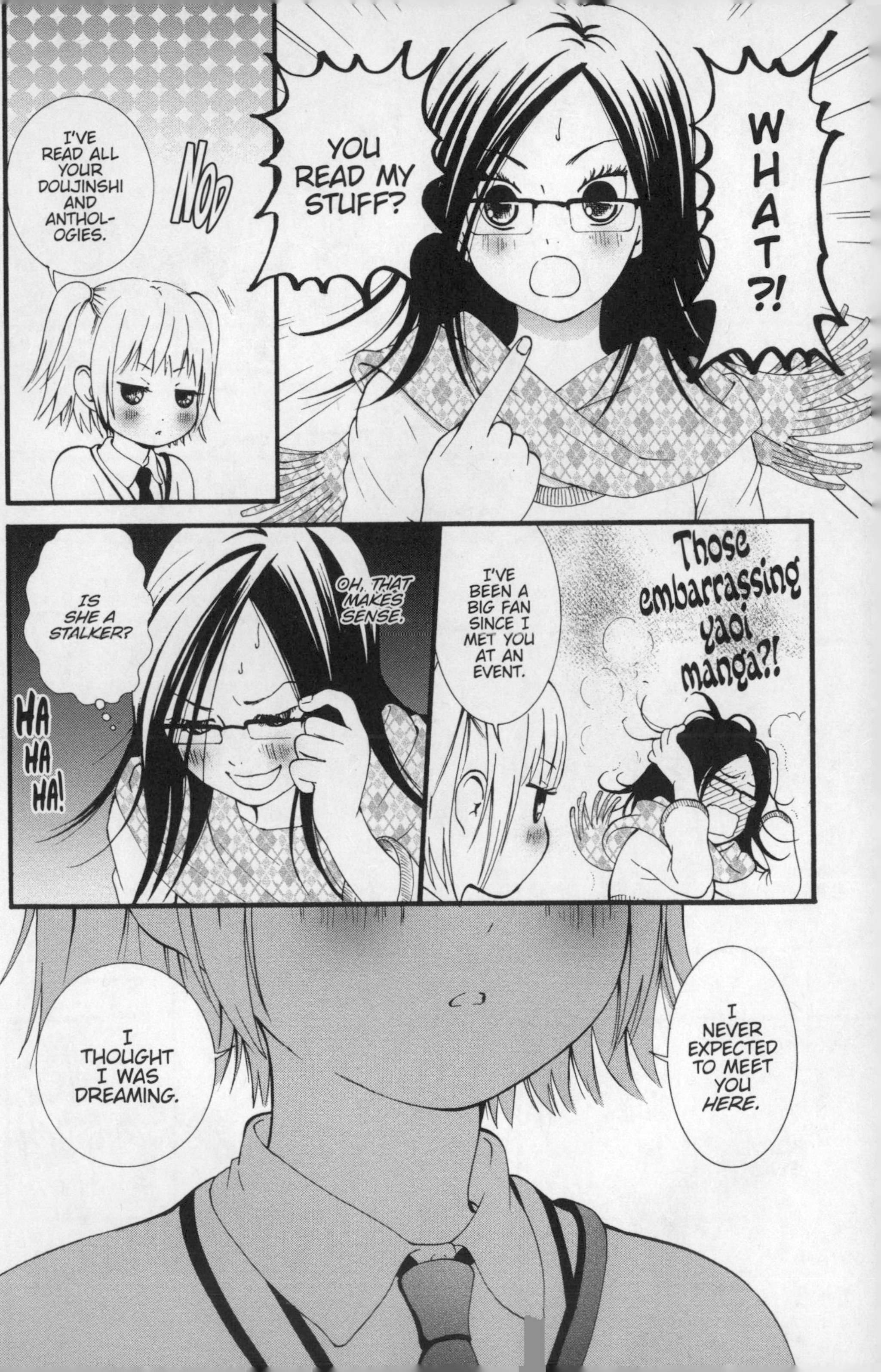
WHAT?!
YOU READ MY STUFF?
I'VE READ ALL YOUR DOUJINSHI AND ANTHOLOGIES.
NOD
Those embarrassing yaoi manga?!
I'VE BEEN A BIG FAN SINCE I MET YOU AT AN EVENT.
OH, THAT MAKES SENSE.
IS SHE A STALKER?
HA HA HA!
I NEVER EXPECTED TO MEET YOU HERE.
I THOUGHT I WAS DREAMING.

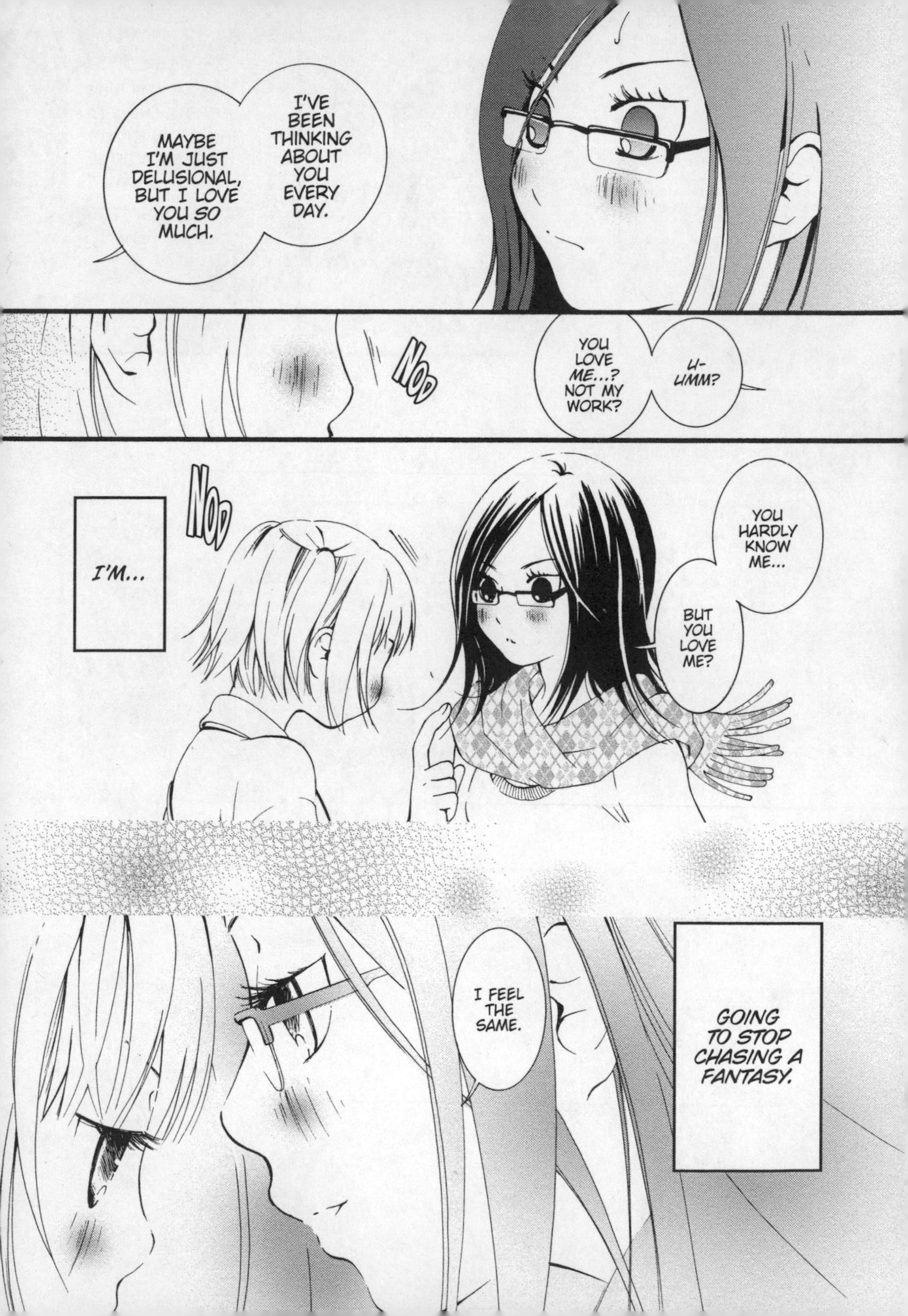
I'VE BEEN THINKING ABOUT YOU EVERY DAY.
MAYBE I'M JUST DELUSIONAL, BUT I LOVE YOU SO MUCH.
U-UMM?
YOU LOVE ME...? NOT MY WORK?
NOD
YOU HARDLY KNOW ME...
BUT YOU LOVE ME?
NOD
I'M...
GOING TO STOP CHASING A FANTASY.
I FEEL THE SAME.

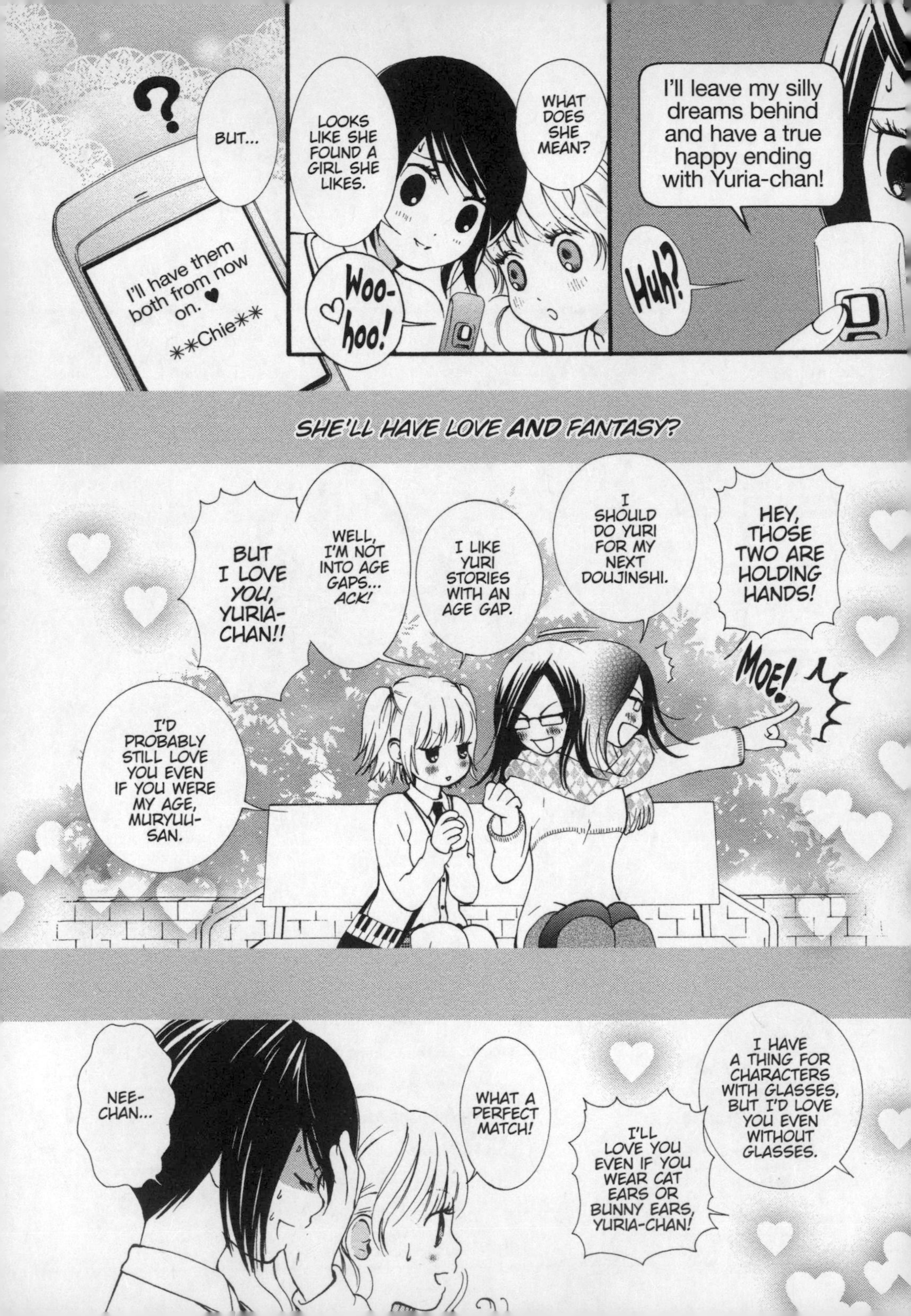
I'll leave my silly dreams behind and have a true happy ending with Yuria-chan!
Huh?
WHAT DOES SHE MEAN?
LOOKS LIKE SHE FOUND A GIRL SHE LIKES.
Woo-hoo!
BUT...
I'll have them both from now on. ♥
Chie
SHE'LL HAVE LOVE AND FANTASY?
HEY, THOSE TWO ARE HOLDING HANDS!
MOE!
I SHOULD DO YURI FOR MY NEXT DOUJINSHI.
I LIKE YURI STORIES WITH AN AGE GAP.
WELL, I'M NOT INTO AGE GAPS... ACK!
BUT I LOVE YOU, YURIA-CHAN!!
I'D PROBABLY STILL LOVE YOU EVEN IF YOU WERE MY AGE, MURYUU-SAN.
I HAVE A THING FOR CHARACTERS WITH GLASSES, BUT I'D LOVE YOU EVEN WITHOUT GLASSES.
I'LL LOVE YOU EVEN IF YOU WEAR CAT EARS OR BUNNY EARS, YURIA-CHAN!
WHAT A PERFECT MATCH!
NEE-CHAN...

ORIGINAL PUBLICATION DATES:

Azure Dreams ....Comic Yuri Hime Volume 13

The Star Prince ....Comic Yuri Hime Volume 11

Honey and Mustard ....Comic Yuri Hime Volume 16

Reminiscence: Nostalgia ....Comic Yuri Hime Volume 15

The Season of the 20-Year Old Virgin .... Comic Yuri Hime Volume 12

Under a Full Moon .... Previously Unpublished

Incomplete Fujoshi ....Comic Yuri Hime Volume 14

Afterword .... Previously Unpublished

Afterword

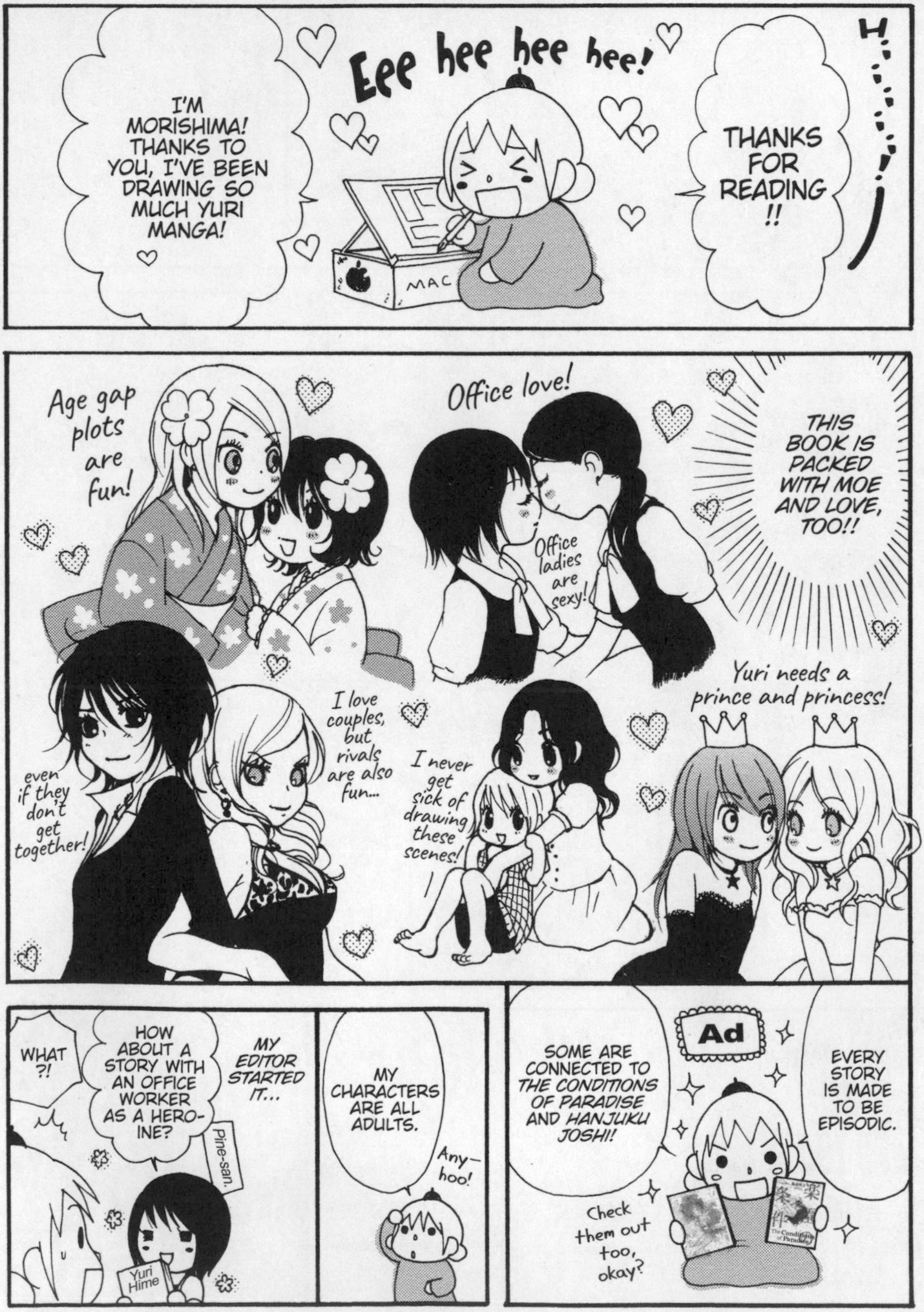

THANKS FOR READING!!
Eee hee hee hee!
I'M MORISHIMA! THANKS TO YOU, I'VE BEEN DRAWING SO MUCH YURI MANGA!
MAC
THIS BOOK IS PACKED WITH MOE AND LOVE, TOO!!
Office love!
Office ladies are sexy!
Age gap plots are fun!
Yuri needs a prince and princess!
I never get sick of drawing these scenes!
I love couples, but rivals are also fun...
even if they don't get together!
EVERY STORY IS MADE TO BE EPISODIC.
Ad
SOME ARE CONNECTED TO THE CONDITIONS OF PARADISE AND HANJUKU JOSHI!
Check them out too, okay?
The Conditions of Paradise
MY CHARACTERS ARE ALL ADULTS.
Any-hoo!
MY EDITOR STARTED IT...
HOW ABOUT A STORY WITH AN OFFICE WORKER AS A HERO-INE?
Pine-san.
WHAT?!
Yuri Hime

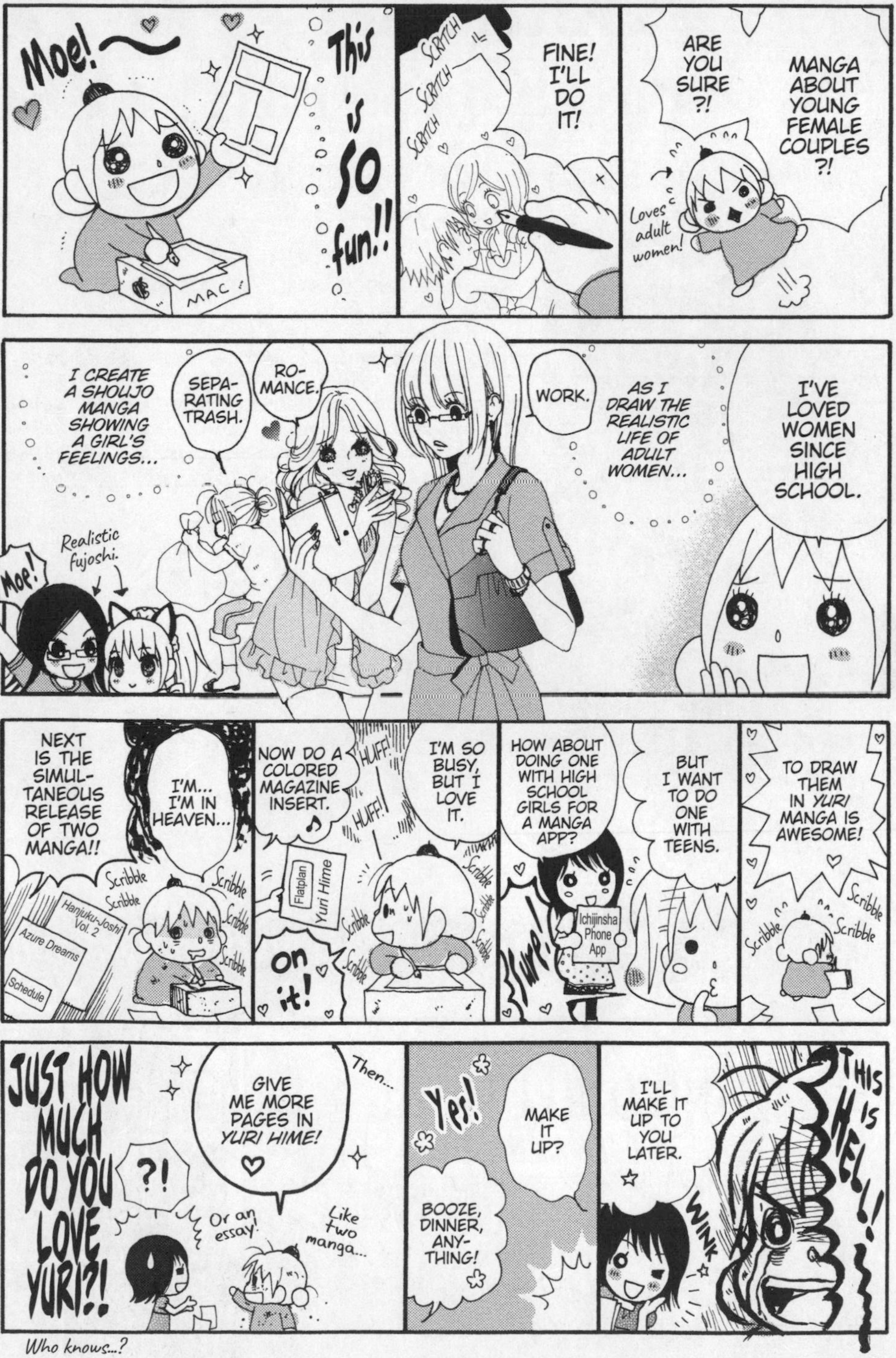
MANGA ABOUT YOUNG FEMALE COUPLES?!
ARE YOU SURE?!
Loves adult women!
FINE! I'LL DO IT!
SCRITCH SCRITCH SCRITCH
Moe!~
This is SO fun!!
I'VE LOVED WOMEN SINCE HIGH SCHOOL.
AS I DRAW THE REALISTIC LIFE OF ADULT WOMEN...
WORK.
RO-MANCE.
SEPA-RATING TRASH.
I CREATE A SHOUJO MANGA SHOWING A GIRL'S FEELINGS...
Realistic fujoshi.
Moe!
TO DRAW THEM IN *YURI* MANGA IS AWESOME!
Scribble Scribble Scribble
HOW ABOUT DOING ONE WITH HIGH SCHOOL GIRLS FOR A MANGA APP?
BUT I WANT TO DO ONE WITH TEENS.
Ichijinsha Phone App
Slurp!
I'M SO BUSY, BUT I LOVE IT.
NOW DO A COLORED MAGAZINE INSERT.
HUFF! HUFF!
Flatplan Yuri Hime
Scribble Scribble Scribble
On it!
NEXT IS THE SIMUL-TANEOUS RELEASE OF TWO MANGA!!
I'M... I'M IN HEAVEN...
Scribble Scribble Scribble Scribble
Hanjuku-Joshi Vol. 2
Azure Dreams
Schedule
THIS IS HELL!
I'LL MAKE IT UP TO YOU LATER.
WINK
MAKE IT UP?
Yes!
BOOZE, DINNER, ANY-THING!
Then...
GIVE ME MORE PAGES IN *YURI HIME*!
JUST HOW MUCH DO YOU LOVE YURI?!
?!
Like two manga...
Or an essay!

Who knows...?

SEVEN SEAS ENTERTAINMENT PRESENTS

The Conditions of Paradise

Azure Dreams

story & art by **AKIKO MORISHIMA**

TRANSLATION
Elina Ishikawa

ADAPTATION
Asha Bardon

LETTERING AND RETOUCH
CK Russell

COVER DESIGN
Nicky Lim

PROOFREADER
Dawn Davis
Danielle King

EDITOR
Shannon Fay

PREPRESS TECHNICIAN
Rhiannon Rasmussen-Silverstein

PRODUCTION MANAGER
Lissa Pattillo

MANAGING EDITOR
Julie Davis

ASSOCIATE PUBLISHER
Adam Arnold

PUBLISHER
Jason DeAngelis

THE CONDITIONS OF PARADISE: AZURE DREAMS

First published in Japan in 2009 by Ichijinsha Inc., Tokyo.
Publication rights for this English edition arranged through Kodansha Ltd., Tokyo.

Seven Seas press and purchase enquiries can be sent to Marketing Manager Lianne Sentar at press@gomanga.com. Information regarding the distribution and purchase of digital editions is available from Digital Manager CK Russell at digital@gomanga.com.

ISBN: 978-1-64505-837-3

Printed in Canada

First Printing: January 2021

10 9 8 7 6 5 4 3 2 1

FOLLOW US ONLINE: ***www.sevenseasentertainment.com***

READING DIRECTIONS

This book reads from ***right to left***, Japanese style. If this is your first time reading manga, you start reading from the top right panel on each page and take it from there. If you get lost, just follow the numbered diagram here. It may seem backwards at first, but you'll get the hang of it! Have fun!!

1
2
3
4
5
6
7
8
9

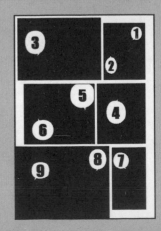